VICTIMS

OAKS

COLLIERY

DISASTER 1847

I dedicate this book to my paternal relations,
Hardys, Baileys and Ostcliffes,
who laboured in the coal mines of the West Riding of Yorkshire.

In remembrance of all mineworkers throughout the ages,
especially victims of colliery disasters or accidents.
Barnsley, like many places, was built on their blood, sweat and tears.

Sculpture by Graham Ibbeson at the National Union of Mineworkers Offices.

VICTIMS OF THE
OAKS
COLLIERY
DISASTER 1847

JANE AINSWORTH

PEN & SWORD
HISTORY

AN IMPRINT OF PEN & SWORD BOOKS LTD.
YORKSHIRE – PHILADELPHIA

First published in Great Britain in 2021 by
PEN AND SWORD HISTORY
An imprint of
Pen & Sword Books Ltd
Yorkshire – Philadelphia

ISBN 978 1 52674 573 6

Typeset in Times New Roman 11.5/14 by
SJmagic DESIGN SERVICES, India.
Printed and bound by CPI Group (UK) Ltd, Croydon, CR0 4YY

Pen & Sword Books Limited incorporates the imprints of Atlas, Archaeology,
Aviation, Discovery, Family History, Fiction, History, Maritime, Military,
Military Classics, Politics, Select, Transport, True Crime, Air World,
Frontline Publishing, Leo Cooper, Remember When, Seaforth Publishing,
The Praetorian Press, Wharncliffe Local History, Wharncliffe Transport,
Wharncliffe True Crime and White Owl.

For a complete list of Pen & Sword titles please contact
PEN & SWORD BOOKS LIMITED
47 Church Street, Barnsley, South Yorkshire, S70 2AS, England
E-mail: enquiries@pen-and-sword.co.uk
Website: www.pen-and-sword.co.uk

Or
PEN AND SWORD BOOKS
1950 Lawrence Rd, Havertown, PA 19083, USA
E-mail: Uspen-and-sword@casematepublishers.com
Website: www.penandswordbooks.com

Contents

VICTIMS OF THE OAKS COLLIERY DISASTER 1847

CONTENTS

Introduction

My interest in coal mining developed from researching my paternal ancestors. My father, John Charles Hardy, escaped that fate and became a secondary-school teacher. I had a huge learning curve to understand properly the lives of my coalmining relations. The National Coalmining Museum provided the invaluable experience, albeit a sanitised and safe one, of going underground in a colliery with former mineworkers as guides.

I felt inspired by various projects undertaken for the 150th anniversary of the Oaks Colliery explosion in 1866, especially the ongoing work to commemorate our mining heritage by the National Union of Mineworkers and People and Mining. We are lucky that so many Barnsley folk are fascinated by our mining history, which is in our genes. It ought to be valued in a town literally and metaphorically 'built on coal', making a vital contribution to the Industrial Revolution and First World War. I am impressed by the commitment of volunteers to preserving our last two surviving colliery buildings at Hemingfield and Barnsley Main, in addition to the important work in Elsecar.

Jane presenting her transcription of the ledger to Paul Stebbing in 2017. (courtesy of Barnsley Archives)

INTRODUCTION

Paul Stebbing, Barnsley Archives Manager, told me in 2017 about the acquisition of a ledger for the minutes of the Colliers' Relief Fund Committee for the Oaks Colliery explosion in 1847. I offered to transcribe it and became curious about the lives of the people referred to in the minutes – widows, orphans and a few survivors.

I was delighted that Pen and Sword were interested in publishing my research and I am extremely grateful to them for extending the deadline several times to enable me to focus on the Barnsley Pals Colours Project. Unfortunately, 'lockdowns' because of the Covid-19 pandemic prevented me from spending more time in archives and churches.

Many of the families I researched have similarities because they all worked hard to survive; they shared harsh working conditions from a very young age, lived in poor quality, overcrowded housing, experienced the death of children in infancy from malnutrition or disease and generally died young. The community in Ardsley comprised fellow-workers, family, relations by marriage, friends and lodgers.

However, the victims were all individuals; their lives were unique and important to their loved ones, whose varied circumstances were changed by their loss. Their different stories deserve to be known and all those involved remembered. There is no memorial for this disaster

Resolutions of a Public Meeting held at the Court House in Barnsley on the 18th day of March 1847 for taking into Consideration the best means to be adopted for relieving the Distress of the destitute Families of the Sufferers at the Explosion at the Oaks Pit or Ardsley Main Colliery on the 5th Instant & a *Record* of the Proceedings of the a Committee elected for carrying out the Objects of such Meeting.—

The first entry in the ledger. (© Barnsley Archives)

and nothing to commemorate the victims, most of whom were buried in communal graves in St Mary's churchyard extension (now Churchfields Peace Gardens). I hope we can remedy this one day.

Some of the victims left little trace and the trail for others went cold, despite my best efforts. However, I was able to research descendants of a few to men who served in the First World War.

As always with family history research, there are some surprises ….

I feel sure that many of the families have descendants still living in Barnsley district, and elsewhere. I would love to hear from any relations.

Barnsley Archives acquired a special set of maps at auction early in 2021, thanks to some generous donations. These maps had been hand-drawn c1800 by Francis Kendray, a linen manufacturer after whom Kendray Hospital was named. Paul Stebbing allowed me a preview then very kindly agreed that I could use a few in my book, their first time in a publication.

Jane Ainsworth

PART ONE

BACKGROUND

Methodology

It proved to be an enjoyable challenge to research the individual victims and their families from basic information for a time when few genealogical records are available. I have taken great care to verify the information used in this book, but I accept that I may have inadvertently 'barked up the wrong tree' in a few cases. However, the stories are based on records and are believable.

My first difficulty was assembling an accurate list of the seventy-three victims from various sources, which had different spellings of surnames and discrepancies in ages.

I was initially dependent on finding parish registers for baptisms, marriages, and burials (BMBs) on subscription websites and in archives. Civil registration of BMBs was introduced on 1 July 1837 but was not compulsory until 1874. Many parents could not afford both and avoided civil registration until it became a legal requirement; baptism was often delayed or arranged for several siblings together. All burials were in churchyards until Barnsley Cemetery opened in November 1861.

Before 1929, a couple had to be over 21 ('full age') to marry without parental consent. If they obtained permission the minimum age was 14 for boys and 12 for girls ('minor'). This seems young to us, but in the early 1800s children were working in factories and collieries by that age.

The introduction of the General Registry Office (GRO) started too late to help with most records for victims, their siblings, parents and spouses, but has been invaluable for their children. BMDs for the Barnsley area were listed under Ecclesfield district until the end of March 1850 and this covered a wider area.

The 1841 Census, taken on 6 June, is the first with personal details and the only one to include the victims. Where these have survived, some writing is illegible, addresses are vague, surnames are spelt inconsistently, ages tend to have been rounded up or down, occupations can be unreliable, birthplaces are only shown for the county and abbreviations were widely used. The 1851 Census for Barnsley suffered from water damage and many entries are no longer readable.

Unfortunately, few early records survive relating to Barnsley or Doncaster Poor Law Union and there are no Workhouse Admission Registers or Censuses for 1841 or 1851.

Wakefield Charities Coroners Notebooks only start in November 1852; they are not comprehensive with some periods missing, but those available are fascinating. I relied on contemporary newspapers for details about disasters and inquests, but the *Barnsley Chronicle* was only established in 1858.

The Principal Probate Registry was established on 12 January 1858 and keeps copies of Wills proved after 1858 in addition to Letters of Administration if intestate. It is much more difficult to find Wills prior to 1858, although it is highly unlikely that the colliery victims would have owned much to bequeath.

The South Yorkshire Miners' Association was founded in 1858 and does not have colliery archives before this.

Writing Up Material

As most victims and their families were baptised, lived, worked, got married and were buried in Barnsley town, I have usually only added the 'township' to addresses elsewhere.

I have provided names for the victims' parents, siblings, spouses and children, including those who died in childhood, whenever I have been able to identify them. The same applies to information about when individuals died and where they were buried. When telling the stories of the victims' grandchildren, I have provided more limited details unless they served in the First World War, were involved in other colliery disasters, or committed any crimes.

I have indicated where I could prove connections between families. However, quite a few surnames kept cropping up, but I could not verify links in the time available.

Where I have written 'in' or 'by' the year, this means by the Census date, which was taken on the following Sundays:

| 6 June 1841 | 30 March 1851 | 7 April 1861 | 2 April 1871 |
| 3 April 1881 | 5 April 1891 | 31 March 1901 | 2 April 1911* |

* includes total children born, how many alive and how many dead (for women)

The 1921 Census is not publicly available until 2022. As the 1931 Census was destroyed by fire during the Second World War and there was no 1941 Census, the 1939 Register, collected on Friday 29 September to produce identity cards, provides the only record between 1921 and 1951.

I have quoted many occupations from the Censuses, some of which are unfamiliar, because I wanted to add some flavour from the enumerators who completed them.

Measuringworth.com calculates relative values and the most recent year is 2019. I mostly used 'labour value' from its range, which is one of the lowest, but I have indicated if based on Retail Price Index (RPI).

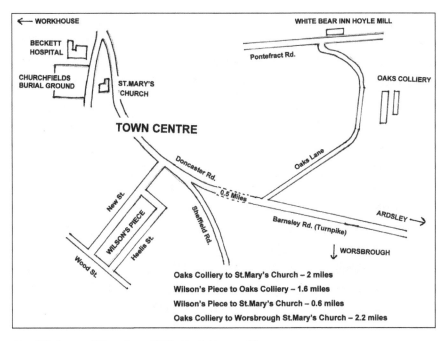

Simplified map of Barnsley c.1847. (Paul Ainsworth)

Acknowledgements

Paul Ainsworth for his constant support and encouragement
Jeff Chambers, Michael Chance, Paul Darlow, Tony Heald, Ken Keen,
    Dan Parker, Doreen Piper, Brian Rowe, Peter Shield, Steven Skelley,
    Chris Skidmore, Paul Stebbing, Steve Wyatt
Barnsley Archives, Derbyshire Archives, BMBC Bereavement Services
National Coalmining Museum, National Union of Mineworkers
The *Barnsley Chronicle* digitised newspapers, the Tasker Trust

Interpretation of the Oaks
explosion by Darren Green
(AKA L. Gold).

Websites

Ancestry, FindMyPast*, the Genealogist – subscriptions (* newspapers)
FreeBMD, GRO.gov, gov.uk/search-will-probate, cemeteries.org.uk, find a grave
TaskerTrust.co.uk
Durham Mining Museum, healeyhero.co.uk,
DVLP website for Oaks 1866 victims
Dearne Memorials Group database, Ardsley Residents Association website
Peter Higginbotham's workhouses.org.uk
Measuringworth.com
Visionofbritain.org.uk
Wikipedia and many general searches for background information

Photographs

Front Cover - "Head to Face" was embroidered by Maureen Livesey and purchased by the Author

Back Cover - both drawings of the Oaks Colliery explosion 1847 were produced for the *Illustrated London News* (Barnsley Archives)

Where the copyright of a photograph is not indicated it is the property of the Author and may not be used without permission

Ledger record of the Annual Meeting 1849. (© Barnsley Archives)

Social and Economic Background

The world in 1847 was different from today. There was no National Health Service, no welfare benefits' system or retirement pension, housing standards for poorer people were generally appalling and education was limited. The Industrial Revolution, between about 1760 and 1840, led to many working people relocating from rural areas to towns and cities in search of employment, but most lived in poverty. Families had few possessions and often lived in one room, sharing beds 'top to toe' and subsisting on meagre, unhealthy diets.

An 1842 report described typical conditions for a worker:

> This house consisted of two rooms. In the first stood a deal table, two chairs and, as a substitute for others, two large stones, a piece of iron rod for poker, a deal fender, an old corner cupboard containing two cups and odd saucers, three basins and parts of others, an old Bible, some old tracts. Upstairs were two old looms, two old bedsteads, chaff-beds, one ragged blanket, an equally ragged quilt; indeed a most miserable and wretched abode.

A collier's weekly wage for an eleven-hour shift was about 15 shillings per week; his sons might earn half that as a hurrier. Rent for a family with six children cost 2/- (2 shillings) per week, coal 1/6 and food: tea 7d (7 old pennies), coffee 5d, sugar 1/-, meat 2/4, wheatmeal 9/-, oatmeal 4/-, yeast 8d, potatoes 1/6, butter 6d, beer ½, soap 1/-. There was little spare for clothing or school fees of 2d per week.

Men had no job security and were at the mercy of employers. Factory or colliery owners took workers on when the market was good, but when it was poor, they were put on short hours or just laid off; wages were also dependent on the market and reductions inevitably led to protests

Above and below: Wellington Street housing. (© Barnsley Archives)

Wellington Street housing. (© Barnsley Archives)

and union involvement. Until John Normansell was appointed as the first miner weighman in Barnsley in 1857 to ensure miners were treated fairly, they had to accept the word of the owner's representatives.

Workers often rented their house from their employer and had to buy their own equipment and candles from them, meaning they could end up trapped in debt and unable to move to another job. Widows and orphans could find themselves homeless, dependent on relations or the much-dreaded workhouse. Working days were twelve to fourteen hours but miners could face long, unpaid, walks to the coal face to begin their shift, while being paid only for the hewed coal and not rock. There were no paid holidays so Christmas Day was a popular day for getting married.

Entertainment

Long working hours for men and endless housework and the raising of large families for women left people with little spare time. Church attendance on Sunday, the only day off work, was expected. Women spent time with supportive family and friends, while most men found camaraderie in the pub. Children could attend school until old enough to work aged 10 but this cost money; they had few opportunities to play and no equipment or games.

Health and Life Expectancy

Free access to doctors, nurses, midwives and medication was many years away. Most working families relied on old-fashioned remedies or cordials and support from friends and relations, with the workhouse infirmary as a last resort. Many diseases, easily curable today, proved fatal. Common causes of death included tuberculosis, typhus, measles, scarlet fever and cholera; outbreaks were spread by insanitary conditions, especially from communal water pumps. Many women died in childbirth and mortality rates were high for children, many dying in infancy. Even by the second half of the nineteenth century, life expectancy was only 40 years – hence my surprise at finding some victims' relations living into their 80s and even 90s.

Support for the Poor

The early nineteenth century saw various campaigns, inquiries, and legislation, most of which were intended to benefit those who had the least – but not all did. For instance, the controversial 1834 Poor Law Amendment Act came about because the old 1601 Poor Relief Act was deemed to have become too generous, allegedly supporting indolence and encouraging large families. This 'New Poor Law' led to new-style workhouses in which conditions were deliberately harsh to act as a deterrent to the 'undeserving poor'. Like many areas in the north, Barnsley initially held out against imposing such a regime but soon fell into line, with the Barnsley Union Workhouse.

The first workhouse in Barnsley for thirty 'inmates' had opened in 1736 in St Mary Place, on the site of alms-houses; Carlton parish had provision for twelve inmates. These were replaced by the new Barnsley Union Workhouse, serving an area similar to the present borough, built in Gawber Road in 1852 with a T-shaped design by Henry F. Lockwood and William Mawson. The building was extended to include a new infirmary in the 1880s and other alterations were carried out. It was renamed St Helen's Hospital in the 1930s, when its purpose changed, and the site was redeveloped as Barnsley Hospital in 1977.

Generally, people had to continue working to support themselves as the first 'old age pension' was not introduced until 1908. Some desperate people turned to crime, risking huge fines or imprisonment for even the smallest offences. Some workers belonged to benefits clubs or friendly societies, paying weekly contributions so they could call on payments in times of hardship or ill-health or to pay funeral costs.

Reform

The country was still governed by wealthy property owners for whom the poor were dispensable. This led to the Radical Movement, campaigning for reform and initially met with forceful opposition (as at the Peterloo Massacre of 1819). The 1832 Reform Act extended male suffrage only to the middle classes, hence the formation of the Chartist Movement in the 1840s, strongly supported in the north. However, it was 1918 before the right to vote was extended to all working men over 21 and some women over 30.

Edwin Chadwick's Sanitary Report of 1842 made several recommendations to improve public health, albeit on economic rather than humanitarian grounds. These were not taken up until after the cholera outbreak of 1848 and even then, the central board of health established under the first Public Health Act had limited powers and no money. Serious reform had to wait until an 1875 Act.

The first Factory Acts to improve working conditions date to the early 1800s, but only started to become effective after 1833 when the Factory Inspectorate was formed to enforce the regulations. In July 1838, disaster struck at the Husker Pit, Silkstone Common, when twenty-six children aged between 7 and 17 years drowned. This led to a Royal Commission investigation into the employment of children in mines and factories and their 1842 report painted a shocking picture of colliery conditions. Women and children, some as young as 5, laboured in the dark for up to fourteen hours a day, earning minimal wages while subject to dangers, physical and moral. The 1842 Mines and Collieries Act prohibited any females and children under 10 from working underground, though some unscrupulous owners did not enforce this. Early attempts to establish Trade Unions for mineworkers failed because of fierce opposition from powerful and ruthless owners. It was not until 1850 that the first safety legislation was passed and it was many years before this became truly effective.

Barnsley in the 1800s

The population of Barnsley district increased dramatically between 1801 (21,363) and 1911 (176,442) as the linen weaving, coal mining and glass making industries developed. In 1841, the population stood at 46,980 and there were 2,380 inhabited houses in the town itself (with 504 more by 1851).

Early manufacturing in the district focused on wire and nails but this was overtaken by the linen trade, introduced in 1774 by William Wilson, a Quaker from Cheshire. Workers wove at home until invention of the power loom around 1842 which enabled one worker to operate four or six looms and saw a move to factory operations. However, the industry was soon superseded by coal mining and glass manufacture.

Ardsley aerial view. (Courtesy of the Tasker Trust)

12

Mining had developed gradually from the late 1600s, and the earliest recorded explosion of gas in a coal mine was on 11 July 1672, resulting in the death of one man. It expanded rapidly with improvements in different means of transporting coal to markets. The Barnsley Canal opened c.1800 and its route, from the town centre to the Aire and Calder Navigation east of Wakefield with a branch north-west to Barnby Colliery, passed through many rich coalfields. New methods of road construction were pioneered by Thomas Telford and John Loudon McAdam, and Barnsley was connected eventually to the railway network in 1851.

Ardsley, Stairfoot and Hoyle Mill

Ardsley was originally an agricultural village, with farms, mills and quarries, within the parish of Darfield. The Dearne and Dove Canal, completed in 1804 and linked to the Barnsley Canal and South Yorkshire Navigation, facilitated growth during the Industrial Revolution. In 1801 the population of Ardsley was 401; this had nearly quadrupled to 1,528 by 1851, when the South Yorkshire Railway arrived at Stairfoot, then again to 6,000 by 1900.

Linen was the first industry to take hold and this needed damp conditions for the flax. Others spread along the canal banks: collieries, tan yards, lime kilns, bleach works, tar distillery, brickworks and glassworks. Just over the border in Barnsley were Beevor Bobbin Works and Barnsley Brewery.

The facilities in Ardsley increased with its population, being well served by pubs, churches and chapels. Some victims' relations managed inns or beer-houses, which provided the focus for socialising; they are a useful landmark for locating addresses. There were more chapels than churches, but the main ceremonies of baptisms, weddings and funerals took place in Church of England premises: All Saints in Darfield, St Mary's in Barnsley town centre, then Christ Church from 1841.

The first school was provided because John Micklethwaite left £30 in 1753 (worth £57,560 today) for a schoolmaster. Ardsley National School opened in 1840 and was replaced in 1910 by the Board School. Kendray Fever (Isolation) Hospital opened in 1890; Stairfoot suffered a typhoid fever outbreak early November 1875. Burials were in churchyards until Barnsley Cemetery opened in 1861.

Three postcards with aerial views over Barnsley centre, the top two from Locke Park and the bottom one from Town End. (Author's collection)

The Doncaster to Saltersbrook Turnpike Road ran through the centre of these communities and its replacement by the dual carriageway, Doncaster Road, led to the destruction of many old properties. Workers' cottages without bathrooms were considered slums and cleared in the 1930s and 1950s. Other historic buildings have been lost and Ardsley House was demolished in 2018, despite objections.

14

The 1842 Royal Commission Report

This referred to the following collieries in Barnsley:

Messrs Day and Twibell's at Mount Osbourne
Messrs Hopwood and Jackson's Barnsley New Colliery
Messrs Traviss and Horsfall's
The Executives of Mr Samuel Thorpe's Gawber Colliery
Messrs Micklethwaite and Co's
Messrs Charlesworth's
Mr Clarke's two in Silkstone
Messrs Field, Cooper and Co's two in Stainborough
Mr Thomas Wilson's Kexborough Colliery at Darton
Gin Pit at Mapplewell.

Drawing of a typical colliery in the 1842 Royal Commission Report. (© National Coalmining Museum)

Testimony from Interviews c.1840

Interviews with owners, managers and workers shared some fascinating details about working conditions, although they were not always truthful.

William Hopwood (No. 80) explained that children usually began work in the mine aged 8 years as Trappers, starting work between 6 and 7am and finishing between 3 and 5pm; they were Hurriers at 10 years then Getters at 16.

> In most of the pits round Barnsley, girls are employed in trapping and hurrying; they do the same work as the boys; and leave the pits at 16 or 17 years old, they are generally employed by their own parents and under their own control. I think no bad result ensues to their morals or their health. They generally work in boys' clothes, but not always.

(Trappers were paid 3 shillings a week, Hurriers 10/- while Colliers could earn 3/9 per day after paying Hurriers).

Sarah Gooder (No. 116) aged 8, admitted to being scared while having to work as a Trapper in the dark; she would sing to herself on occasions when she had a light but was too afraid without.

Mr George Traviss (No. 84) stated that,

> hurrying is tolerably hard work... Our present corves are six and a half cwt when full, but we are going to make them larger, when they will weigh nine cwt. [One hundredweight was probably double the weight of a 10-year-old child, who might have to push twenty corves a day over a considerable distance; the corves at Gawber Colliery weighed 12.5 cwt]. I do not think the children are over-worked so as to hurt them. They always appear to me to be very cheerful and run and play about when they come out of the pit in the evening.... Colliers' children are generally well fed … they take their dinner with them, they bring out great pieces of bread in their hands and meat or cheese.

However, <u>Maria Gooder</u> (No. 112) aged 12, disagreed:

> It is hard work and tires me a good deal in my back mostly.... It is very cold often.... We have dry bread for dinner and nothing else. We don't have cheese or butter nor meat. There is water in the pit but we don't sup it. Sometimes the men let us have a little beer, but not always.... When we come up we go and have our dinner, sometimes it's meat and potatoes, and sometimes pudding... I don't like being in the pit. I am tired and afraid.

<u>A collier</u> (No. 94) confirmed that workers got an hour for their lunch (unpaid) during their twelve-hour shift as the engine stopped.

> It would be very awkward for children to come out before the men. It would be too much trouble to draw them up and down twice as often, and there would be more chance of accidents.... Sometimes the pits work at night but not generally. The children get but little schooling.

<u>Eliza Coats</u> (No. 115) aged 11, said that she had never been to school because she had no shoes and, like many of the children tested, had little understanding of religion: 'I think God made the world, but I don't know where God is. I never heard of Jesus Christ.'

<u>Mrs Fern</u> (No. 144) a collier's wife who had herself worked in a pit for eleven years, explained that her stepdaughter Ann worked in a colliery because she had been unable to get her into service. Ann had not attended Sunday School that winter because, 'I wanted her to stay at home and learn some jobs at house ... she can read pretty well at Testament ... Ann can knit very well and sew middling.'

<u>The agent for Gawber Colliery</u> (No. 118) reckoned that only three of his men out of fifty could sign his own name.

There were mixed opinions about whether girls should be allowed to work in pits but some men felt very strongly that it was wrong.

<u>John Thorneley</u> (No. 96) JP with forty years' experience in the management of collieries, condemned it as 'a most awfully demoralising practice. The youths of both sexes work often in a half-naked state and the passions are excited before they arrive at puberty. Sexual intercourse decidedly frequently occurs in consequence. Cases of bastardy also frequently occur.'

<u>Dr Michael Thomas Sadler</u> (No. 139) surgeon with eighteen years' experience in Barnsley, had come across diseases of the heart associated with the 'violent exertions' of miners, who looked pale through absence of natural light and did not have long lives, although they generally lived well. Their children looked strong but he felt light was 'essential to perfect health', and 'ventilation of pits of the greatest importance to health'. Dr Sadler stated: 'It is a brutalising practice for women to be in collieries, the effect on their morals is very bad.... It is impossible to prevent accidents altogether, but they might be much diminished with more care and prudence.' Dr Sadler subsequently became the Medical Officer of Health for Barnsley and, in his report in 1866, he highlighted 'the deplorable standards of housing and of sanitation in large areas of the south and south western parts of the town', with 'the relatively high death rate among tenants of the crowded courts' and 'the highly objectionable back to back houses'; he advocated the building of public baths.

<u>Another Surgeon</u> (No. 99) with twenty-four years' experience was aware of a number of women who continued to work in pits after getting married and even when pregnant, close to confinement.

Illustration of female colliers in the 1842 Royal Commission Report. (Courtesy of the National Coalmining Museum)

A meeting of Yorkshire Coal Owners was held in May 1841 to discuss the recommendations of the Royal Commission. They protested that any legislation and the appointment of an Inspector were a 'violation of every maxim of civil and commercial freedom'. They believed that keeping a register of children with medical and educational entries would cost them time and money, they objected to keeping records that could incriminate them and the 'vexatious system of espionage which is fundamentally interwoven with any provision of the Act'. They 'deny that there is anything in the nature of the employment in coal or iron mines that affects the health, since in this respect miners may be favourably contrasted with the general population', but they conceded to the exclusion of females and boys under 8 from working underground.

The 1842 Report also provided details of pay rates in Yorkshire: (1 shilling is worth £40 today) Trappers received 6d a day; Hurriers aged 11 years old earned 5 shillings a week, aged 14+ 8 shillings, and aged 17+ 12 shillings; men's wages varied according to 'their industry and strength', but a young able-bodied man earned between 20 to 25 shillings a week. Colliery owners and managers took advantage of their employees by operating a 'truck system' whereby workers received at least some of their pay in tokens or vouchers that had to be spent in their 'tommy shop', restricting choice and competition.

The White Bear Inn at Hoyle Mill, where inquests were held. (Courtesy of the Tasker Trust)

The Oaks (Ardsley Main) Colliery and 1847 Explosion

The land was owned by Richard Micklethwaite of Ardsley and the first colliery shaft was sunk in 1824. Deeper shafts were sunk in 1838/9 at great expense to reach the Barnsley Seam. By 1847, Ardsley Main Colliery was owned by William Micklethwaite and let to Messrs Firth Barber & Company. Repairs and structural alterations were carried out after the 1847 explosion and another shaft was sunk. Ardsley Main became the Oaks by 1851, known as the Old Oaks after the 1866 explosion.

The mine was renowned for having areas where inflammable gas (firedamp or methane) accumulated and, while workers were not supposed to use naked flames nearby, this was not adequately enforced and the Oaks Colliery was notorious for its number of accidents.

The Explosion on Friday 5 March 1847

Owing to the depth of the coal seam being worked, the Oaks Colliery had two shafts, one that was used for winding men, boys, and materials, and the other for ventilation. A fire had damaged the headgear of the ventilation shaft on 4 December 1845 and repair work was underway there in March 1847. The terrific explosion occurred at about 3pm, when the ninety-five men and boys working underground or in the air shaft were approaching the end of their shift.

Reports in contemporary newspapers described vividly the huge explosion that 'shook the whole neighbourhood like an earthquake ... a blaze of fire arose from the pit to a considerable height above the head-gearing and was followed by a dense body of sulphurous smoke', 'resembling the eruption of a volcano', 'smoke, dust, bricks, coals and timber were thrown up into the air from the mouth of the pit, to the height of 30 or 40 yards'. 'Frantic wives and weeping children' rushed towards the pit head, to be

The explosion and the pit head in the *Illustrated London News*. (Courtesy of Barnsley Archives)

joined by thousands of people from Barnsley and surrounding villages in addition to miners from miles around who wanted to 'render assistance to their unfortunate brethren.' They had to wait to descend until it was assessed as safe and the partition between the two air shafts had been rebuilt.

At the time, this was one of the biggest colliery disasters in the country with its huge loss of life. Seventy-three victims were killed either by 'choke damp' (a suffocating gas, usually carbon dioxide) or burns and injuries resulting from the explosion. There were thirty-one boys, aged from 10 to 18, and forty-two men, the oldest of whom was 50. Several families lost more than one member.

Some detailed accounts of the tragedy published in newspapers included gruesome details of the miners trapped underground, the escape of some survivors and the difficult recovery of the bodies, many 'scarcely identifiable' because of burns. It had a huge impact on families involved and their community because they knew each other well.

The names of twelve of the nineteen survivors were mentioned and some of them, plus Michael Haigh, were connected to victims or referred to by the Colliers Relief Committee (underlined):

William Ayre	Edward Burrows	William Charlesworth
William Cooke	William Drury	William Hare
William Hewitt	Bernard Morgan	William Peach
Joseph Simonds	Thomas Steel	Bernard Wogan
George Yates		

Top of the shaft in the *Illustrated London News*. (Courtesy of Barnsley Archives)

The *Illustrated London News* sent an artist to Barnsley to produce drawings of the scene to accompany its description of the explosion, the aftermath and its cause, in its edition of 13 March 1847. 'On Tuesday morning the pit was very full of sulphur, and in the evening it was impossible to descend. At that time there remained in the pit three individuals, Abraham Matthews, John Wroe, and William Walton.' Abraham and William had been working close to James Whiteley and his two sons; they all perished.

J.D. Barker esquire, deputy coroner, opened the inquest at the nearby White Bear Inn, Hoyle Mill, on Monday 8 March. The jury were sworn in and viewed about sixty-four bodies of the victims who had been brought out, before adjourning to the Court House in Barnsley. The names of the fifteen men on the jury were listed in some of the newspapers with a transcript of the inquest:

Edward Bromley	Jonathan Carneley	John Gelder
John Harrison	Timothy Hepworth	W.J. Hindle
George Johnson	Rev. Alfred Lambert	Edward Parker (foreman)
Rodgers	John Scales	George Scorah
James Taylor	William Wood	William Wordsworth, junior

The inquest continued the following day to view four more bodies brought out overnight so that they might be interred without delay. It was then adjourned to 16 March so that 'the mine might be viewed and other evidence elicited'. After listening to the testimony of managers, survivors and experts brought in to inspect the pit, it became clear that the explosion was caused by William Walton using a candle, but the verdict was 'Accidental Death'. The jury added 'that efficient regulations are not enforced in the district to prevent the use of naked lights in those parts of coal mines where inflammable gas is known to exist', and they forwarded their verdict to the government in the hope that it would review the regulations to prevent such accidents recurring.

Most of the funerals took place on the afternoon of Monday 8 March. Forty-five men and boys were conveyed – some carried in the usual way and others on a dray – in a mile-long procession to St Mary the Virgin's Church in Barnsley town centre. 'Two of the graves were made to hold about 18 bodies each. There were likewise two small graves, for the remaining 8. ... The other bodies were conveyed to the church yards at Ardsley, Worsbro', Darton, and Tankersley.'

Parish registers confirm that the victims were buried in churchyards at St Mary the Virgin, Barnsley (45), Christ Church, Ardsley (14), All Saints, Darton (4), St George, Barnsley (3), St Mary, Worsbrough (3), St Peter, Tankersley (2), All Saints, Darfield (1) and St Paul, Monk Bretton (1).

The parish registers for St Mary's highlight the victims by the addition of two vertical lines at the side of the pages, and a separate typed list of all seventy-three killed in 'Explosion at Oaks Pit, Ardsley' was attached. The Vicar of All Saints' Church, Darton, wrote underneath the four names in the parish registers: 'The above from more of the numbers of the unfortunate 73 persons who lost their lives in the Oaks coal mine at Ardsley on the fifth Inst: Friday last about three o'clock in the afternoon.'

The churchyard was extended in 1823 and closed in 1859. After a period of neglect, it was tidied up in the 1970s with undamaged headstones being laid round the edge of four lawns in what became Churchfields Peace Gardens. Noticeboards in the public gardens explain the history of the site, there is a plan of surviving headstones and a list of individuals interred; their bodies remain here.

Newspapers claimed that the colliery proprietors had 'done all they could to comfort and console the widows and children of the deceased and defrayed the expenses of the coffins and interments'. There was no legal requirement for colliery owners then to provide any financial assistance to their employees following accidents at work.

Funeral at St Mary's in the *Illustrated London News*. (Courtesy of Barnsley Archives)

The Colliers' Relief Fund and its Administration

The South Yorkshire Miners' Association, founded in 1858, fought for mineworkers and their families to receive compensation from colliery owners following an injury or death at work. Before this, any allowances or funeral costs depended on whether workers could afford to join one of the many 'Secret' (Friendly) Societies in existence at the time.

One that was mentioned in the newspapers was the Ancient Order of Free Gardeners, which was established in Scotland in the mid-seventeenth century before spreading to England; it had similarities to Freemasonry. Three others referred to for later disasters included the Oddfellows, Ancient Order of Foresters and the Ancient Order of Romans. The Barnsley Cordwainers' Society was established in 1747 and is the oldest surviving Friendly Society; its membership included mineworkers early on.

The only 'safety net' for the destitute was the punitive Poor Law and the workhouse.

In 1847, it was agreed that a Public Subscription Fund should be set up, primarily to provide financial support for the colliers' widows and dependent children, whom they called 'orphans'.

The ledger donated to Barnsley Archives is a rare and precious record to have survived for 170 years and it allows us an insight into the administration of the Colliers' Relief Fund. It contains the minutes of the Committee for a period of nearly five years, from its inception in March 1847 until the end of 1851. Unfortunately, there are no further minutes from January 1852 and the last entry is for a special meeting called on 25 February 1857 to discuss the Lundhill Colliery disaster.

About seventy local dignitaries, comprising vicars, colliery owners, solicitors and other notable people, were named in the ledger and from

Illustration of female colliers at Wigan Collieries. (Author's Collection)

these the Subscription Committee was formed. Edward Newman, a well-known and highly respected solicitor, was elected secretary of the committee from the first meeting and he took minutes for all of them. Attendance varied by other committee members, several of whom had given testimony to the Royal Commission in 1839.

Members of the Colliers Relief Committee

Chairman: Edward Pearson Tee
Treasurer: Samuel Linley
Secretary: Edward Newman, solicitor

Members:

Thomas Allen	Charles Bailey	William Bailey
Edward Brady	Edward Bromley	David Byrd
Joseph Canter	Thomas Cope	P. Dearshale
William Hopwood, colliery owner	Robert Ibeson	James Ibeson
Richard Inns	Francis Johnson	Edward Parker

C.I. Mence, solicitor for proprietors	John Ostcliffe	Richard Pybus
Joseph Parkinson	George Pitt	Charles Tee
John Shaw	James Steel	
John Tyas	John Whitworth	

Revd John Waters Banks
Revd Henry Joseph Cooke
Revd C. Maxwell
Revd R.G. Micklethwaite   Christ Church, Ardsley
Revd R Readow
Revd R.E. Roberts   St George's Church, Barnsley
Revd Tiley
Revd Robert Willan   St Mary's Church, Barnsley

The committee made considerable efforts to collect money for the fund, dividing up Barnsley and the surrounding area and nominating 'Gentlemen' to solicit donations. They sent subscription forms to 'Banks in the West Riding of the County of York – to the Dudley & West Bromwich Banking Co. at Bromwich, and to the Mayor of Newcastle – and that one be left at the Royal Hotel & one at the Kings Head in this Town'; they also made a direct approach to Queen Victoria, her mother the Dowager Queen, Prince Albert, the Archbishop of York and the Bishop of Ripon. They reported back to Mr Micklethwaite, owner, and Messrs Firth & Barber, lessees, that their contributions were inadequate.

An amount of £2,100 was pledged to the fund (worth £1.7 million) but, according to an article in the *Leeds Mercury* on 29 January 1848 affixed to the ledger, only £1,982 14s 9d appears to have been collected. The sum of £1,200 was invested in the Midland Railway Company on debentures bearing interest at five per cent, with the balance in Barnsley Banking Company.

At their meeting on 29 March 1847, the Committee 'Resolved that the Names of all Parties subscribing £20 (worth £16,000) and upwards be advertised three times in two successive weeks in the *Times News Manchester Guardian* and the *Doncaster Gazette'*.

Initially, the beneficiaries were thirty-four widows and fifty-seven children, of whom five were orphans, in addition to three surviving miners who were injured. The Committee used their discretion to

Above and below: Postcards of women mineworkers in Wigan. (Author's collection)

include other relations, such as parents who were dependent on wages from children killed. Children were only supported until they reached 10, unless there were exceptional circumstances, and they had to attend school. They were then expected to go into service or become an apprentice, at which stage they were provided with an 'outfit' (see chapters for Day page 87 & Hartley page 140).

The numerical and alphabetical register has not survived, but reference numbers were noted against some names in the minutes. The cash book with details of payments has been lost.

At each Annual Meeting a statement included the number of beneficiaries, total payments made during the year and the remaining balance.

Date	Widows	Orphans (aged 1 – 10)	Payments	Fund
January 1848	34	57	Not known	Not known
January 1849	21	52	£307 8s 6d	£1,350 1s 0d
January 1850	14	40	£263 1s 3d	£1,149 16s 9d
January 1851	12	37	£195 4s 5d	£1,005 15s 4d
January 1852	6	32	£174 1s 7d	£831 13s 9d (net of interest)

In the first year, £15 13s 5d was spent on administration:

> printing – £8 0s 5d
> lithography for circulars etc – £1 16s 6d
> stamps and carriage of parcels – £5 16s 6d.
> (£1 is now worth £800).

Christmas Dinner for 'participants in the Charity' in 1847 cost £5 11s 5d, of which 10d was paid to Mrs Batty (matron of the workhouse) 'for her trouble' in preparing the meal. The meal of roast beef and plum pudding was provided in the large room at the Court House for the widows and children. Rev. Maxwell said grace and Rev. R.E. Roberts of St George's Church addressed the women and children after dinner. The children were given a spiced bun as they left.

The ledger does not record what the initial payments were for widows and children, but on 24 June 1847 they resolved that,

> the allowances to Widows be reduced to two shillings per week [worth £80] and to Children to one shilling per week. That it be imperative upon the Mothers of Children between the ages of three and ten, except under peculiar circumstances to send them to School and that the Expense of so doing be paid by the Committee.

At the Annual Meeting of the Committee on 28 December 1848 it was recommended that 'after the 21st day of June next the Payments to Widows be reduced to one shilling per Week preparatory to its being discontinued altogether at the next general Annual Meeting.' They confirmed this at their General Meeting on 11 January 1850 because they believed the widows 'are all now in positions to be able to do without it, but more especially because they deem the Children to be the first objects of the Charity.' However, the Report to the Annual Meeting on 27 December 1851 stated that the allowance of 1/- per week had been continued and it was agreed at this meeting that it should be continued for another year. It is not known when the payments ceased other than if widows died, got married again or 'misbehaved'.

The Committee was powerful and comprised wealthy men. Their disapproval of the behaviour of some of the widows led to loss of financial support. On 22 April 1848, they 'Resolved – that in consequence of Reports unfavourable to the Characters of Mrs [X etc] that the Allowance to them and their families be suspended.' On 4 May 1848, they,

> Resolved unanimously – That the Allowance to the Widows who have by their conduct rendered themselves so truly undeserving of sympathy be wholly withdrawn but that the Payments be continued to their Children on its being proved to the Committee that they regularly attend some School – that the fortnight's pay to the Children which was withheld on the 22nd Ult. be paid up to-morrow – and that the same course be adopted with regard to all Parties who shall grossly misconduct themselves.

The back of Graham Ibbeson's Oaks 1866 sculpture.

There is no explanation in the ledger for the discontinuance of minutes of meetings. At the end of 1851, £831 remained in the fund (worth £700,000) and payments were ongoing to six widows and thirty-two orphans.

The *Barnsley Chronicle* reported on 5 January 1867:

> in the opinion of this Committee [1866 explosion], it is desirable that a permanent fund should be raised to be invested in the names of trustees, for the relief of sufferers by Colliery Accidents in South Yorkshire district. That the sum appropriated to the South Yorkshire district out of the Hartley fund, the existing surplus of the Oaks fund of 1847, and any surplus which may arise from the present Oaks Colliery subscription be available for the above purpose. That the coal owners and miners in the district be invited to cooperate in furthering this object; and that this resolution be communicated to the Lord Lieutenant with a view to securing his sanction and support.

The Hartley Colliery disaster in 1862 in Northumberland killed 205 miners and public donations were extremely generous. A large surplus not paid out in relief was invested, resulting in people's reluctance to make donations for new disasters, such as the 1863 Edmunds Main explosion. The committee agreed that the surplus should be used towards relief in other disasters. However much the surplus was in the Oaks 1847 fund, it may have been used for the 1866 disaster.

Interviews with Key Barnsley Residents in 1839 for the 1842 Commission

Thomas Wilson, owner of three pits, advocated the introduction of a general club for collieries in the district; he had introduced a scheme for his own workers in 1833 and it was still well supported in 1839. Members earning less than 7 shillings a week paid ½d per week and received 3/6 if unable to work because of illness or injury, whereas those earning more than 7/- paid 1d and received 7/- each week – one shilling in 1833 was worth about £43 in 2019. During the first seven years, membership varied from 107 to 270 each year; a total of £334 was collected of which £321 was paid out and there were 261 chargeable accidents.

Edward Newman, solicitor, had explained in 1839 that he was familiar with seeing colliery workers but did not know any; he was concerned about the number of girls employed and described seeing them,

> washing themselves naked much below the waist as I passed their doors ... talking and chatting with any men who happen to be there with the utmost unconcern.... The moral effect of the system must be exceedingly bad. They dress, however, so well after their work and on Sundays that it is impossible to recognise them... There is a great deal of slang and loud talk between the lads and girls as they pass along the street ... Their dress when they come out of the pit is a kind of skull-cap which hides all the hair, trousers, without stockings, and thick wooden clogs: their waists are covered... A general prohibition is indispensably necessary to this practice.

John Ostcliffe, registrar of Barnsley district for twenty years, confirmed that,

> children in the pits earn the highest wages but work harder than the weavers' children. I think the collier class upon the whole more healthy than the weavers. The colliers are, however, not more long-lived, which I attribute generally to harder labour and to chronic diseases arising from 40 to 50 years of age. They suffer chiefly from asthma, rheumatism etc arising from their subterranean employment. The weavers are more affected by consumption. The colliers drink a good deal of malt liquor [ale] ...I am aware that girls working in pits have left them to walk the streets, but so have weavers' girls become prostitutes, and I cannot say which are the worst.

John Micklethwaite, proprietor of the Oaks Colliery, entrusted

> ... the entire management of the pit to an agent; and I merely come and ride over here as an amusement, and do not interfere with the pit at all. The coroner's inquest will give the best information about the rope being broken, when two men were killed about the 6th of January. It is impossible to take any precautions against such accidents. There is not a doubt that the rope broke through the frost; and there is no doubt the rope was sufficiently strong. I have never been in the pit and never will go. We have no children under eight or nine years, as far as I know. I don't know whether there are lasses or not working in the pit, but I must refer you for all information to the underground steward.

William Duckworth (No. 120) who had been underground steward for about six months, had testified that no females worked in the Oaks Colliery and that the boys got little schooling. There had been no explosion since he had started and, although there was much black damp, there was 'not so much danger with it, because when the lights are put out the men leave the place'. He was there when the rope broke at 3pm and he explained what had happened to the two victims, who had

Oaks Colliery explosion 1866 in the *Illustrated London News*. (Courtesy of Barnsley Archives)

been ascending the shaft with a full corve: 'One was killed on the spot, the other lived until a quarter past twelve at night; they were half way up the shaft when the rope broke, and the shaft 115 yards deep.'

Revd Richard Earnshaw Roberts, Vicar of St George's Church, was concerned at the deficient education of the children of miners and weavers who were working. Few children attended church or Sunday School, which he put down to 'general indifference of the parents' and 'early employment of their children', resulting in an 'absence of moral example' as well as religious instruction.

Revd Richard Willan, Chief Minister of St Mary's Church for twenty-two years, felt that the morals of the working classes in Barnsley were 'in an appalling state', weavers and miners, but that the migratory workers were worse than local inhabitants. 'The master-sin amongst the youths is that of gambling', even on a Sabbath, followed by 'promiscuous sexual intercourse', which was induced by families having to share beds:

I have known a family of father and mother and 12 children, some of them grown-up, sleeping in a kind of sacking and straw bed, reaching from one side of the room to the other, along the floor.

Then drinking ensues and this is the vortex that draws in every other sin. Few of the colliers are habitual drunkards, and their houses are generally better, and they have good nutritious food. In these respects the colliers are better off than the weavers.... A master-weaver who has a four or six loom shop and can work most of his looms by his own family, has a better income than any of the clergy in this town.

Rev. Willan also expressed concern at the children's lack of education and attendance at Sunday School; sometimes because they had no suitable clothes. He was aware of some men, too 'aged or crippled' to work, who acted as peripatetic teachers visiting families to carry out some basic instruction for a livelihood and he wished that the church had the means of visiting, since 'Those who most need our advice and admonitions never come near us at all.'

Corves near St Mary's church

Information about other Relevant Colliery Disasters and Accidents

Some victims and survivors of the 1847 explosion had relations who suffered accidents or were killed in Barnsley collieries prior to this disaster and afterwards. Details were reported in contemporary newspapers and I have included any relevant information about individuals in the appropriate chapters. This chapter provides some general information about disasters referred to in the ledger or relevant to victims' families.

The 1842 Report on the Condition and Treatment of Children Employed in Mines and Collieries was written following a three-year investigation for the Royal Commission. This was established because Queen Victoria had been distressed to learn that twenty-six children had drowned in Huskar Pit on 4 July 1838, following a four-day unpaid holiday to celebrate her coronation. It listed,

> …the chief accidents to which persons employed in coal mines are exposed:
>
> 1. Falling down the shaft, whether of a pit in work, or of one now abandoned.
> 2. The falling of something on the head while descending or ascending the shaft.
> 3. The breaking of the rope or chain.
> 4. The falling of something from the roof of the mine.
> 5. The being drawn over the pulley and dashed to the ground or precipitated down the shaft from the neglect of the engine-man.
> 6. Being crushed by a mass of coal unexpectedly falling while hewers are 'undergoing'.

7. Suffocation by carbonic acid gas.
8. Suffocation or burning, or both, from the explosion of carburetted hydrogen gas.
9. Drowning from the sudden breaking in of water from old workings.
10. Minor accidents from falls in the mine, and injuries from the horses and carriages.

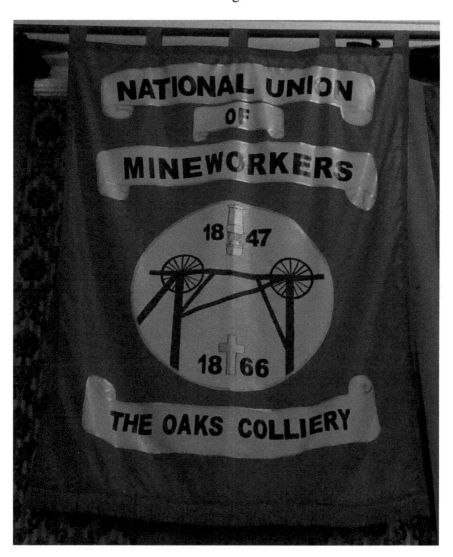

Oaks Colliery banner in the Miners' Hall. (Courtesy of the NUM)

Hopwood's Colliery, Barnsley, Explosion on 22 February 1842

This colliery was near the town centre; four girls were killed, including:

Mary Day, daughter of Peter Day and sister of John Day, victims in 1847.

Darley Main Colliery, Worsbrough Dale, Explosion on 29 January 1847

(Owned by G. Jarrett.) Six men were killed by smoke suffocation when coal caught fire underground.

John Gilberthorpe was brother of George and Joseph Gilberthorpe, victims in 1847.

Darley Main Colliery, Worsbrough Dale, Explosion on 24 January 1849

(Owned by G. Jarrett). This tragedy led to the deaths of seventy-five men and boys, leaving thirty-one widows and fifty-five children, with twenty-seven survivors of the 107 miners at work. Most victims died from serious burns and injuries, making identification difficult, rather than after-damp (a toxic mixture of gases including carbon monoxide and carbon dioxide). Bodies were taken to local homes or nearby pubs for inspection prior to the inquest, which was opened on 26 January by Coroner Thomas Badger at the Masons Arms. Most of the funerals took place on the next day and most victims were interred in an unmarked mass grave in Worsbrough churchyard. The report of the Inspector of Mines provided details of the cause of the explosion and recommendations for prevention in future. There was insufficient evidence to charge anyone with criminal negligence, but they felt 'the ventilation had not been managed with all the care and skill that the circumstances of the colliery demanded', especially because a similar explosion had occurred in February 1847 in which six people had died.

The 1847 Committee met on 25 January 1849 and agreed to offer £50 to William Newman Esq. of Darley Hall (a solicitor and older brother of

Edward Newman, secretary) towards immediate relief of survivors and victims' widows and children. The Committee subsequently reported that this amount had been declined because a public subscription fund had been well supported; Queen Victoria and Prince Albert, as well as the Queen Dowager, respectively contributed £25, Earl Fitzwilliam £50, and F.W.T. Vernon Wentworth £100 (£25 is now worth £20,250).

The *Leeds Intelligencer* noted that: 'Several of the sufferers are those who escaped the disastrous explosion which occurred on the 5th of March 1847, at the Oaks.'

Relations of 1847 Victims:

Amos Harper was a first cousin of John Harper and brother-in-law of John Riley.

Edward Billington and **William Billington** were brothers of George Billington.

Oaks Colliery Accident on 10 September 1849

William Johnson was killed, husband of Sarah, widow of George Billington, victim in 1847.

Oaks Colliery Explosion on 9 June 1851

The ledger recorded that the request from James Marshall, colliery manager, for the widows of the three men killed to be added to the list for the 1847 fund was refused on 11 July 1851. Two of the three victims were married, one being:

Thomas Billington, brother of George Billington, victim in 1847.

Lundhill Colliery, Wombwell, Explosion on 19 February 1857

This disaster resulted in the deaths of 189 men and boys, aged from 10 to 59; it also left ninety widows and 220 children. Fire raged underground rendering it unsafe for rescuers to remove bodies for several months; four were never found. 185 bodies were interred in a mass grave in All Saints' churchyard, Darfield, marked by a memorial obelisk with a dedication that ends: 'PREPARE TO MEET THY GOD'. The inquest found that the mine was inadequately ventilated, allowing a build-up of firedamp (methane), and safety rules were not properly enforced to prevent the use of candles. Without sufficient evidence to pinpoint the cause, the jury returned a verdict of accidental death rather than criminal negligence. A special disaster fund was established to which both Queen Victoria and Prince Albert made substantial donations.

The 1847 Committee met on 25 February 1857 and agreed that if any application were made for relief, they should await the outcome of their public appeal, when they would consider it favourably if insufficient funds were raised.

Old Silkstone (Higham) Colliery Explosion on 15 February 1860

(Owned by Messrs Charlesworth). Thirteen men and boys lost their lives, eleven underground 'charred and scarcely recognisable', with two succumbing to injuries after being brought to the surface.

John Wilson, husband of Martha Steel, widow of Joseph Steel, victim in 1847.

Joseph Wilson, John's son.

Henry Wilson, John's brother; his son was injured badly but survived.

Wombwell Main Colliery Accident on 29 September 1865

In a 'freak' accident, the wire rope used for hauling corves up the shaft, inspected that morning, broke, struck the banksman on the head and dragged him down the shaft.

William Henry Banks, brother of Charles Haigh, a victim in 1847.

Mount Osborne Colliery Accident on 13 April 1866

(Owned by William Day [see chapter for Buckley page 78].) Two brothers were killed by a fall of coal in No. 1 Pit.

Charles Gardner and **James Gardner,** brothers of Henry Gardner, victim in 1847.

Oaks Colliery Explosion on 12 December 1866

The first huge explosion occurred at 1pm on 12 December followed by two more early the next morning. Fire raged underground and 361 men and boys were killed, including twenty-seven volunteer rescuers. Twenty-one victims were brought out of the pit alive, but most died soon afterwards. Victims were difficult to identify because of horrific burns, being crushed and losing limbs. There were 167 widows, 366 children under 12 and a significant number of parents supported by sons. They received relief from a public subscription fund of about £48,000 (worth over £30 million). It was the worst colliery disaster in the UK until more miners were killed in Wales in 1913; it remains the worst in England.

The inquest was opened by Coroner Thomas Taylor on 14 December at the White Bear Inn in Hoyle Mill, before proceeding to the Court House in Barnsley. Mining experts from around the country visited to inspect underground and the Yorkshire Miners' Association was involved. The verdict was not conclusive and petitions were sent to the government requesting an inquiry. This resulted eventually in the 1872 Coal Mines Act.

Children of the victims were given a special Oaks Bible, and several commemorative ceramic items, such as mugs, teapots and bowls, were created with images of the disaster. A memorial to the victims, paid for by public subscription, was erected in 1879 in Christ Church churchyard, where thirty-five were interred. Samuel Joshua Cooper donated money for a memorial to the rescuers in 1913 and there is a stained-glass window in St Thomas' Church, Worsbrough, in memory of Thomas Parkin Jeffcock, a colliery engineer.

Graham Ibbeson's Oaks Colliery Explosion 1866 memorial. (Author's collection)

Barnsley artist Graham Ibbeson created the magnificent sculpture to commemorate the 150th anniversary in 2016. This stands near St Mary's Church with the woman facing the site of the Oaks Colliery.

Explosion at the Oaks Colliery in 1866 in the *Illustrated London News*. (Courtesy of Barnsley Archives)

Relations of 1847 Victims

Peter Day, son of Peter Day and brother of John Day.

John Everett, husband of Mary Ann Scales, son-in-law of William Scales.

John Harper, nephew of John Harper and John Riley.

Walter Hazle, son of Elizabeth and Robert Hazle.

James Rayner, husband of Elizabeth, widow of Robert Hazle.

James Rayner junior, son of James and Elizabeth Rayner.

Matthew Scales, son of William Scales.

Ephraim Sellers, father of Ephraim junior who married Fanny, sister of George Parker.

Thomas Walton, son of William Walton, brother-in-law of John Riley.

Henry Wilby, husband of Jane, widow of William Scales.

Winter: John, Thomas, Duncombe (Duncan), Joseph, William (sons of William) and **Henry** (son of Benjamin) were all cousins of Ezra Winter.

Haigh, John and Matthew, brothers of Charles Haigh, helped with the rescue and gave evidence.

Swaithe Main Colliery, Worsbrough, Explosion on 6 December 1875

(Owned by Mitchell, Bartholomew, Tyas and Company, with Edmunds Main and Mitchell Main Collieries in Worsbrough.) Swaithe Main was under the management of Joseph Mitchell junior, eldest son of Joseph Mitchell, senior partner, when the explosion of methane gas occurred. The disaster resulted in the deaths of 143 men and boys with approximately eighty miners managing to escape. Local newspapers suggested that some of the funds raised for the 1866 Oaks explosion should be used to provide relief. The inquest opened at the Masons Arms, Worsbrough, on 9 December, but the cause was not established.

A memorial was erected in St Thomas' churchyard, Worsbrough, where most bodies were buried in a mass grave; it includes the phrase: 'IN THE MIDST OF LIFE WE ARE IN DEATH'. A bone china memorial plate was produced in 1994; featuring John Normansell, secretary of Yorkshire Miners' Association, with names of victims round the rim; on the back are details of the explosion and: 'Boast not thyself of tomorrow, for thou knowest not what a day nor an hour may bring forth'.

Swaithe Main
Colliery explosion in
1875 memorial plate.
(Courtesy of NUM)

Relations of 1847 Victims

George Banks, nephew of Charles Haigh.

James Denton, brother of Matthew Denton.

Leonard and Frederick Galloway, nephews of James Galloway.

James McCullough, connected to Charles Haigh.

Bernard Wogan, survivor in 1847, was injured in an accident at this colliery in 1878.

Edmunds Main Colliery, Worsbrough, Accident on 16 November 1878

(Managed by Joseph Mitchell junior.) A colliery labourer was crushed between two wagons in the yard on the 15th and died in hospital:

Charles Harper, related to John Harper and John Riley, victims in 1847.

PART TWO

THE VICTIMS

Brothers:
Richard Beardshall (1828–1847) and
Thomas Beardshall (1834–1847)

Richard and Thomas were the eldest of the five children of George and Elizabeth Beardshall. George, son of William Beardshall, a 'Clotheer', was a weaver until at least 1834, after which he worked in a colliery. Richard was baptised on 21 September 1828 at St Peter's Church,

Recreation of miner's cottage in National Coalmining Museum.

Hoyland Nether. Thomas, born on 28 February 1834, was baptised on 28 October 1838 at St George's Church, Barnsley, at the same time as his younger sister Mary, born on 25 July 1837.

In 1841, George, a coal miner aged 35, was residing in Heelis Street with his wife Eliza, the same age, and their three children: Richard, Thomas and Ann; Mary died in infancy. The two brothers would have started work at the Oaks Colliery with their father. They were both killed in the 1847 explosion; Richard was 18 years old and Thomas 13. They were interred three days later in one of the communal graves in St Mary's churchyard.

The ledger recorded on 24 June 1847 'That a further Grant of one pound (worth about £803) be made to the Father of Thomas and Richard Beardshall'. The loss of two working sons would have caused financial hardship for the family without this grant.

George had changed his occupation again to labourer in gas works by 1851, when he and Elizabeth resided at 132 Primrose Hill with two children: Ann and William. George died in 1852, aged 50, and was buried on 12 July in All Saints' churchyard in Silkstone. Elizabeth died early 1868, aged 69.

Richard and Thomas' Sister

Ann Beardshall (c.1838 – ?) married William Wyke in 1865 at St John the Baptist Church, Royston; he was a widower, aged 41, and worked as a colliery labourer then banksman. They moved from Carlton to Kendray Row, Ardsley, with their only son William Charles, who died in spring 1874, aged 5. Their lodger, George Boothroyd, moved with them to Dove Row, where they all remained. By 1891, Ann had died, William was a 'cow-keeper (milk)' and George, a 'colliery engine shunter', had married. William died early 1899, aged 75.

George Bedford (1829–1847)

George was baptised on 27 December 1829 at St Mary's Church, where all three children of William Bedford and Sarah (née Walker) were baptised: Joseph on 18 March 1838 and Elizabeth (Eliza) on 19 April 1840.

William, a 'stone getter' aged 35, resided at Hoyle Mill by 1841 with his wife Sarah, the same age, and their three children: George, Joseph and Elizabeth; they also had a lodger. They were next door to William's two brothers: Richard, an agricultural labourer aged 50, with his family and his unmarried brother, John, the same occupation, aged 65. Richard, a labourer in bleachworks in 1851, was still in 'Oil Mill', with his wife, their six children and his brother John, a pauper. William died in spring 1845, aged 40.

George Bedford was killed, aged 17, in the 1847 explosion and was buried three days later in Christ Church churchyard, Ardsley.

George was married, but I have been unable to identify his wife. The ledger recorded on 24 June 1847 that 'two pounds and ten shillings [worth £2,007] be allowed to the Widow of <u>George Bedford</u> towards defraying the Expenses of Administration to the Effects of her late Husband.'

George's mother, Sarah, got married again on 23 August 1847 in St Mary's Church to Samuel Seddon, a coal miner aged 24. By 1851, they were living in Hoyle Mill with Eliza, aged 11, who was a domestic servant in Garden Street, Wakefield, for Martha Watson, proprietor of houses, by 1861. Sarah Seddon died in 1859, aged 53, in Sheffield.

George Billington (1823–1847)

George Billington was born on 2 June 1823 to Martin Billington, a linen weaver, and Ann née Walton, who may have been related to William Walton. George was baptised on 2 November 1823 at St John the Baptist's Church, Royston, at the same time as his older brother, John. Martin and Ann had married in Darfield in 1812. After several moves within the Barnsley area, they settled in Worsbrough Common, where they had five sons by 1841 – Thomas, John, George, Edward and William, all miners at the Oaks Colliery. John appears to have died young.

On 26 August 1844, George married Mary Brown, aged 16, at St Mary's Church. They had two daughters: Ann, born late 1844, and Sarah, born late 1846. George was killed in the 1847 explosion, aged 23,

Old and New Oaks collieries. (© Barnsley Archives)

and was interred three days later in one of the communal graves in St Mary's churchyard.

By cruel coincidence, George's parents suffered the tragic loss of three more sons, Edward, William and Thomas, in colliery accidents within four years of his death. Ann Billington died late 1850, aged 64. In 1851, Martin, a widower and hand loom linen weaver, resided at Wilcock Row, Worsbrough, with a lodger. He died in summer 1853, aged 64.

Edward Billington and William Billington were both baptised at St Mary's Church; Edward on 11 August 1825 and William on 19 September 1828. They were killed together on 24 January 1849 in an explosion at Darley Main Colliery; Edward was 24 years old and William 21. They were interred together along with most of the victims in a mass grave in Worsbrough churchyard. (see chapter Information about Other Relevant Colliery Disasters page 46)

Thomas Billington was baptised on 7 April 1819 at St Mary's Church. He got married on 28 May 1849 at St Mary's Church, Worsbrough, to Sarah Brown, a widow fifteen years older than him and daughter of William Wigfield, farmer. (Wigfield Farm in Worsbrough has survived and is a popular tourist attraction with a farm shop.) In 1851, they were living at 'Late W Taylor Houses' with her two children, Sarah and Thomas Brown, and a lodger. Thomas was killed soon afterwards in an accident at the Oaks Colliery on 9 June 1851, aged 32.

The Leeds Times' headline read 'DREADFUL COLLIERY EXPLOSION NEAR BARNSLEY'

A fearful explosion from fire-damp took place about a mile from Barnsley, on Monday last, at the works called the Oaks Colliery, which proved fatal to three persons. On the evening of the 1st of May the sides of the upcast shaft fell in, which put a stop to the working of the pit …. The three men who have lost their lives were employed in clearing the downcast shaft, which is now doing duty as an upcast shaft….

Shortly after twelve o'clock at noon, as the unfortunate miners were being let down the shaft, 286 yards deep, and when about eighty yards from the bottom, a terrific explosion suddenly took place, the fire-damp rushed up the shaft with frightful violence, and issued at the top like the eruption of a volcano. Two of the poor fellows on being brought to the surface were found to be dreadfully burned, and quite dead. Their companion, however, had been thrown from the basket and precipitated to the bottom, from whence there is little hope of his recovery, at all events for some time to come, as the water at the bottom is more than twelve feet deep.

The unfortunate men were Charles Pickard, aged 24, single; James Bell, aged 28, who has left a wife and two children; Thomas Billington, aged 28, a married man, and who remains in the pit. It is somewhat remarkable that Billington is the last of four brothers who have lost their lives by explosions... Thomas Billington was not regularly engaged to work in the pit but had gone as a substitute on Monday in lieu of a companion who was attending a club dinner. With respect to the cause of the explosion, it is thought that the miners in sinking the shaft had opened up a fissure communicating with some old workings. Through this the foul air that had been there accumulating found a vent into the new shaft, and on coming in contact with the lighted candles of the workmen, ignited.

An inquest was held on Wednesday at the White Bear Inn, Ardsley, by Coroner Thomas Lee, on the two men whose bodies were recovered. The jury returned the verdict: 'Accidentally burnt in a coal pit.' They were interred in St Mary's churchyard.

The Sheffield Independent reported that Thomas' body had been removed from the pit on Friday morning 13 June and the inquest was held on 14 June.

James Hunt was the only witness heard. It appeared by his evidence that Billington was found, contrary to expectation, on the stage in the shaft, which is 110 yards from the surface. His body could scarcely be identified as that of a human being, the head and arms having been consumed by fire; and witness states, that had it not been for his legs and shoes, which he first discovered, he would have left it – not thinking it was deceased. Nothing more could be brought forward to throw any additional light on this painful occurrence. The Jury returned a verdict of 'Accidental death.'

Mary Billington (c.1828–1865) was just 19 when widowed with two young daughters to raise alone. She was dependent on relief from the committee. Mary suffered a further loss when 3-year-old Ann died soon after her father.

On 12 June 1848, Mary got married again to William Johnson, a miner aged 22. Tragically, William was killed on 10 September 1849 in an accident at the Oaks Colliery. *The Sheffield and Rotherham Independent* reported:

> On Tuesday an inquest was held by T. Lee, Esq. Coroner, at the White Bear Inn, Hoyle Mill, Barnsley, on the body of Wm. Johnson, collier, who was killed by a quantity of coals falling upon him, on Monday, while at work in the Oaks Colliery. Verdict – Accidental death.

Twice widowed by the age of 21, Mary had one daughter, Sarah, with George, but no children with William. She was subsequently referred to three times in the ledger. In October 1849, she applied to be re-admitted on the Charity (her relief having stopped on her second marriage) and this was agreed, subject to confirmation at the annual meeting in January 1850, when relief was restored at the reduced rate. However, Mary's payments were stopped in January 1851 because she had given birth to an illegitimate child, Charles, father unknown, who died in infancy.

Mary married for a third time in early 1856 to James Johnson, aged 28, William's younger brother. They had four children: Eliza, William, Elizabeth and James. The family, including Sarah Billington, a linen weaver aged 14, were still in Worsbrough Common in 1861.

After a difficult, short life, Mary Johnson endured a painful death at home on 18 October 1865, aged 38. She suffered from bleeding and uterine phlebitis for fifteen days after giving birth to a son, who also died. James, widowed at 37 and left with four young children to raise, got married again to widow Betty Wood (née Fitton).

George and Mary's Daughter

Sarah Billington (1846–1892) married Robert Hoyle, a miner, in spring 1866. They lived in Moss Square, Worsbrough, and had four children: James, Eli, who died in 1872 aged 1, Mary and Walter. Sarah died in summer 1892, aged 46, soon after her daughter Mary's wedding. Robert was a stonemason's labourer by 1901, when he was living with a married son in Barnsley. In 1911, he was a labourer for the Council and boarding at 8 Ship Inn Yard, Worsbrough. Robert Hoyle died late 1924, aged 79.

James Hoyle (1868–1945), a coal hewer, married Minnie Dougherty in 1899 and they had one son, Frank. They occupied four rooms at 78 Cope Street until they died. Frank, an iron foundry worker, left home after he married Hilda Wortley in 1922; they had one son James. Minnie died in 1943, aged 66, and James died in summer 1945, aged 76. Their son Frank achieved 85 years.

Mary Hoyle (1873– ?) married coal hewer William Smith in spring 1892 and they lived first at Dumfries Road, Worsbrough, then in five rooms at Villa Square, Barugh. All four of their children had died by 1911.

Walter Hoyle (1880–1953), a coal miner trammer, married Margaret Greenoff early 1901. They had five children in Worsbrough: Sarah, William, Ernest, Emily and John. By 1911, the family occupied three rooms at 19 Back Howard Street, Worsbrough Common. Walter was a builder's labourer in 1939, when he lived at 3 California Terrace with William, a 'steelworks general labourer', and John, a 'machine hand in glassworks'. Ernest, a colliery hewer, was married and living at 6 George Square. Margaret Hoyle died in 1946, aged 64, and Walter died late 1953, aged 73.

The Children of Mary and James Johnson

None of their descendants would have existed had George not been tragically killed, but his widow's life story is a poignant one; Mary died before any of her children got married so she did not meet any of her many grandchildren. I have provided details about some of her family to show how things change or remain the same down the generations and to commemorate those who served in the First World War.

Eliza Johnson (1854–1914) got married in 1874 at St George's Church to George Traviss Howe, a butcher of Shambles Street, aged 21, and they had seven children: Annie Traviss, Mary, Walter, Herbert, Albert, Percy and Harry. The family moved from 44 Grace Street to 30 Highstone Lane, Worsbrough Common, by 1891, when George had his own business as a tripe dresser, in which several of his sons worked.

Herbert Howe (1884–1947) worked in his father's tripe dressing business after leaving school. He enlisted on 9 December 1915, aged 30 years and 11 months, as a Private in the 3/IX East Anglian Brigade of the Royal Field Artillery. He was 5ft 6in tall, weighed 124 lbs, had a 35½in chest and vision in both eyes was 6/6. After a period in the Army Reserve and a temporary exemption of six weeks granted by the Worsbrough Military Tribunal because of his occupation, Herbert was mobilised on 23 June 1916 as a Gunner in the 3rd Battalion of the Bedfordshire Regiment. He was transferred from 10 September to Private in the 57th Battalion of the Machine Gun Corps. He embarked on 11 February 1917 at Southampton for Le Havre and was promoted to Lance Corporal that August. Herbert spent nearly two years in France before being demobilised on 24 January 1919; he was subsequently awarded the Victory and British War Medals.

Herbert married Mary Ellen Gleaden in summer 1922 and they had four children: George Travis, Irene, Mary and Nellie. In 1939, he was a tripe dresser master, aged 55, living at 105 Highstone Road with Mary, aged 40, their four children and Mary's widowed mother. Having served from 1915 to 1919, Herbert experienced war at home from 1939 to 1945, anxious for his son George who had been called up to serve in the Army. Herbert died at home on 13 February 1947, aged 62.

Harry Howe (1894–1957) also joined the family tripe dressing business. He was called up at Barnsley on 30 October 1916, aged 22 years and 3 months. He was 5ft 3¼in tall with a 34in girth. Harry joined as a Private in the 3rd Battalion of the York and Lancaster Regiment and transferred to the 2nd Battalion on embarking for France on 28 January 1917. He was promoted to Lance Corporal in the 8th Battalion from 8 August 1917. Herbert received a severe gunshot wound to his right arm on 24 October 1917 and this led to his discharge on 8 November 1918, after an Invaliding Board at Wharncliffe War Hospital. (This was in the asylum in Wadsley, Sheffield, that became Middlewood Hospital before being converted into private apartments). Harry was awarded a weekly pension of 19/3 (worth £203) subject to review in fifty-two weeks and issued with a Silver War Badge on 31 May 1919.

Harry married Mabel Dunn in spring 1919 and they had two daughters: Eva and Elsie M. He was a master tripe dresser and general dealer in 1939, residing at 91 Highstone Road with Mabel, aged 44, housewife and assistant in business, and their two daughters: Eva, housemaid and assistant in business aged 19, and Elsie, at High School aged 15. Harry died at home on 31 May 1957, aged 62; he left Mabel an amount worth £169,900 based on RPI.

Mary Johnson (1886– ?) was a weaver residing at 62 Pond Street, when she married Ernest Cherry, a carter, at St John the Baptist's Church on 20 August 1910. Their first home was in two rooms at 14 Back Howard Street, Worsbrough. Ernest was imprisoned for two months early 1911 for stealing a cart and this was his second offence. They had three children: Robert, who died in infancy in 1912, a second son named Robert in 1913 and Mary in 1915.

Ernest Cherry (1888–1917) was the son of Robert Cherry, coal miner, and Mary Ellen, who took over the management of a pub in Wood Street. Ernest enlisted at Barnsley on 11 December 1915 as a Private in the York and Lancaster Regiment, when his daughter was about 6 months old. He was transferred to the 8th Battalion of the Machine Gun Corps. The Attestation Form records that Ernest was a hawker of 6 Park Row, 27 years and 9 months old, 5ft 2in tall, weighing 124lbs and with a 34½in chest. Defects that did not prevent his enlistment were 'slight flat feet, mole above right nipple, bow leg, scar left groin'. Ernest committed a serious offence on 22 August 1916, while on Active Service at Home, when he overstayed his pass until apprehended by Civil Powers on 2 September, for which he was deprived of twenty-eight days' pay. There is no evidence for where he was staying, but the loss of pay would have made things difficult for his wife and young children.

Ernest went to France with the 35th Company of the Machine Gun Corps. He suffered two periods of sickness in October 1916 then, from 16 March 1917, he had gangrenous appendicitis. Ernest died in No 2 Canadian General Hospital at Le Treport at 1.10am on Saturday 24 March 1917, aged 29, of peritonitis following an appendectomy.

Ernest Cherry. (Courtesy of the *Barnsley Chronicle*)

Captain Leeming of the Canadian Army Medical Corps carried out a post-mortem: 'Abdominal cavity was filled with haemorrhagic fluid, part of the blood being organised into a clot, considerable amount of pus was found in the ileo-caecal fold. The intestines were much congested. Liver and spleen: normal. Heart and lungs: normal.'

Ernest was buried in Mont Huon Military Cemetery in Le Treport (Grave IV C II). Mary, his widow, paid to have words added to his headstone: 'WE CANNOT LORD THY PURPOSE SEE, BUT ALL IS WELL THAT'S DONE BY THEE'.

The *Barnsley Chronicle* reported Ernest's death on 14 April 1917 as being from wounds received the previous month. Mary also gave this as the cause of death in the notice she had published in the same edition, along with a poem:

Sleep on, dear husband, as the days go by,
We cannot see the grave where you lie;
For the waters of the ocean keep us apart,
But your smiling face shall shine in our hearts.

Farewell, dear wife, my life is past,
You loved me dearly to the last;
Mourn not for me, nor sorrow take,
But love my children for my sake.

Ernest had made a Soldier's Will on 21 September 1916 leaving all his property and effects to his wife. Three months after her husband's death, Mary Cherry was sent £2 12s 1d (worth £721) pay owed and she also received a weekly pension. In November 1919, she received £3 War Gratuity (worth £510 one hundred years later) for his death in service; in 1921 she was sent Ernest's Victory and British War medals and the Memorial Plaque and Scroll.

Mary got married again on 9 June 1918 at St John the Baptist's Church to John Richard Crossland.

<u>John Richard Crossland</u> (c.1880 – ?) was the son of Annie and John Thomas Crossland, a coal miner. He worked as a labourer in the glass works then a carter before enlisting at Barnsley on 26 February 1908, aged 18 years and 9 months, for six years as a Private in the 3rd Battalion (Special Reservists) of the York and Lancaster Regiment. John had dark brown hair, brown eyes and a fresh complexion; he was 5ft 6in tall, weighed 132lbs, with a 35in chest and a wart on his left forearm. He was a Wesleyan, 'teeth cavious, but recruit is very well nourished; has had no trouble in regards toothache or digestive troubles'.

He committed four offences: in June 1908 he got seven days' 'CB' for overstaying his pass, the next two in July 1909 he got day days' 'CC' for not complying with an order and having a dirty rifle on parade. He was living at 60 Commercial Street when he was arrested and convicted of assault on 28 April 1910; he was sentenced to one month's imprisonment with hard labour.

John was mobilised on 5 August 1914 at Pontefract, but his First World War Service Records were destroyed in the Second World War. When John and Mary got married in 1918, he was a Private in the 2nd Battalion of the York and Lancaster Regiment. They continued to reside at 6 Park Row, where they had six daughters: Doris, Violet, Irene M., Edith, Evelyn and Barbara P.

<u>Elizabeth Johnson</u> (1891–1959) married Harry Ellis on 18 July 1918 at St Peter's Church.

<u>Harry Ellis</u> (1886–1964) was one of twelve children of Charlotte and William Ellis, a coal miner then coal merchant. The Ellis family occupied for many years three rooms at 12 King Street, where his mother became a grocer after being widowed in 1903. Harry worked in the glass works before he enlisted during the First World War, serving as a Private in the 4/5th Black Watch Royal Highlanders, but his Service Records have not survived. He was awarded the Victory and British War medals.

Elizabeth and Harry had two children after the war ended: Harry and Hilda, who died in infancy in 1922. In 1939, Elizabeth and Harry, general labourer, shared their home with their son Harry, an apprentice plumber aged 19. Harry junior married Violet Keeton in 1942 and they had one daughter, Pamela. Elizabeth died in summer 1959, aged 68, and Harry died early 1964, aged 77.

Francis Birtles (c.1835–1847)

Francis Birtles was born c.1835 in Westmeath, Ireland, the illegitimate son of Mary Connor. Mary, aged 22, married John Birtles, a spinner aged 26, in Manchester Collegiate Parish Church (Cathedral) on 28 September 1837. Although baptisms, marriages and funerals had to be carried out in the Established (Church of England) Church then, the family were Roman Catholic and attended the small church in Barnsley that opened in 1832 with a schoolroom in the cellar. (This replaced the original building constructed in 1824 and would be rebuilt on a different site as Holy Rood Church, consecrated in 1919 and still in use.)

The family relocated to Barnsley soon afterwards and Francis' seven half-siblings were all born there: Ann, Ellen, Jane, John, Francis, James and Mary. In 1841, John, a linen weaver, resided with Mary in a shared house in Union Row with three children, including Francis, aged 6. His first job would have been as a pony driver or 'trammer' at the Oaks Colliery, where he was killed in the 1847 explosion, aged 12. Francis was buried three days later in St Mary's churchyard in one of the communal graves.

John and Mary Birtles had moved to Taylor Row by 1851 and their sixth child, born about a year later, was named Francis after his older brother. They remained there and John worked as a hand loom linen weaver, as did his daughters. By 1871, Mary was a laundress and several sons worked at the bobbin works, making the wooden thread-holders used in the weaving of textiles. John died early 1878, aged 71, and his widow Mary went to live with her married daughter Jane. Mary died early 1886, aged 71.

Francis' Six Half-Siblings

Ann Birtles (c.1838–1915) married Robert Godfrey, an Irish born weaver, on 7 September 1856, aged 19, at All Saints' Church, Silkstone.

They had five children: Robert, Mary Ellen, Sarah, John and Arthur, who were baptised at St Mary's Church, and lived all their lives in Taylor Row. Ann worked as a linen weaver when necessary, while Robert had various jobs, such as lamp repairer at the colliery and linen bobbin winder, before going blind in the 1890s and being unable to work. Their sons worked in the bobbin works and glassworks. Robert died at home on 22 August 1901, aged 70. Annie Godfrey died in spring 1915, aged 78.

Ellen Birtles (c.1840–1883) was a hand loom linen weaver aged 19, when she had an illegitimate daughter, Jane Ann. She subsequently married coal miner William Carr and they had five children: Maria, Francis (Frank), Mary, Clara and William. William died early 1876, aged 40, at 37 King Street and Ellen had five young children to support. She had moved by 1881 to 2 Cordeaux Road, Union Street, next door to her sister Jane. Ellen Carr died in spring 1883, aged 43.

The four youngest children were orphaned between the ages of 7 and 18, but they supported each other. Francis died late 1890, aged 25. Mary and Clara, who both worked in a bobbin mill, went to live with their married sister, Maria Meade, at 1 Union Street. William was a miner and stayed with his married sister Jane at 3 Union Street, next door to Maria. Mary, Clara and William all subsequently got married and had families of their own.

Barnsley General Hospital 1928 incorporating the workhouse. (© Barnsley Archives)

Jane Ann Birtles (1859–1914) assumed her stepfather's surname of Carr when she got married to James Hogan in spring 1881. They lived in Hoyland Nether, where they had six children. James had a responsible job as coal miner's checkweighman until he died in 1909, aged 56.

In 1911, Jane was an 'inmate' in Barnsley Union Workhouse in Gawber Road; unfortunately, the reason for her admission and details of treatment are unknown. Jane Ann Hogan died in the workhouse in summer 1914, aged 57.

The Census Summary provides general information about the workhouse in 1911. The chief resident officer was Samuel Johnson Crawshaw and he was assisted by thirteen officials (four males, nine females). There were 264 residents (152 males, 112 females) and these were categorised as 'Inmates (Workhouse)': 144 (ninety-one males, fifty-three females), 'Sick (Infirmary)': forty-three (eighteen males, twenty-five females), 'Imbeciles': fifty-six (thirty-one males, twenty-five females) and 'Vagrants': eight males. There is also a breakdown of the rooms in the building:

	Rooms	Males	Females	Persons
Workhouse	40	94	58	152
Vagrant wards	2	8	-	8
Infirmary	32	50	54	104
Old Imbecile wards	15	-	-	-
Fever Hospital	7	-	-	-

Jane Birtles (1842–1916) was a hand loom linen weaver when she got married in summer 1876 to Bartholomew Mitchell, a coal miner with Irish parents. They had one son, Thomas, and resided at 6 Cordeaux Row, Union Street, then 118 Pontefract Road. Bartholomew found employment at the bobbin mill, where his son became foreman. After Bartholomew died in 1903, aged 57, Jane stayed with Thomas and his wife at 18 Oakwell Lane. Jane Mitchell died in spring 1916, aged 73.

John Birtles (1846–1929) trained as a sawyer when he left school. He married Mary Ellen Hampshire in summer 1868 and they had nine children, baptised at Holy Rood Church. The family resided at

21 Buckley Street then 24 Albion Terrace before relocating to Kirkdale, Liverpool by 1891, where John died on 18 January 1929, aged 85.

Francis Birtles (1848–1922), a 'bobbin works tool maker', married Elizabeth Crawford in summer 1871; they had nine children, six of whom died young. Frank had been promoted to foreman at the bobbin works by 1881, when they lived at 14 St Thomas Street, and he was manager by 1891, the family occupying five rooms at Beevor Villas, 104 Pontefract Road. A daughter was a millinery saleswoman and a son was at teaching college. When Frank died at home on 12 January 1922, aged 73, he left a will worth £307,000. Elizabeth died early 1928, aged 79.

Francis Birtles (1899–1982) was Frank's grandson, the only son of John, a clerk for the Co-operative Society, and Lavinia Ann (née Hoyland). He was an elementary schoolteacher and married Nora Atkinson in 1927; they did not have any children. In 1939, Francis, a teacher and air raid precaution warden for the Second World War, and Nora resided at Newlands Bungalow, Barnsley Road, Dodworth. Francis died there on 8 September 1982, aged 82.

James Birtles (1850–1901) was a 'knocker off' in the bobbin mill by the age of 10, but he was a wood-turner when he married Emily Hawley in spring 1872; they had six children. In 1881, James was a 'commercial traveller timber and bobbins', living at 41 Buckley Street with his family. Their children worked in the bobbin mill, glass works or as domestic servants, and most of them got married. Frederick, a wood turner aged 41, got into debt and was committed to HM Prison Wakefield Prison for ten days over Christmas 1913. The family moved to Park Road by 1891 and were still there when James died in 1901, aged 50. Emily then supported herself by becoming housekeeper for two unmarried coal miner brothers; she died in 1922, aged 72.

Mary Birtles (1855–1917) a linen weaver, got married late 1875 to George Henry Steele, a stonemason labourer aged 23, and they moved permanently to Halifax, where they had seven children. Mary worked as a filler in a carpet printing works in the early years and their children worked in the worsted industry, brickyard and toffee factory. After George died in 1909, aged 57, Mary stayed with her two youngest daughters. Mary Steele died in summer 1917, aged 62.

James Brown (c.1797–1847) and His Nephew Thomas Brown (c.1829–1847)

Brown is a common surname, but I feel sure that James and Thomas were related in some way. James and Thomas' father William may have been brothers.

James Brown, a miner aged 42, married Sarah Bennett, a widow aged 27, in spring 1838. In 1841, they lived in Worsbrough Common with two daughters: Mary, aged 3, and Ellen, 3 months, as well as a lodger, Joseph Mitchell, another miner at the Oaks Colliery, aged 22. Sarah's son by her first husband, Thomas Bennett, aged 11, was living elsewhere. James and Sarah had two more daughters, who were baptised at St Mary's Church, Worsbrough: Martha Ann on 4 June 1843 and Charlotte on 6 September 1845. James was killed in the 1847 explosion, aged 50, and he was interred three days later in Christ Church churchyard in Ardsley.

Sarah Brown (c.1817– ?) was widowed for the second time aged 37 and left to raise four children. She would have been dependent on relief from the subscription fund. The Colliers' Relief Committee referred to her children at three meetings. On 4 May 1849, they ordered that the eldest child, Mary, continue at school until a further order was made. On 11 July 1851, they recorded that clothes had been provided, costing £1 15s 3d (worth £195 based on RPI). They reported on 27 December 1851 that payments were discontinued to Ellen because she was 10 years old on 17 April and expected to work. In 1851, Sarah, a widow receiving parochial relief, was living in Worsbrough Common with all five of her children and a lodger. Thomas Bennett was a coal miner aged 21, Mary, a staymaker aged 12, and the three youngest at school.

Thomas Bennett (c.1830–1897) continued to live in Worsbrough. He got married to Lucy Turner in 1852 and changed his occupation to beer-house-keeper in Johnsons Terrace; they had one daughter, Elizabeth. Lucy died in 1874, aged 40, and Thomas got married again two years later to Zillah Oxley, a widow who had taken over as innkeeper at the Masons Arms in East Street when her husband Henry died. (The Masons Arms was used for the inquests on the victims of the 1849 Darley Main Colliery Explosion. Zillah Oxley was referred to in the coroner's records of the 1875 Swaithe Main Colliery Disaster also held there). Zillah Bennett died in 1885, aged 50, and Thomas got married for a third time the following year to Mary Dickinson; he remained at the Masons Arms until his death in 1897, aged 69.

Three Daughters of James and Sarah

Ellen Brown (1841–1919) married William Hough, a miner aged 21, at St George's Church on 30 May 1859; both parties resided in 'Steel Mills'. They were lodging with the Simmons family at Turnpike Road in 1861 with their firstborn John, aged 1. The family had moved by 1871 to Methley, near Leeds, where they had another eight children, the four survivors of nine being: John, George Herbert, Benjamin and Dennis. The brothers joined their father in the local colliery, two got married but all died young, William died late 1903, aged 64. Ellen Hough died in 1919, aged 78, and was interred in St Oswald's churchyard in Methley on 29 March.

Martha Ann Brown (1843–1919) was baptised on 4 June 1843 at Worsbrough Church. She was a housemaid for John Brown, a civil engineer, and his family at Harbrough House by 1861. Martha married John Chapman, a miner, on 4 June 1865 at St Thomas' Church in Gawber. They lived at different addresses in Barugh and had seven children, three of whom had died by 1911. John retired before 1901, when he was living on his own means. He died on 27 March 1908, aged 70, leaving an estate worth £34,440 to his widow. Martha occupied four rooms at Bake House Yard, Gawber, by 1911 with an unmarried, a married daughter and a grandson. Martha Ann Chapman died on 12 March 1919, aged 76, about a fortnight before her sister Ellen. She left most of the money she had inherited to her children.

Jack Chapman. (Courtesy of the *Barnsley Chronicle*)

John (Jack) Chapman (1877–1916) was a coal miner and he got married on 23 January 1905 at St Thomas' Church to Emma Wood, aged 22, whose father George was a shopkeeper in Gawber. They had seven children, three of whom died in infancy. In 1911, John and Emma occupied two rooms at Low Carr Green, Mapplewell.

John enlisted as a Private in the 14th Battalion (Second Barnsley) of the York and Lancaster Regiment. He was one of many of the Barnsley Pals who were killed in action on 1 July 1916, the first day of the Somme Offensive in France; he was 38 years old.

Emma received £2 15s 7d pay owed to John more than a year after his death; she was also awarded a war gratuity of £4 10s because he was killed in service (worth £1,246). She was subsequently sent his two medals, Victory and British War, and the Memorial Plaque and Scroll. According to the Commonwealth War Graves Commission, John Chapman was initially buried as an unknown soldier, but he was identified from his uniform, boots and 'titles' when he was removed to Serre Road Cemetery No. 2 in 1931. His 'titles, "FF", knife, toothbrush stamped 14 YL 1007, and piece of denture (found in grave)' were forwarded to base to be returned to his next of kin.

The *Barnsley Chronicle* recorded on the front page on 21 April 1917: 'Local Men in the July 'Push' Missing at the Roll Call, now Officially Reported Killed', among whom:

> Private John Chapman, Y and L, whose home was at Church Street, Gawber, is officially reported killed. He was 38 years of age and leaves a wife and 4 Children. The deceased, who was better known by the name of 'Jack', worked at North Gawber pit before enlistment.

His name is on the granite cross war memorial in St Thomas' churchyard and his photograph is on the 'Light Lines' commemorative sculpture created for the centenary of the 1 July 1916, when 300 Barnsley men were killed on the Somme.

THOMAS BROWN (c.1829–1847) was baptised on 31 August 1832 at St Mary's Church in Barnsley, the son of William, a plumber aged 31, and Sarah Brown, aged 31.

William Kay Brown (c.1798–1871) was baptised at St Mary's Church on 20 February 1800, son of John and Sarah Brown. He had qualified as a plumber when he married Sarah Gilson on 6 July 1817 at All Saints' Church, Darton. They lived in Back Lane, Regent Street, where they remained, and had ten children: Sophia, Sarah, Harriet, William, Fanny, Thomas, Henry, Eliza, Emma and Frederick. No occupations were recorded on the 1841 Census for any of the children although some of the four oldest would have been working.

Thomas would have started work at the Oaks Colliery soon after the Census. He was 18 years old when he was killed in the 1847 explosion and interred in Christ's churchyard three days later.

Sarah died in 1866, aged 61. In 1871, William, a plumber and glazier employing four men and a boy, lived at 5 Back Regent Street with three children: Harriet, aged 44, William, aged 42, who had his own plumbing and glazing business, and Eliza, aged 34; they employed a domestic servant. William died on 29 December 1871, aged 73, without making a Will and probate was granted to Harriet and Frederick, a plumber.

Replica of a memorial plaque for those who died in the First World War.

John West Buckley (1809–1847)

There are discrepancies in John's age in different records; he was 24 or 36. I only found details of a John Buckley, aged 36.

John Buckley was born on 20 November 1809 and baptised at St Mary's Church. He was a bleacher living in Beevor, between Beevor Hall and Junction Lock House, Silkstone, in 1841 with his parents: William, a bleacher aged 55, and Martha, aged 50, plus two sisters baptised at St Mary's: Jane on 20 July 1823 and Anne on 14 August 1825. Anne married in 1844 and Jane married William Ward, a civil engineer, on 3 April 1845 at St Mary's; his father Jacob was a farmer in Wath
    John was killed, aged 36, in the 1847 explosion and interred in one of the communal graves in St Mary's churchyard three days later. His father died in spring 1854, aged 67.

Anne Buckley (1825–1905), married William Day, a surveyor of coal mines, on 21 July 1844 at St Mary's; his father, Benjamin, was a farmer in Monk Bretton. They lived in Monk Bretton, where they had seven children: William H., Jane S., Thomas Cooper, Martha B., Mary A., Agnes Maud and Mildred A. In 1851, Anne, aged 35, and William, a coal proprietor aged 38, resided at Town End with three children and two domestic servants. They had moved to Osborne House, next to the Sun Inn, by 1861, with four children, three servants and a governess. William owned Mount Osborne Colliery 'employing 505 men and 309 boys' in 1871, when two children were at Osborne House, a niece, Frances Caukwell, whose father managed a bleachworks, was staying with them and they had four servants. William died in 1882, aged 60, and Anne, living on her own means, moved to Park Mount, Scriven, Knaresborough, with a servant. Anne Day died on 1 October 1905, aged 80.

William Carlton (c.1837–1847)

Some individuals throughout the ages leave only limited information about their lives. Despite my best efforts and tenacity, I was unable to flesh out the stories of some victims of the 1847 explosion.

William Carlton was killed, aged 10, in the 1847 explosion and he was buried in one of the communal graves in St Mary's churchyard three days later.

Illustration from the 1842 Royal Commission Report. (© National Coalmining Museum)

Brothers:
Robert Chadwick (1830–1847) and
James Chadwick (1882–1847)

Robert and James Chadwick were sons of John Chadwick and Mary (née Walton), who had married on 8 August 1824 at All Saints' Church, Silkstone. John Chadwick was born in Bury, Lancashire, but had moved to Barnsley by 1824, when he worked as a linen weaver. He and Mary, born in Barnsley, had nine children: Jane, Robert, James, Ruth, who died early 1843 aged 7 years, Ann, Feargus, William, who died in infancy,

Illustration from the 1842 Royal Commission Report. (Courtesy of the National Coalmining Museum)

Gas Nook. (© Barnsley Archives)

and two more children named Ruth and James Robert after their older siblings who had died.

The brothers were both baptised at St Mary's Church: Robert on 4 September 1831 and James on 10 September 1833. In 1841, the family were living at Gas Nook, where John, Mary, aged 35, and their oldest children, Jane, aged 15, and Robert, aged 10, were linen weavers. Robert subsequently went to work in the local colliery and was joined later by his brother James. They were both killed in the 1847 explosion: Robert was 17 years old and James was 15. They were buried three days later in St Mary's churchyard in one of the communal graves.

John and Mary Chadwick resided at Primrose Hill by 1851, when he was a weaver and grinder, while his wife was a winder; Ann worked in a factory and Feargus was at school. New additions to the family were Ruth, aged 8 attending school, and James Robert, aged 4; they were also looking after their nephew David Cooke.

John and Mary moved to the Courts in Pontefract Road before 1861 and remained there until they died. John became a knife then scissor grinder and locksmith, while Mary raised their children then some grandchildren, taking in lodgers to supplement their income. Mary died late 1874, aged 72. John continued to work until he was at least 80 years old; he died early 1884, aged 83, in Barnsley.

Robert and James' Five Siblings

Jane Chadwick (1826–1902) worked as a linen weaver until she got married on 8 November 1847 at All Saints' Church, High Hoyland, to George Turner, a cordwainer. They had seven children: William, Elizabeth, John, Ruth, Samuel, Walter and Mary Ann. Between 1871 and 1891, they moved from Race Common Road to Kingstone Road then Keresforth Road, and all of their sons worked in a colliery. George died in summer 1891, aged 71, and Jane Turner died in spring 1902, aged 77.

Ann Chadwick (1838–1916) worked in a linen factory. She had two illegitimate daughters: Agnes in spring 1856 and Emma late 1859, who were both baptised at St Mary's Church on 23 December 1860. Ann and her daughters were supported by their grandparents, with whom they lived until Ann got married on 12 October 1861 at St Mary's to Christopher Dryden; a plasterer, who had been boarding with her parents in 1861. They moved from Pontefract Road to five rooms at 86 Doncaster Road, where they remained until they died. Christopher established his own business employing three men. They had eleven children together but five died in infancy (identified with *): John*, Mary, Fanny Jane*, Elizabeth*, Jane Jenny, Elizabeth*, Robert, Sam, Ada, Laura and Walter*. Their nephew, Fred Fox, came to live with them and worked as a plasterer for his uncle. Christopher died on 15 December 1906, aged 65, but he left Ann well provided for with effects worth £128,400. Ann continued to share her home with Fred Fox, and, in 1911, a granddaughter, aged 17, was a domestic servant. Ann Dryden died early 1916, aged 77.

Feargus O'Connor Chadwick (c.1840–1908) was baptised at St Mary's Church on 6 June 1847, aged 7, at the same time as his three younger siblings: Ruth, William, and James Robert. As this was only three months after the deaths of their older brothers Robert and James, the tragic loss may have encouraged their baptisms as well as the naming of the youngest son. Feargus began working in a colliery and was a coal miner when he got married to Emma Addy. They moved from Duke Street by

1881, when Feargus changed career to become a beerhouse keeper at the Cherry Tree Inn, 21 Copper Street. They had five children, including a son called Robert. Emma died early 1895, aged 52, and Feargus got married again on 4 August 1897 at St John the Baptist Church to Fanny Brook, who was also widowed. Feargus was still the publican of the Cherry Tree Inn when he died late 1908, aged 66.

Ruth Chadwick (1843–1924), baptised aged 4, worked in a linen factory until she got married on 30 December 1861 at St Mary's Church to William Atkinson, a miner. They had eight children, but one had died in infancy: Mary, Sarah, Jonas, Edward, James, George and John. All their sons became coal miners. They moved from Blucher Street to five rooms at 38 Thomas Street in Worsbrough, where they remained for the rest of their lives. William died in the 1890s and Ruth shared her home with her youngest son then three grandchildren. Ruth Atkinson died in summer 1924, aged 81.

James Robert Chadwick (1847–1936) was baptised as a baby; he worked in a colliery and became a coal miner hewer. James got married on 7 January 1871 at St Mary's Church to Hannah Barraclough, whose father John was a locksmith. James and his wife had two children, Mary and Alfred. The family moved from the Courts in New Street to Wood Street then Grace Street, where James continued to reside after Hannah died in summer 1899, aged 46. When Mary got married in 1906, he and Alfred boarded with Arthur Theaker, a miner hewer, and his family. James died in spring 1936, aged 89.

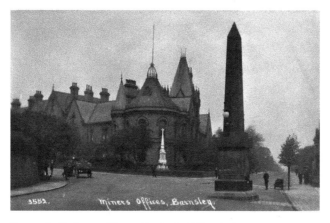

Postcard of miners offices. (Author's Collection)

Richard Cooke (1821–1847) and John Cooke (1826–1847)

It is possible that Richard and John were first cousins.

Richard Cooke was baptised on 20 May 1821 at St Mary's Church, the son of William Cooke, a weaver, and Elizabeth; his father subsequently became a miner. He got married on 13 November 1843 at All Saints' Church, Silkstone, to Hannah Yates, a winder. They had one son John in 1844. Richard was killed in the 1847 explosion, aged 25; his father, William Cooke, and Hannah's brother, George Yates, were listed among the survivors. Richard was interred on 8 March in one of the communal graves in St Mary's churchyard.

Hannah Cooke (c.1818–1861) was baptised on 9 August 1818 at St Mary's Church; her parents were John Yates, a miner, and Ann. She was widowed at the age of 28 and left with a young son to raise. Hannah would have been dependent on the relief from the Subscription Fund. She was referred to in the ledger on two occasions. On 22 April 1848, she was one of the women who had her payments suspended because of 'Reports unfavourable to the Characters'. However, on 11 July 1851 they approved 'the supply of Clothes … to Widow Cooke's Boy £1. 10. 0' (worth £165 based on RPI).

Hannah gave birth to an illegitimate daughter, Emma, who was baptised on 29 September 1850 at St George's Church. In 1851, a widow and pauper, she resided at Croft Ends with her two children: John, aged 7, and Emma, aged 3, who seems to have died in childhood. This was the home of her mother Ann Yates, also a pauper and widow. The household comprised three other grandsons, all miners in their teens: James Yates, William and Joseph Woodcock.

Hannah got married again on 12 September 1853 at All Saints' Church in Silkstone to Samuel Simpson, a coal miner. Hannah Simpson died late 1861, aged 42. Samuel appears to have died in summer 1863, aged 30, in Barnsley Union Workhouse.

Richard and Hannah's Son

John Cooke (1844–1900) was baptised on 25 July 1847 at St George's Church. He was a coal miner hurrier in 1861, when he was staying with his aunt Mary, her husband Thomas Ashat, a colliery labourer, and their four children at 12 Pall Mall. John's grandmother, Ann Yates, a pauper, was also living with them and she died there in 1865, aged 81.

John married Jane Duffey, aged 18, on 24 August 1863 at St John the Baptist Church; they had four children: Richard, Elizabeth, Charles and Hannah (Anna). In 1871, John, a colliery engine worker, resided at 20 Boundary Street with Jane, a fish hawker, and two children. They moved by 1881 to 48 Melton Square in Wombwell. Jane died early 1894, aged 48, at 17 John Street, Barnsley, and John died in spring 1900, aged 56.

Elizabeth Cooke (1867–1930) left home soon after 1881 to work as a servant for Robert Marshall Christie, a travelling draper born in Scotland, at 8 Court 3 Nelson Street, next to the Eagle Inn. She had an illegitimate son, Robert Marshall Cooke, whose father was her employer. Elizabeth and Robert got married on 14 June 1891 at St John the Baptist's Church. They moved by 1901 to two rooms in Calcutta Street, Bradford, where they remained with the five survivors of their ten children. Robert was a maltster at a brewery before becoming a 'general labourer corporation'. Elizabeth Christie died in summer 1930, aged 61, in North Bierley, Bradford.

Charles Cooke (1880–1968) was a miner, residing at 5 Joseph Street, when he got married on 10 February 1901 at St John the Baptist's Church to Ada Scales, aged 21, who lived next door. They began married life in a lodging house at 14 Court, 3 New Street, and this was just a few doors away from Ada's widowed father Matthew Scales, a coal miner hewer, and her three siblings. In 1911, Charles and Ada occupied two rooms at 7 Park Road with their only surviving child out of five, Ada's father and nephew Walter. Ada Cooke died late 1930, aged 52 and Charles died late 1968, aged 87.

Hannah Cooke (1884–1948) was born in Wombwell and, by 1901, was employed as a bobbin borer, boarding with brother Charles. Hannah married Frederick Richard Botham, aged 22, on 13 April 1902 at St George's Church. In 1911, Hannah and Fred, a coal miner hewer, occupied four rooms at 8 Poplar Row, Canal Wharf, Chesterfield, with their three young children; a baby had died. They had another seven children after this, but five of them died in infancy. In 1939, Fred was a coal mine packer underground. Hannah Botham died early 1948, aged 63, and Fred died early 1969, aged 88.

JOHN COOKE (1826–1847) was baptised on 24 September 1826 at St Mary's Church, the son of James Cooke, a weaver aged 30, and Mary, the same age. In 1841, they resided in Pall Mall with their four children: William, a collier aged 20, Ann, a domestic servant aged 15, John, and Jane, aged 5. John was killed, aged 20, in the 1847 explosion and interred in one of the communal graves in St Mary's churchyard three days later.

Ann Cooke married Joseph McKenzie on 22 January 1843 at All Saints, Silkstone. They and their daughter Mary, aged 2, resided with Ann's widowed father in Pall Mall in 1851. They moved to Scott Hill, Clayton West, by 1861, when Joseph was a cotton dyer and they had four children: Mary, George, Isabella and Fred. James Cooke died in summer 1864, aged 77.

William Cooke got married in summer 1848 to Sarah Ann Rushforth, a 'factory girl', who had an illegitimate son aged 13. They were living with her widowed grandmother Ann, a pauper, in Brown's Yard by 1851 with their 6-day-old daughter Elizabeth. They resided at 4 Court Sevenhill Fold Road in 1861 with Sarah's grandmother and their four daughters: Elizabeth, Mary, Sarah and Emily, aged 7 months. Sarah's parents and siblings lived either side of them: George Rushforth, a linen hand loom weaver aged 57, his wife Mary Ann and their seven children at 5 Court; Samuel Rushforth, a blacksmith's labourer aged 25, at 2 Court with his wife Sarah, their three sons and his mother Ann, a 'house nurse' aged 53.

Peter Day (c.1802–1847) and His Son John Day (c.1832–1847)

Peter Day, aged 27, got married to Esther Moseley, aged 28, on 10 February 1829 in Rotherham. In 1841, Peter, a coal miner, was residing at West Gate North Pavement with Esther and their five children: Elizabeth, aged 17, Mary, aged 15, John, aged 8, Esther, aged 3, and Peter, aged 1. The Census did not record that both Elizabeth and Mary worked in a colliery, but both gave evidence in 1841 to the Children's Employment Commission, whose report was produced in 1842. Several members of this family were tragically killed in different colliery explosions.

Peter Day, who witnessed his daughter Elizabeth's wedding in 1846, was killed in the 1847 explosion, aged 45, along with his son John, who was 15. They were buried three days later in one of the communal graves in St Mary's churchyard in Barnsley. The *Leeds Intelligencer* reported that solicitor Benjamin Marshall 'appeared on behalf of Peter Day, and those of the rest of the sufferers, and asked if the men had complained about the ventilation'. Mr Mence, Solicitor for the proprietors, said 'there was no objection to Mr Marshall asking any questions he thought proper,' but he 'waived asking any questions'.

Esther Day senior (1800–1883), the daughter of John and Elizabeth Moseley, was widowed at 46 and left with three children to support, being dependent on relief from the Subscription Fund. The Day family were referred to in the ledger on three occasions. On 4 October 1850, 'Esther the Daughter of Peter Day gone into the Service of Mr Vincent Moxon of the Hoyle Mill Bleachers. Ordered that she be provided with a suitable Outfit at the discretion of Mrs Ed. Newman.' A detailed list of items was made for the total cost of £3 19s 11½d (worth £431 based on RPI) and, according to a note at the side, 'Mrs Day made up all the

Things save the Cloak & the frocks.' On 30 November they 'Resolved that the Outfit provided for Esther Day is approved & that it be now presented to her.' On 28 December 1850, the records confirm that relief had been stopped because Esther senior was no longer a widow.

Esther got married again on 25 February 1850 at Ardsley Church to John Depledge, a colliery labourer at the New Oaks Colliery in Ardsley, aged 50. They resided at 52 Pontefract Road until they died. John continued to work until his death late 1881, aged 81. Esther Depledge died in April 1883, aged 82; and she was buried on the 11th in Barnsley Cemetery.

Peter and Esther Day's Four Children

Elizabeth Day (1824–1849) worked in Messrs Hopwood's Colliery (see chapter Information about Other Collieries page 46) from about 8 years old. She was interviewed for the 1841 Commission as a hurrier, aged 17; the Sub Commissioner reported that he believed this witness to be 'respectable and credible', and she gave evidence 'with much good feeling and propriety'. Elizabeth's work was 'rendered more severe by her having to hurry part of the way up hill with loaded corves, a very unusual circumstance'.

> I have been nearly nine years in the pit. I trapped for two years when I first went, and have hurried ever since. I have hurried for my father until a year ago. I have to help to riddle and fill, and sometimes I have to fill by myself. It is very hard work for me at present. I have to hurry by myself; I have hurried by myself going fast on three years. Before then I had my sister to hurry with me. I have to hurry up hill with the loaded corves, quite as much up as down, but not many have to hurry up hill with the loaded corves. When I riddle I have to hold the riddle, and shake the slack out of it, and then I throw the rest into the corf. We always hurry in trousers as you saw us today when you were in the pit. Generally I work naked down to the waist like the rest. I had my shift on today when I saw you, because I had had to wait and was cold, but generally the girls hurry naked down to

the waist. It is very hard work for us all. It is harder work than we ought to do a deal. I have been lamed in my ankle, and strained my back; it caused a great lump to rise on my ankle-bone once. The men behave well to us and never insult or ill-use us, I am sure of that. We go to work between five and six, but we begin to hurry when we get down. We stop an hour to dinner at 12; we generally have bread and a bit of fat for dinner, and some of them a sup of beer; that's all; we have a whole hour for dinner, and we get out from four to five in an evening; so that it will be 11 hours before we get out. We drink the water that runs through the pit. I am not paid wages myself; the man who employs me pays my father; but I don't know how much it is. I have never been at school. I had to begin working when I ought to have been at school. I don't go to Sunday-school. The truth is, we are confined bad enough on week-days, and want to walk about on Sundays; but I go to chapel on Sunday night. I can't read at all. Jesus Christ was Adam's son, and they nailed him on to a tree; but I don't rightly understand these things.

Elizabeth got married on 3 May 1846 at St Mary's Church to Edwin Rock, who was a stonemason. They lived in Barebones, where Edwin owned a house and tenement. Elizabeth Rock died there on 1 December 1849, aged 25, of phthisis (tuberculosis or TB). She was interred on the 3rd in St George's churchyard.

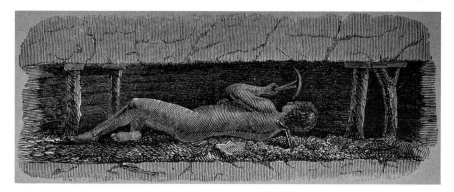

Illustration from the 1842 Royal Commission Report. (Courtesy of the National Coalmining Museum)

Edwin Rock (c.1824–1887) got married again late 1850 but served a three month sentence in HM Prison Wakefield for 'larceny' (theft) from 6 March 1851, leaving his new wife Sarah, aged 20, to support herself as a house servant for John Raynor, a pork butcher and bacon factor, and his family in Queen Street. In 1861, Edwin, stonemason, was lodging in Wood Street with his widowed mother, a few doors away from his brother Abraham and family, while Sarah was living elsewhere with their only son, George, aged 2. They were all together by 1871 at Barnes Green in Ecclesfield, where George became a stonemason. Edwin died on 29 November 1887, aged 63, leaving a small personal estate to his son George. Sarah Rock died in 1889, aged 60.

Mary Day (c.1826–1842) started work at the Hopwood Pit aged 10 and she gave evidence in 1841, when she was a hurrier like her older sister.

> I am going on 16. It is six years since I first went to the pit. I work in trousers and sometimes with my shift on and sometimes off. I have been hurrying about four years. I have my little brother [John] with me, who is not nine years old; he helps me. We have to hurry the loaded corves up hill a little way sometimes, as well as along the level. It is not such very hard work, nor so very easy. The getter or collier shovels, and I riddle and help to fill. I work for my father. I never hear bad language or swearing in the pit. If I had anything to do out of the pit, and had good wages, I should like it better. I go regularly to the Methodist Sunday-school. I can read little words only. I hear about religion there. I have heard of Jesus Christ, but 'please, Sir, we haven't taken a deal of notice of that'. 4 times 5 is 20, 5 times 6 is 40. I don't know how many weeks there are in the year. I have never been badly; I look pale, but I am very hearty.

Mary was killed in an explosion at Messrs Hopwood's colliery on 22 February 1842, aged 16, and the *Leeds Times* reported the details. Workers were reluctant to descend early that Tuesday morning because water had collected at the bottom and the engine had stopped working. Two men and four girls went down in a corve carrying candles and they managed to get over the water, but the girls' candles were blown

Illustration from the 1842 Royal Commission Report. (Courtesy of the National Coalmining Museum)

out. However, the candle of the young man in the lead 'caused the gas to ignite and a terrific explosion ensued'. Mary's was one of the four 'blackened corpses, three being girls', carried out of the pit.

Esther Day (1838–1909), baptised on 5 March 1838 at St Mary's Church, went to work for Vincent Moxon, as arranged, while continuing to live with her mother. She got married late 1856 in Doncaster to James Stocks, a bricklayer, and they had four children: John William, Sarah Ann, James and Jesse; Sarah Ann died early 1873, aged 13, but her siblings all got married and had children. James died in 1903, aged 67, and Esther Stocks died in summer 1909, aged 71, in Doncaster.

Peter Day (1841–1866) tried to avoid working in a colliery by becoming apprenticed to Joseph Taylor, a Sheffield grinder, but he was badly treated; magistrates agreed in 1855 to set aside the indentures and he became a coal miner [#1]. Peter got married on 19 January 1863 at St Mary's Church to Ann Hiland. Peter was one of the 361 victims of the Oaks Colliery explosion on Wednesday 12 December 1866, aged 25. (see chapter Information about Other Collieries page 46). Peter's body was one of the first group of men to be brought out of the pit and identified. The *Leeds Mercury* on 17 December 1866 published a list of men from information gathered by the Oaks Branch of the South Yorkshire Miners' Association, who had visited families of members to identify who had died and their status, i.e. children, single, married and whether they left any dependents. Peter, who left a widow and three children, was interred in Barnsley Cemetery on Saturday 15th in a communal grave with nine other victims.

#1 Information from Dearne Valley Landscape Project website. Denise Bates' *Pit Lasses: Women and Girls in Coalmining c.1800–1914*

Esther Day's Outfit

Mrs Mason reported that she had '2 Chemises, 2 Cotton Petticoats 2 Pinafores, 1 pair of Stockings. 1 pair of Shoes. 2 Frocks 1 Bonnet, and one pair of Stays.'

Postcard of female mineworker in Wigan. (Author's Collection)

Articles supplied agreeably to the above resolution & the Cash of them

3 Chemises of unbleached Cotton	3. 4
1 Wolsey Petticoat	2 – 5½
1 Cobourg Do	3 – 7½
2 Flannel Do	5 – 6
1 Stuff Frock	5 – 3½
1 Print Do	3. 0
1 Cloak	10 –4 ½
1 Pair of Boots	4 – 9 -
1 Do Shoes	4. 3
4 Checked Pinafores	4 6½
2 Harding Do	1 10½
1 Bonnet	5 6½
4 Pairs of BR Worsted Stockings	4 6
Calico for lining	1 . 3
One pair of Stays	3 . 3
4 Pocket Handkerchiefs	1 0
Calico for night Caps	. 5
Dress makers Bill	5 – 6
Box	10 – 0
	£3. 19. 11½

They also provided a Bible.

Children in
Cawthorne.
(Courtesy of the
Tasker Trust)

Matthew Denton (1832–1847)

Matthew Denton was baptised on 29 July 1832 at St Mary's Church, the eldest of eight children of Thomas and Frances Denton. Thomas Denton, aged 22, had got married on 20 December 1831 at All Saints' Church in Silkstone to Fanny Barnes, aged 20; banns were also read at the Chapelry of Barnsley (St Mary's Church). In 1841, Thomas, a linen weaver, resided at Greenwood Square with Frances and five children: Matthew, aged 8, Ellen, aged 7, Martha, aged 5, Thomas, aged 3, and 7-month-old Ann. James and Mary were born later. Matthew was the first member of the family to work in a colliery. He was killed, aged 15, in the 1847 explosion and interred three days later in St Mary's churchyard in one of the communal graves.

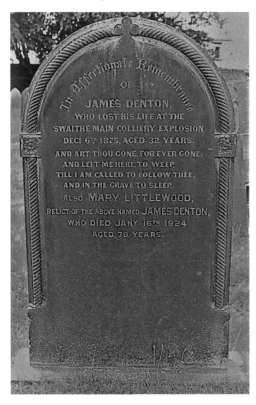

Thomas, a linen bleacher, and Frances had another son in 1851 and named him Matthew, but he died at 11 months old and was buried on 27 June 1854 in St George's churchyard. The family had moved to Thomas Street by 1851 and they remained there. Mary died in July 1867, aged 16, and she was interred in Barnsley Cemetery with

Denton family headstone.

84

other relations, William and Ann Denton. Fanny also died in 1867, aged 58, and she was interred on 26 November in Barnsley Cemetery. Thomas died in September 1876, aged 71, and he was buried with his wife.

Matthew's Five Siblings

Ellen Denton (1834–1896) was baptised on 2 March 1834 at St Mary's. She married George Boocock, a coal miner aged 23, late 1858 and their first home was in Low Valley, Wombwell, before relocating to Joseph Street in Barnsley, where they remained. They had nine children: Thomas, Charles, George, William, Benjamin, Hannah, John, Henry and Fred. Ellen Boocock died in March 1896, aged 61, and George died in August of the same year, aged 63. They were buried in Barnsley Cemetery in the plot adjacent to where two sons had been interred: Fred in 1887, aged 4, and Thomas in 1891, aged 32.

Martha Denton (1836–1887) was baptised on 10 April 1836 at St Mary's and, late 1853, she married William Lee, a coal miner from Worsbrough. They lived for most of their lives there and had eight children: Ann, Matthew, Henry, Fanny, William, John, Sarah and James. In 1871, William was a beerhouse keeper in Goodworth Street, but they had moved to 54 Corporation Street in Barnsley by 1881, when William and his sons were mineworkers. Martha Lee died in 1887, aged 51, and she was buried on 13 November 1887 with her parents in Barnsley Cemetery. William stopped working by 1891, when he occupied three rooms at 6 Dumfries Row, Worsbrough, with five sons. William died in April 1913, aged 80, and he was interred in Barnsley Cemetery in a communal grave.

Thomas Denton (1838–1904) was baptised on 20 July 1838 at St Mary's. He worked as a wire drawer then bleacher. Thomas got married on 21 September 1856 at All Saints' Church, Silkstone, to Rebecca White; they were both 17. Their first home was at Court 7 Wilson Street No.2, where they had the first five of their ten children: Mary, Matthew, Elizabeth, Martha Ann, John William, Sarah, Thomas, Frances (Fanny), Alfred and Alice. They moved to 24 Heelis Street then 52 Joseph Street, where Thomas died on 31 March 1904, aged 65, of 'volvolus, [sic] partial obstruction then recovery, then cardiac failure'. (Volvulus is a loop of intestine that twists round itself and causes bowel obstruction causing abdominal pain, vomiting and constipation). Thomas was interred on 4 April 1904 in Barnsley Cemetery, where Rebecca joined him after her death in summer 1909, aged 70.

Matthew Denton (1861–1940) became a miner and married Margaret Johnson on 13 November 1880 at St John the Baptist Church. By 1911, they occupied five rooms at 25 Arthur Street, Worsbrough, where they remained. They had thirteen children, the nine survivors being: Alice, Lily, Agnes, Matthew, James, Thomas, Annie and two not identified. In 1939, Matthew, a retired colliery packer, and Margaret were next door but one to his married brother James. Mathew died in summer 1940, aged 73.

Ann Denton (1840–1868) was baptised on 28 October 1840 at St Mary's and she attended school until at least 10 years old. She got married on 24 April 1859 at St Mary's to John Hatfield, a coal miner aged 25. By 1861, Ann and John had moved from Wilson Street to 6 Court, Number 2 Albert Street, with their son Joseph. They had two more children, Christine and Ellen, before moving to Sheffield, where Ann Hatfield died late 1868, aged 28. John, left with three young children, got married again.

James Denton (1843–1875) was baptised on 22 May 1843 at St Mary's. He worked in a colliery after leaving school. He married Mary Linsley, aged 19, on 13 October 1864 at St John the Baptist Church. They resided at 16 Mitchell Street, Worsbrough, where their only daughter Annetta was born in spring 1871. James was killed on 6 December 1875, aged 32, in an explosion of gas at Mitchell & Company's Swaithe Main Colliery, where there were 143 victims, men and boys (see chapter Information about Other Collieries page 46). The inquest opened the following day, when James was included on the first list of names, but it was adjourned at least twice with additional lists of names. Testimony from relations and fellow mineworkers ran to many pages of records.

Wakefield Charities Coroners Notebooks 1875 –
At the house of Zillah Oxley,
the Masons Arms Inn, Worsbrough,
on Tuesday the 7th day of December
1875 on view of the bodies of ....

James Denton
Henry Wood of the Park in Worsbrough, Colliery Banksman, on his oath says, …. I have also been acquainted with the dec'd Jams Denton for the last 4 years. He was 32 years old & a Coalminer. I saw him last Sunday afternoon and his body this afternoon.

Details of the disaster at Swaithe Main Colliery, victims, the inquest and burials were reported in several editions of the *Barnsley Chronicle* throughout December and January in addition to many other local and national newspapers. James was one of the earliest to be identified. He was interred in St Thomas' churchyard with an impressive headstone that includes the poignant words:

AND ART THOU GONE FOR EVER GONE
AND LEFT ME HERE TO WEEP
TILL I AM CALLED TO FOLLOW THEE
AND IN THE GRAVE TO SLEEP.

Mary was widowed at 30 and left with her young daughter to support. She got married again, less than a year after James' death, to widower John Crossley, a colliery deputy, who lived in Mitchell Street with his young son, William. By 1891 they had one daughter, Annice, and had moved to the White Horse Inn, 9 Shambles Street. John, the innkeeper aged 45, Mary and their three children shared their home with three nephews and three nieces, one employed as a domestic servant. John, publican of Peel Square, died on 26 October 1897, aged 52.

Annetta Denton, aged 27, married William Rushforth, a drayman (railway) aged 25, on 11 March 1899 at St George's Church. They were both at 21 Castlereagh Street, which became their first home.

Mary, aged 56, got married for a third time soon after her daughter to John Littlewood, aged 55, who was the innkeeper 'own account' at the California Inn, Darton Lane Head. They combined families there with John's two children and Mary's younger daughter, Annice Crossley, aged 17. By 1911, John and Mary occupied four rooms in High Street, Darton, where they had three boarders. Mary Littlewood died on 16 January 1924, aged 70, and she was interred in the same grave as her first husband, James Denton.

Memorial plate for the Swaithe Main disaster. (Courtesy of the NUM)

George Dyson (1810–1847)

George Dyson was killed in the 1847 explosion, aged 37, and was buried in one of the communal graves in St Mary's churchyard three days later.

Although George Dyson was not a common name I found four possibilities, but none led anywhere. Details are provided to illustrate how difficult it could be to identify victims.

Illustration from the 1842 Royal Commission Report. (Courtesy of the National Coalmining Museum)

1. George was born on 28 April 1810 and baptised the next day at St Mary's Church, the son of James, a bleacher, and Mary Dyson.
2. George married Mary Myers, aged 17, on 5 October 1838 at All Saints Church, Silkstone.
3. In 1841, George, a weaver aged 30, resided in Duke Street with his parents, William, a weaver aged 55, and Mary, aged 55, plus four siblings: Mary, aged 25, Bessie and Joseph, both 15, and Eliza, aged 9.
4. In 1841, George, a weaver aged 31, resided in Full Lane, Hoylandswaine, with his wife Sarah, a weaver aged 23, and their five children: John, aged 11, Charles, aged 7, Vincent, aged 5, Maurice, aged 2, and Salina, aged 2 months. They were next door but one to his parents: Andrew Dyson, a farmer aged 58, and Ann, aged 45, with two children, Hannah, aged 8, and Sarah, aged 4, and farm servant Martha Wright, aged 15.

Miners at the shaft top. (Courtesy of the Tasker Trust)

Joseph Fearnley (c.1827–1847)

Joseph Fearnley's mother Ann, aged 45, was widowed by 1841. She, Joseph, aged 14, and his older brother John, aged 15, were all linen weavers living at 4 Old Mill Lane, where they remained. Joseph probably started working in the local colliery to earn higher wages. He was killed in the 1847 explosion, aged 20, and was buried three days later in one of the communal graves in St Mary's churchyard.

<u>Ann Fearnley</u> (c.1794–1866) was referred to in the ledger: after reducing allowances for all widows on 24 June 1847, they decided on 4 May 1849 'that the Pay to the following Parties be henceforth discontinued altogether they being merely Widows who lost Children upon whom it is considered they did not much depend viz- to Widows Fearnley etc'.

By 1861, Ann, a washerwoman, was living with her unmarried son John, a labourer, who died in April 1864, aged 41, and was interred in St George's churchyard. Through poverty, age or ill health, Ann was admitted to the Barnsley Union Workhouse. (Between 1861 and 1871, John Wright was the workhouse master and his wife Mary Ann was the matron. There were 226 to 246 'inmates': 128 to 148 males and 98 females). Ann died there of 'general decay' on 5 May 1866, aged 75, She was buried in Barnsley Cemetery in the consecrated area but in an unmarked communal plot.

Postcard of the main entrance to Barnsley Cemetery in 1904. (Author's Collection)

Thomas Foundhere (1832–1847)

Thomas Foundhere was born in York and baptised on 23 January 1832 at St Margaret's Church there. He was the son of George Foundhere, a linen weaver, and Frances (née Eden), who had married on 30 August 1819 at All Saints Pavement and St Peter the Little Church in York. George, aged 40, and Frances had moved to Stairfoot by 1841 with three of their six children: Elizabeth, aged 15, Thomas, aged 9, and George, aged 7. William, aged 20, lodged elsewhere and two infants had died: Sarah and Francis (who was baptised at St George the Martyr Church in Southwark on 1 March 1826, when his parents were living in the workhouse). Frances died soon after the 1841 Census was taken,

Barnsley Main Colliery. (© Barnsley Archives)

From Wellington Street to Holy Rood RC church. (© Barnsley Archives)

aged 40. Thomas would have started work in a colliery by the age of 10 and his wages were much needed to help support his family. He was killed, aged 15, in the 1847 explosion and interred three days later in one of the communal graves in St Mary's churchyard.

George Foundhere (c.1801 – ?) was born in Nottinghamshire or 'London in the Burton', and lived in different places, especially in Yorkshire. Although he got married in York in 1819, his and Frances' first child was born in 1821 in Barnsley. Their other children were born and baptised in York, Barnsley and London.

Records of Quarter Sessions in 1825 and 1826 reveal that the family were living in poverty and, typical of the times, no one wanted to accept responsibility for them under the Poor Law. Barnsley seemed to be especially zealous in their attempts to deny them poor relief. They must have been desperate as they travelled round the country seeking work or relief.

At Doncaster Sessions on 19 January 1825 it was,

> ordered that the Appeal of the Churchwardens and Overseer of the poor of the Township of Fewstone [Harrogate] in the said Riding against an adjudication and order under the Hands and Seals of Godfrey Wentworth Wentworth Esquire and Stuart Corbett Doctor of Divinity two of his Majestys Justices of the peace in and for the said Riding bearing date the fifteenth day of December last made for the removal of George Foundier Frances his Wife and William and Elizabeth their Children from the Township of Barnsley in the said Riding to the said Township of Fewstone be respited until the next General Quarter Sessions of the peace to be holden at Pontefract in and for the said Riding-//-

It was decided at Pontefract on 11 April 1825 to respite it to Rotherham, meanwhile the family went to London.

A year after the first Sessions, the following decision was made at the Quarter Sessions in Doncaster on 18 January 1826:

> upon hearing the Appeal of the Churchwardens and Overseer of the Poor of the Township of St George's in the Borough of Southwark London against an adjudication and order under

Shambles Street. (© Barnsley Archives)

the Hands and Seals of Godfrey Wentworth Wentworth and
Joseph Beckett Esquires two of his Majestys Justices of the
peace in and for the said Riding bearing date the twenty
eighth day of September last made for the removal of George
Foundier Francis his Wife and William and Elizabeth their
Children from the Township of Barnsley in the said Riding
to the said Township of St Georges. It is ordered that the
said Order of Removal be Discharged-//-

Unfortunately, there are no surviving records of poor relief in Barnsley
for this period. By 1851, George, a widowed linen weaver, aged 57, was
lodging in Union Row with his son George. He appears to have died
before the 1861 Census.

Thomas' Four Siblings

William Foundhere (1821–1876) was baptised on 23 December 1821
at St Mary's Church. He had left home by 1841 and was employed
as a linen weaver, lodging in overcrowded accommodation in Union

Row, then Barebones by 1851. William subsequently moved to Leeds, where he worked as a canvas weaver. He got married to Eliza Thrush, who was ten years younger, in spring 1870, and their first home was at 27 Chesham Street, Holbeck. Their time together was short as Eliza died early 1875, aged 43. William died a year later in Holbeck, aged 56.

Elizabeth Foundhere (1823–1884) was baptised on 4 June 1823 at Bedern Chapel in York. She got married on 25 March 1842 in Otley to John Harper, a tile and brick maker, with whom she had eight children: Martha, Joseph, Eliza, Mary, Thomas, Henry, George and Elizabeth. They moved from Ardsley to Worsbrough by 1861, when they lived at Fifty-Four No. 50, near to her brother George and family. John became the innkeeper at Pindar Oaks Hotel, 162 Doncaster Road, by 1871, when son Joseph was a brickmaker. The accommodation at the hotel was large enough to share in 1881 with their children, two grandsons, a boarder and a domestic servant. John continued to work as a brickmaker as well as innkeeper while sons Joseph and George worked in a colliery. John died in June 1884, aged 67, at Pinder Oaks Terrace, Measbrough Dyke, and Elizabeth Harper died five months later, aged 65; they were buried in the same grave in Barnsley Cemetery.

George Foundhere (1834–1918) was born in Ardsley but baptised at St Margaret's Church in York. He started work in a colliery young and was a coal miner when lodging with his father in 1851. George moved to Worsbrough by 1861, lodging at Fifty-Four No. 3, near to his sister and family. He got married in 1872 in Mexborough to Harriet Foster. They had four children: Thomas, Herbert, Matilda and William. The family moved from 4 Court 3 Buckley Street to 53 Waltham Street by 1891, when all their children were working, aged from 25 to 13: Thomas, a miner, Herbert, a pupil teacher, Matilda, a dressmaker, and William, an errand boy. As their children left home, George and Harriet moved several times but they remained at 82 Spring Street from 1902 to at least 1915 according to Electoral Registers. George Foundhere died in November 1918, aged 82, at 15 Nursery Street and he was buried on the 11th in Barnsley Cemetery. Harriet died in October 1930, aged 87, at 10 Spencer Street and she was interred on the 7th in the same grave as her husband.

Thomas Foundhere (1866–1945) was born on 30 March 1866. He worked at a glass bottle works and was a 'packing base marker' by 1891. Thomas was living in Grace Street when he got married on 11 November 1894 at St John the Baptist's Church to Alice Nunn, aged 27, of Honeywell Street. They had moved to 14 Pretoria Street in Sandal Magna by 1901 and Thomas was a 'plating machine worker' in a box factory. In 1911, Thomas, a 'machinist box-making' in glass bottle works, and Alice occupied four rooms at 20 Gordon Street, Sandal, with their 9-year-old son, Herbert; their younger son Edgar had died in infancy in 1908. In 1939, Thomas, wood working machinist (retired), and Alice resided at 56 Barkerend Road, Bradford, close to several shops. Thomas died there in spring 1945, aged 79. Alice died in Bradford in spring 1955, aged 83. Their only son Herbert Foundhere died there late 1967, aged 64.

St John the Baptist church and school. (© Barnsley Archives)

James Galloway (1820–1847) and John Galloway (c.1824–1847)

James and John may have been cousins.

Richard Galloway (1796–1864) was born on 5 October 1796 and baptised thirteen days later at St Mary's Church, the son of Richard and Ann Galloway. He married Anne Emsall on 1 March 1818 at St Mary's Church and they had two sons: William then James, who was baptised there on 2 April 1820. After his first wife died, Richard married again on 9 July 1826 at All Saints' Church, Silkstone, to Margaret Baker Walsh, with whom he had another nine children: Edward, John, Sarah, Jane, Thomas, Leonard, Richard (who died in infancy in spring 1839), Cordelia and George. In 1841, Richard, a weaver aged 45, resided in Worsbrough Common with Margaret, seven children, ages ranging from 20 to 1, and a lodger; James was a labourer, while three half-siblings were weavers. William was living elsewhere.

James Galloway, now a miner at the Oaks Colliery, married Elizabeth Myers on 7 January 1844 at All Saints' Church, Silkstone; they both lived in Kingston Place. They had a son, William, who was born in spring 1842. James was killed, aged 26, in the 1847 explosion. The *London Morning Post* reported: 'One poor man named James Galloway had his legs broken and was much burnt.' The *Illustrated London News* explained that James was brought out alive on Saturday 6 March but died soon afterwards. He was buried two days later in one of the communal graves in St Mary's churchyard.

James' father lived in Cooke Row, Worsbrough, by 1851 with Margaret, five children and a lodger. Margaret died late 1859, aged 55, and their son Leonard died early 1860, aged 19. By 1861, Richard had moved to 7 Park Row, which was a property shared with two other households, one being his brother Thomas Galloway, a weaver, and his wife Hannah. Richard died in 1864, aged 70, and was interred in Worsbrough Church on 31 August.

Elizabeth Galloway (c.1824– ?), daughter of Richard Myers, was 23 when James was killed, leaving her a widow with a child to raise alone and dependent on relief. Elizabeth was referred to twice in the ledger in April and May 1848 along with several other widows for whom payment of relief was stopped because of their behaviour; allowances for children continued on condition that they attended school regularly. In 1851, Elizabeth, a weaver and servant, resided in Baker Street with William Horsfield, a weaver aged 29; she was recorded as unmarried while William, aged 9, was a lodger. He was a miner by 1861, lodging with Maria Rothwell and family at 1 Court, 1 Oak Street. By the 1891 Census, William was a widower and coal miner, boarding at 15 Wilson Street with Emily Newton, provision dealer.

James' Brother

William Galloway (c.1818–1875) was baptised at St Mary's Church on 17 July 1818. He married Ann Walker on 1 May 1836 at All Saints' Church, Silkstone, and they had two children: Sarah Ann and George, who died in summer 1846, aged 6. Both William and Ann worked for some time as linen weavers. In 1841 the family were sharing his grandmother Sarah Galloway's home in Park Row; she was 65, widowed and of independent means. They were next door but one to his uncle Thomas Galloway, another linen weaver. William, a labourer, and Ann, a power loom factory worker, had moved from Nook to 4 Court, 9 Shambles Street by 1861 and were looking after Sarah Ann's 2-year-old illegitimate daughter, Mary Ellen; she remained with them for more than ten years. By 1871 William was a drayman, and they lived at Blucher Street Court 12, No.13. William Galloway died late 1875, aged 58, and Ann died in summer 1879, aged 67.

Sarah Ann Galloway (1837–1915), baptised on 26 September 1837 at St Mary's, had a daughter, Mary Ellen, before getting married on 13 October 1860 at St George's Church to David Rogers. They went to live at Westgate with David's widowed mother Mary, who was a servant.

By 1871, Sarah Ann, a linen weaver, and David, an engine tenter in a colliery, had moved to Higham Common, Barugh, where they remained and had nine children: William James, Ann, Bertha, George, Lucy, David, Maria, Mary E and Walter. David died in spring 1888, aged 54. At the time of the 1911 Census, Sarah, aged 77, occupied four rooms at No. 8 Giggal Row, Higham, with three of her children and a grandson, all of the men being coal miner hewers: Bertha, aged 45, George, aged 40, David, aged 34, and Walter Rogers, aged 23. Sarah's married daughter Maria Stead, aged 30, who had lost two of her four children, was visiting her from Halifax with her 3-year-old daughter Ivy. Sarah Ann Rogers died in summer 1915, aged 88.

James' Seven Half-Siblings

James' half-brothers and sisters were baptised at St Mary's Church, some in Worsbrough and others in Barnsley; most of them worked as linen weavers. They appear to have enjoyed close relationships, sometimes lodging with siblings or living nearby.

Edward Galloway (1827–1876) was described as a 'Cripel' but the nature of his disability is not known. He did not work early on, but by 1861 was employed as a carter and was staying with his married sister Sarah. In 1871, Edward was a labourer in a coal mine, lodging with his brother John. Edward died aged 48.

John Galloway (1830–1906) was a weaver when he married Ann Hurst, aged 19, on 20 August 1848 at All Saints' Church, Silkstone. They lived at 8 Dumfries Row, Worsbrough, for most of their lives and had ten children: Mary, Francis, Silverton Silvester, Leonard, Frederick, George, John, Cordelia and two who died in infancy. In 1851, the family resided next door to John's married sister Sarah. In 1861 they had two lodgers: Ann's widowed father and their granddaughter Louisa, a winder aged 16. John and Ann shared their small home with six children and two lodgers by 1871: his brother Edward and nephew William; all males over the age of 10 worked in a colliery. John returned to working as a linen weaver in his sixties and had retired by 1901, when only son John was still at home. John senior died in spring 1906, aged 76, and Ann died late 1908, aged 78.

Leonard Galloway (1860–1875) and Frederick Galloway (1862–1875) both joined their older brothers in Swaithe Main Colliery and were killed in the explosion on 6 December 1875 (see chapter Information about Other Collieries page 46); Leonard was 16 years old and Frederick was 13.

The Wakefield Charities Coroners Notebooks recorded details of the inquests on the 143 victims, men and boys, carried out by Coroner Thomas Taylor, whose main purpose was to identify individuals in order to issue death certificates. The inquests on Leonard and Frederick were held on Tuesday 14 December and their mother gave evidence:

> Ann the wife of John Galloway of Worsbrough Common, Colliery Underground labourer, on her oath says The dece'd Leonard Galloway and Fred'k Galloway were my sons. Leonard was 15 years old & Fred'k was 13 years old. Leonard [was bruised – crossed out] was burnt all over & bruised about the back of his head. Fred'k was burnt all over but not bruised. They are in the Gardeners Brief.

Local newspapers added that Ann had identified her sons on separate occasions, Leonard on the 9th by his shirt and a bruise on his forehead, which had been there on the Monday, and Frederick on the 14th. Both boys were 'drivers' and both were insured with the Ancient Order of Free Gardeners' Society, a friendly society that would have helped

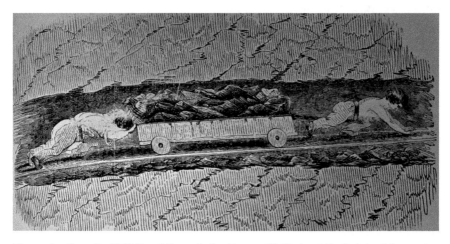

Illustration from the 1842 Royal Commission Report. (© National Coalmining Museum)

with funeral costs. Her husband, John, was employed at Swaithe Main Colliery, but he had not gone to work on the day of the explosion.

Leonard was one of twenty men and boys interred in St Thomas' churchyard, Worsbrough Dale, on Saturday 11 December 1875, another nineteen, including Frederick, having been buried there the previous day with a similar number to follow on Sunday. Processions of mourners from Swaithe Main and Worsbrough Common met at the church gates for the services for groups of about seven victims at a time; local newspapers reported the scene as 'indescribably sad'.

Sarah Galloway (c.1831–1865) married George Edson on 17 February 1850 at St Mary's Church and they had five children. She died aged 34.

Jane Galloway (1833–1867) got married on 8 July 1850 at All Saints' Church, Silkstone, to William Oxley, a brickmaker, and they had no children. They relocated to Ashton-under-Lyme in Lancashire by 1861. Jane Oxley died aged 34.

Thomas Galloway (1835–1869) married Eliza Twibel, aged 18, on 13 November 1854 at All Saints' Church, Silkstone. They resided in Worsbrough, where they had five children. After Thomas died, aged 34, Eliza continued to work as a weaver and took in boarders to support the family; her sons George and John worked as coal miners. Eliza died aged 69.

Cordelia Galloway (1842–1887) moved to Bradford and was working as a wool weaver by 1881. She died there aged 44.

George Galloway (1846–1915) was a coal miner and he married Mary Hyde in the summer of 1867 in Wortley. They had twelve children, six of whom had died young: James, Joseph, Grace, George, Frank and another. They lived in Chapeltown then Marine Row, Racecommon Road, Barnsley, where they remained, occupying three rooms, for at least forty-four years. George was a platelayer's labourer at 55, but no longer working by 65; he died, aged 70, and Mary died in 1924, aged 76.

John Galloway (c.1824–1847) was baptised on 20 August 1826 at St Mary's Church, the son of James Galloway, a weaver, and Hannah. In 1841, he was a miner residing in D Row, Worsbrough, with his

Postcard of St Mary's church, Worsbrough. (Author's Collection)

widowed mother Sarah aged 40, a weaver aged 32, and four siblings: Sarah, aged 15, Sampson, aged 5, Eleana, aged 3, and 4-month-old Robert; they had two lodgers, both weavers. His mother, the daughter of John Hutchinson, a weaver, got married again on 23 May 1849 at All Saints' Church, Darfield, to John Ward, a labourer aged 38. John Galloway was killed in the 1847 explosion, aged 23, and buried in Christ Church churchyard, Ardsley, three days later.

Henry Gardner (1834–1847)

Henry Gardner was baptised on 26 July 1835 at Manchester Parish Church (Cathedral), son of Thomas (a labourer) and Ann Gardner. By 1841, Henry, aged 8, resided in Wilson Street, Barnsley, with his parents, Thomas, a linen weaver aged 40, and Ann, aged 36, as well as his two siblings: Mary, aged 14 and 8-month-old Charles. Henry was killed in the 1847 explosion, aged 13, and was buried in one of the communal graves in St Mary's churchyard three days later.

Thomas Gardner (c.1801–1872) was born in Warwick and he relocated to Manchester then Knaresborough before settling in Barnsley by 1840. In 1851, he was living in New Street with Ann, a bobbin winder born in Wigan, and their two children: Mary and Charles, a scholar. Their son, James, was born after the Census was taken, but he was not with his family in 1861 when they moved to 25 Union Street. Ann died in summer 1865, aged 60, and Thomas, a hawker of smallware, went to live with his married daughter Mary in Speddings Fold. Thomas died in 1872, aged 70, and was buried on 20 April in Barnsley Cemetery.

Henry's Three Siblings

Mary Gardner (c.1829–1891) was born in Knaresborough. She worked as a steam loom weaver and got married on 2 February 1852 at All Saints' Church, Silkstone, to Thomas Prestage, a weaver aged 32. They had two children: Henry and Ann Harriet. Thomas was a coal miner in 1861 and they lived at Speddings Fold. By 1871, Mary's widowed father shared their home and their surname was first recorded as 'Preston'; they may have changed it because of difficulties in spelling their surname correctly. Thomas was unemployed, either because of ill health or an injury, and he died in spring 1880, aged 62. Mary moved to 1 Albert Street East with two children, Harriet, aged 14 at school, and Henry with his wife Elizabeth and their three young children. By 1891, Mary was a general domestic servant for Samuel and Lucy Gill in a shared house at 12 Wellington Street. It must have been a lively household as Lucy was a pianist and other occupants were in the entertainment business, from different areas of the country: Harry Lester, a music hall pianist, Oliver Conroy, a professional vocalist, with his family, and Fred Sansom a comic vocalist. Mary Preston died in 1891, aged 72.

Henry Prestage (Preston) (1852– ?) was registered as Charles Henry Prestedge in summer 1852. He worked as a shoemaker after leaving school and got married c.1874 to Elizabeth, with whom he had six children. In 1881, the family resided with his widowed mother and they had moved to 8 Albert Street by 1891. Henry was a shoe and boot riveter, and the five children, aged from 16 to 1, who lived with them were: Alfred, a glass blower's apprentice; Thomas, taker-in at glassworks; Henry, Agnes and Charles were at school; 1-year-old Mary. Alice, aged 14, was elsewhere.

Charles Gardner (c.1840–1866) was born in Barnsley and worked in a colliery after leaving school. He was a coal miner when he was killed in an accident in Mr William Day's No 1 Pit at Mount Osborne Colliery on Friday 13 April 1866, aged 25. An inquest was held at the Shoulder of Mutton Inn, Speddings Fold, the following day and Charles' father, Thomas, a weaver of Baker Street, was present. Jeremiah Stott of Worsbrough Common explained that he was working with Charles on the Barnsley Thick Bed seam:

> Dec'd & I were getting coal in a Bank there yesterday. We had finishing holing the coal about noon & we were wedging it to bring it down. The Bank was between 17 & 18 yards long. As the Coal did not come down with wedging I went to one end of the Coal & dec'd & his brother who was his hurrier went to the other end with an iron Crowbar. On putting in the bar the Coal came down very suddenly & fell forwards & knocked down the timber props wch were nearly 4 feet from the face. 8 or 10 props fell & the roof &

stone came down at the same time as the coal. My hurrier was in the Bank gate. Dec'd's hurrier was holding a light. He & dec'd were buried with the Coal & stone from the roof. I made an alarm & assistance came. We had not any chocks set. Only 5 yards out of the 17 were holed under. The coal fell for the length of the 5 yards. There was a Pack wall at each end of the bank. John Robinson came whilst we were wedging. Dec'd was not uncovered for nearly three quarters of an hour & he was quite dead.

John Robinson, the Under Manager, was nearby 'between 11 & 12 o'clock yesterday morning' and gave evidence, as did Charles Morton, Inspector of Mines. The verdict was 'accidentally killed'. Charles 'Gardiner' was buried on 15 April 1866 in Barnsley Cemetery.

James Gardner (c.1851–1866) worked as a hurrier for his brother and was injured in the same accident that killed Charles. The *Barnsley Chronicle* reported on 21 April 1866 that he 'lies in a very precarious state, though his medical attendant is not without hope of his recovery'. However, James succumbed to his injuries and died in spring 1866, aged 15.

Albert Street being cleared for redevelopment. (Courtesy of the Tasker Trust)

John Gelder (c.1836–1847)

John Gelder was the son of Thomas Gelder and Ellen (née Best), who had seven children: Mary Ann, William, Louisa, John, George, Harriet and Thomas. Thomas and Ellen had married in 1827 at St Peter's Church in Hoyland, where Ellen and their eldest child Mary Ann were born and baptised. Thomas and Ellen had relocated to Barnsley by 1833, when Louisa was baptised at St Mary's Church. Four of their children died before the age of 4: Mary Ann and Louisa, who were buried in St Peter's Churchyard, Harriet and Thomas.

In 1841, Thomas was a coal miner residing in Worsbrough Common with Ellen, aged 30, and three sons: William, aged 10, John, aged 4, and George, aged 1. Harriet was baptised on 2 July 1843 at St Mary's Church, but she died in January 1847, aged 3, and was buried in St George's

Postcard of St George's church. (Author's Collection)

Churchyard. John was killed in the 1847 explosion, aged 11, and he was interred three days later with his sister.

Thomas Gelder (1806–1855) was one of the ten children of George Gelder, a weaver, and Elizabeth (née Ditch) of Ardsley. The family initially attended the New Street Methodist New Connexion Chapel in Barnsley, where some of the children were baptised, until the Wesleyan New Connexion chapel opened in Ardsley in 1806. George was a founder member and the chapel leader.

Thomas was a linen weaver until 1837, when he worked at the Oaks Colliery, where, by tradition, his sons would accompany him as they attained 10 years. Thomas and John worked different shifts on 5 March 1847 and the former had returned home when the explosion occurred; he subsequently gave evidence to the inquiry about conditions in the pit during his shift. The shock of losing his young son in the colliery would have been compounded by the recent loss of his infant daughter.

Thomas was tried at Rotherham Sessions on 3 July 1848 for larceny (theft) on 14 June. Thomas had stolen one brass candlestick valued at one shilling (worth £5 today) from William Mason, innkeeper at the Wire Trellis in Barnsley, observed by John Hardcastle, a customer, and arrested by Constable George Kershaw. Thomas was given an extremely lenient sentence: imprisoned 'at the rising of the court', which meant he had a criminal record but was free to go. All seventeen cases heard that day were for larceny as misdemeanour; eight men were found guilty with sentences ranging from one week to one month, and eight men and one woman were found not guilty.

Thomas was tried at York Castle on 10 July 1850 for burglary; he had broken into the home of Aaron Bent and stolen a ham weighing 20lbs worth 10 shillings, a bacon joint worth 10 shillings, a tea pot worth 3 shillings, 'a quantity of wearing apparel, blankets, sheets, pillowslips, bolsters, a quantity of books, a quantity of glass and china and a large quantity of other articles', (one shilling then is worth about £40 today). His sentence of fifteen months with hard labour, served in Wakefield House of Correction, appears to be lenient for the times.

In 1851, there were 851 prisoners, 804 males and 47 females, with five children under the age of 12 months being looked after there. Edward Shepherd, aged 42, was governor and he was accompanied by his wife, five children and three servants. Other staff, several of whom had

Above: Postcard.
(Author's Collection)

Right: Nelson Street.
(© Barnsley Archives)

families, were a deputy governor, chief warder, eleven prison warders, six nightwatchmen, six matrons, a chaplain and a resident surgeon. The original West Riding House of Correction had been built in 1595 and was replaced in the 1760s then again in 1847. In 1874, it became part of the national prison service, known as HM Prison Wakefield, which is still in use as a maximum-security establishment.

Thomas Gelder died in 1855, aged 49, of phthisis (TB) and he was interred on 8 July in St George's Churchyard.

Ellen Gelder (1807–1875) was widowed at the age of 48 and she continued to reside in the courts in Nelson Street for the remainder of her life. While her husband was in prison, Ellen was a charwoman and George was at school, supported by her older son William and taking in lodgers. William may have started work in the Oaks Colliery but, after his brother's death there, he became a cordwainer. Ellen witnessed the death of her sixth child when William died of asthma and heart disease at their home in February 1872, aged 41. He was buried in Barnsley Cemetery, where he was joined by his mother when Ellen died in January 1875, aged 67.

John's Surviving Brother

George Gelder (1840–1900) was baptised on 7 June 1840 at St Mary's Church and he was the only one of John's siblings to outlive both parents. George was living in Sheffield by 1861, working as a spring knife cutler, and he married Esther Frost, aged 22 from Rotherham, on 21 April 1862 at St George's Church, Barnsley. They settled in Sheffield and had eight children between 1863 and 1876: Lucy Ann, William, Mary Jane, Florence Esther, George Frederick, who died in infancy, Rose Frost, who died in infancy, Elizabeth Ellen and Selina, who died aged 2.

In 1871, they lived at 41 Leicester Street, where George had an apprentice; this was next door to William Westby, a master cutler employing eighty men, twenty boys and eight girls. George became a plumber and gas fitter by 1881, after which he and Esther separated. George resided at the Ball Inn, 50 Lambert Street, for the rest of his life. On 10 August 1893, he stood trial in Wakefield for being drunk and was sentenced to seven days' imprisonment or a fine of 15/8 (worth £362 today); he was 5ft 4in tall with brown hair.

George died in 1900, aged 60, and he was interred on 17 January in Burngreave Cemetery, Sheffield.

Esther, a nurse, was living in one room at Back of 15 Pea Croft in 1891, after which she went to stay with her married daughter Elizabeth. Esther died at 2/7 Hodgson Street in 1902, aged 61, and she was buried on 4 November in Burngreave Cemetery, in the same grave as her husband.

Lucy Ann Gelder (1863–1908) married Harry Straw, a cutler and blade grinder, in 1882 and they remained in Sheffield, where their four children were born: Harry, Selina, William and Elizabeth, who died in 1892, aged 3. Harry died in March 1908, aged 48, leaving an estate worth £757,100; Lucy died later that year, aged 45.

Harry, Selina and William started work in the cutlery industry; they all got married and continued to live in Sheffield. Harry had four children – Hilda, Harry, Frank and Clarissa – with Clarissa Elizabeth (née Ward), but was only 37 when he died. Selina married George Frederick Bramhall, a breadboard manufacturer, and she celebrated her 80th birthday. William and Clara (née Wigglesworth) had one daughter Edna.

William Gelder (1865–1938) married Sarah Fagan, aged 17, in summer 1883 at St Vincent's Roman Catholic Church, Sheffield. They had three daughters, baptised at St Vincent's: Maria Beatrice in 1885, Lucia (Lucy) Anna in 1895 and another in between who died in infancy. In 1891, William was a horse-hair carder living at 16 St Thomas Street with Sarah, a silver finisher aged 30, and their daughter Maria. William was an executor to his father's will in 1900. By 1901, Sarah, a spoon and fork buffer, was head of the household occupying five rooms in Lambert Street, with her two daughters: Maria, also a cutlery buffer, and Lucy. William had deserted his wife and daughters.

Maria Gelder married Edward Hobson in 1906 but died less than a year later, on 10 November 1907, aged 22, being interred in St Michael's Roman Catholic Cemetery in Sheffield. By 1911, Edward, a 29-year-old widower and furnace man in a steel rolling mill, and his brother John, a yard man for a saw-maker aged 26, were residing with Sarah and Lucy Gelder. Lucy married William Steel in 1925 in Sheffield and they had three children by 1931: William, who died in infancy, Joan and Sheila. Sarah Gelder died in 1937, aged 73. In 1939, Lucy was a spoon and fork buffer residing at 4 Haslehurst Road, Sheffield, with one of her young daughters. Lucy Steel died on 16 May 1975, aged 80, leaving an estate worth about £144,000 today.

William left his wife and relocated to London as a horsehair carder by 1901, when he was living at 24 Westminster Bridge Road, Southwark, with Jane Knightley, a cook, described as a boarder. Jane was born in 1870 in Southwark, where her father George was a brush maker, but by 1881 she was staying with her grandfather, James Taylor, a horsehair carder from Middlesex, and his family in Sheffield. William probably knew James and his sons, Thomas and Samuel, as they all shared the same occupation.

Jane Elizabeth Knightley, a servant aged 31, was admitted to Newington Workhouse in Southwark on 10 April 1901 and she left at her own request on 3 May 1901 with her 2-week old son George. It was customary for poor women to use workhouse infirmaries when unable to afford medical fees. In 1869, Southwark St George and Newington St Mary Poor Law Unions amalgamated with St Saviour and became the Southwark Union in 1901; the detached infirmary at Newington was replaced in 1887 by a modern hospital in Dulwich, designed to allow plenty of light and air into the wards.

The 1911 Census shows William Gelder occupying one room at 232 Union Street, Blackfriars, with Jane and their son, George; he changed their surnames to Gelder on the form, which states that they have been married for twelve years. George continued to reside in Southwark and had two children with Emily Pinchen. Jane died in 1934, aged 63, in Southwark and William died in 1938, aged 73, in Lambeth.

Mary Jane Gelder (1867– ?) got married late 1886 to Thomas Richard Smith, aged 24 from London; they had eleven children but seven died young. In 1901, Mary and Thomas, both 'fibre dresser[s] hemp', resided at 269 Hallam Lane, Sheffield, with three children, William, Selina and Ada. By 1911, Thomas, owner of a feather dressing business, and Mary occupied four rooms at 17 Godfrey Street, Abbey Lane, with four children: William, a handbag maker aged 20; Selina, a feather dresser aged 18; Ada, a scholar aged 10; and Bernard, aged 5. The common surname Smith in combination with common first names provided too many options for most of the family. Selina Smith married Thomas Emmott (or Emmett) in 1921 in Sheffield and they had a daughter, Doreen, in 1934. In 1939, Selina and Thomas Emmott, a 'saw parer', lived in the courts in Portland Street with their daughter.

<u>Florence Esther Gelder</u> (1868–1893) was a general servant, aged 13, for George Marshall, a pork butcher, and family at 49 West Bar Green. Florence married James Frederick Chambers in spring 1890 but she died only three years later, aged 25, and was buried in City Road Cemetery on 26 July 1893. James, who got married again, died in 1932, aged 62.

<u>Elizabeth Ellen Gelder</u> (1874–1962) married Thomas McDonald in spring 1892, but he died in summer 1898, aged 41. Elizabeth got married again later that year to William Jarvis, a horn presser cutler aged 28. They had ten children: Emily, Annie, Lily, Holly, William and five others who had died by 1911. In 1901, the family resided at 9 Bennett Lane, Sheffield, and Elizabeth's widowed mother Esther was staying with them. By 1911, they occupied three rooms at 2 Court 8 House, Weston Street, with their five surviving children. William Jarvis died in summer 1926, aged 57. In 1939, Elizabeth resided alone at 175 Emerson Crescent, Sheffield. Her surname was crossed out and Kirkham added as she got married for a third time on 18 March 1944 to Joseph Kirkham. Elizabeth Kirkham died early 1962, aged 87, in Sheffield.

With thanks to Michael Chance for sharing information about his ancestors.

Postcard of Southwark Union Workhouse (used as First World War Military Hospital). (Author Collection)

Brothers:
George Gilberthorpe (c.1822–1847) and Joseph Gilberthorpe (c.1828–1847)

George and Joseph were sons of William and Susannah Gilberthorpe. William, a shoemaker, married Susannah Hyde on 5 February 1822 at All Saints' Church, Silkstone and they had eleven children, all baptised at St Mary's Church, but several died young: George was baptised on 4 August 1822; Joseph on Christmas Day 1828; Isaac on 17 March 1839, dying early 1852, aged 13; Harriet in 1840, dying under 1-year-old; and Sarah on 20 July 1845, dying in spring 1847, aged 2.

In 1841, William and Susannah, both aged 40, resided in Rich Lane with ten children aged from 18 years to 6 months. Several brothers worked in the local colliery, George being the eldest while Joseph was 10 years old. George got married on Christmas Day 1846 at All Saints' Church, Silkstone to Ann Beley, widow. George would not have known that Ann was pregnant.

George Gilberthorpe, aged 24, and **Joseph Gilberthorpe**, aged 18, were both killed in the 1847 explosion; they were interred three days later in St Mary's churchyard in one of the four communal graves. Their mother Susannah died late 1847, aged 47; she must have been grief-stricken at the loss of four children in spring 1847. William Gilberthorpe died in spring 1849, aged 53.

Ann Gilberthorpe (1824– ?) was baptised on 10 April 1825, aged 10 months, at All Hallows Church, Kirk Burton, the daughter of Francis Watton. She had only been married to George for two months when she was widowed and would have needed relief, especially in the later stages of pregnancy. Their daughter was born at the end of 1847. The ledger

Illustration from the 1842 Royal Commission Report. (Courtesy of the National Coalmining Museum)

recorded on 28 December 1850: 'Since the last General Annual Meeting the following Parties have gone off the List of Participants, viz:- <u>Widow Gilberthorpe</u> on her marriage, & her <u>Daughter</u> on her death.'

George and Joseph's Six Siblings

<u>John Gilberthorpe</u> (c.1824–1847) was killed in an explosion at Darley Main Colliery, Worsbrough, on 29 January 1847, aged 23. Six men were killed by smoke suffocation when coal caught fire underground.

<u>William Gilberthorpe</u> (c.1825–1855) became a cordwainer like his father and married Esther Shepherd in summer 1844; they had two children: Susannah and Walter. They were living in Albert Street in 1851 and William died there late 1855, aged 30. Esther gave birth to an illegitimate child, George, in 1857 but she died in 1858, aged 30, being interred in St George's churchyard. Her three orphaned children were admitted to Barnsley Union Workhouse, where they would have been separated by gender. Both sons died there in 1861 within about a month of each other; Walter aged 9, and George, aged 4, were buried in St George's churchyard.

Susannah Gilberthorpe (1848–1923) was recorded as 'Susan', aged 11 and a scholar, in 1861 in the workhouse. She would have been expected to go out to work soon afterwards. Susannah got married on 1 January 1868 at Leeds Parish Church (Minster) to George Ward, a blacksmith, with whom she had four children: Mary, George, Esther and Walter. George Ward died in Leeds in 1876, aged 37. Susannah got married again on 20 November 1880 at Beeston Hill to Thomas Barrass, another blacksmith, and they continued to live in Leeds, where she had another child, Maria. Thomas died in summer 1895, aged 50, in Holbeck and Susannah worked as a charwoman to support herself and family. In 1911, she occupied three rooms at 36 Balloon Street with Maria, a tailor aged 29, and her illegitimate 4-year-old daughter Martha, at school. Susannah Barras died early 1923, aged 74, in Holbeck.

Elizabeth Gilberthorpe (c.1826–1892) got married on 14 May 1848 at St Mary's Church to William Roberts, a coal miner. In 1851, Elizabeth, aged 24, and William, aged 34, resided at Greenwood Square with their two daughters: Martha, aged 2, and Mary Ann, who was 2 months old. Elizabeth's orphaned siblings, Susannah and Isaac, were staying with them. William appears to have separated from his wife, but divorce would have been too expensive then. In 1861, Elizabeth was recorded as married while residing in Leeds with Robert Sutton, aged 34, a gas maker, her two daughters, and Emma Sutton, aged 9. Another daughter, Elizabeth Sutton, was born in spring 1861, but Elizabeth and Robert only got married in summer 1871 in Bramley, Leeds. They would have had to wait until William died. They remained in Bramley, where Robert continued to work as a labourer or stoker in the gas works and they looked after two grandchildren. Elizabeth Sutton died in summer 1892, aged 48, and Robert died in spring 1896, aged 69.

James Gilberthorpe (c.1831–1901) worked in a colliery and, after his parents died, he lodged with Robert Warhirst, a miner aged 39, and his wife at Hoyle Mill. James got married in summer 1853 to Charlotte Lockwood, aged 18, and they lived in Cannon Street, where they had six children: George, John, Annette, Walter, Elizabeth and Emily. Charlotte worked as a power loom linen weaver. However, by 1881 they were living apart. James was at 17 Albert Street, with Elizabeth, aged 11 and at school, and Emily, aged 4, while Charlotte was at 33 Britannia Street with John, a colliery labourer aged 21, Annette, a linen weaver aged 18, and William, a scholar aged 7. Charlotte had moved to Thomas Street by 1891, when she was a grocer, assisted by her daughter Elizabeth; William and Emily were also with their mother and they had a boarder. By 1901, James was a watchmaker, lodging at 15 & 17 Park Row, while Charlotte was living alone at Hayes Croft, New Street. Coincidentally, they both died that year; James in spring 1901, aged 70, and Charlotte in autumn, aged 67.

Martha Gilberthorpe (1833–1902) was baptised on 10 February 1833 at St Mary's Church. She got married on 19 August 1855 at All Saints' Church, Silkstone to Edwin Wood, a warehouseman. They had relocated by 1861 to Manchester, where Edwin was employed as a linen warehouseman and where most of their five children were born: James Arthur, Hannah Maria, Annie Elizabeth, Herbert and Emily. Edwin died late 1869, aged 37, and Martha became a draper to support herself and young children. By 1881, Martha had four children still at home: Hannah, a dressmaker aged 22, Annie, a confectioner aged 20, Herbert, a tailor aged 16, and Emily, aged 11 and attending school. Herbert subsequently became a salesman and Emily a clerk for the Council while Martha was their housekeeper. She moved to Bolton by 1901 to live with her married daughter Hannah, her husband John Rice, athletic sports manager, and their two children. Martha Wood moved back to Barnsley by 1902 and lived at Church Street, Darton, where she died in spring 1902, aged 71.

Susannah Gilberthorpe (c.1835–1861) lived with her sister Elizabeth after their parents died. She married Isaac Roberts, a miner aged 31, on 14 November 1853 at All Saints' Church, Silkstone.. They resided in Worsbrough Common when Susannah died in summer 1861, aged 25. Isaac died in spring 1870, aged 45.

Charles Haigh (c.1824–1847)

Charles Haigh was the sixth of seven children of Charles Haigh, a linen weaver, and Ann (née Bowns), who married c.1810. Charles' siblings were baptised at St John the Baptist's Church, Royston: Mary, Harriet, William, John, Sarah, and Matthew. Their mother died before 1841, by which time the three oldest children had married and left home.

In 1841, Charles, a linen weaver aged 17, resided at Measbrough Dyke with his father, aged 60, and three siblings: John, a collier, Sarah, a linen winder, with her illegitimate baby daughter Ann, and Matthew, a collier. Charles subsequently joined his younger brothers at the Oaks Colliery. Charles died on 6 March 1847, aged 23, because of injuries sustained in the 1847 explosion the previous day. The *Illustrated London News* reported that Charles was brought out alive on Saturday 6 March but died soon afterwards. He was interred two days later in St Mary's churchyard in one of the four communal graves.

Charles Haigh senior, born in Royston c.1778, continued to work as a hand loom linen weaver until he was at least 83 years old, when he was living at 11 Measbrough Dyke with his son Matthew and family. Charles died there in February 1869, aged 91, and was buried on the 25th in Barnsley Cemetery.

Charles' Five Siblings

Mary Haigh (1811–1869) got married on 16 July 1832 at St George's Church to Jonathan Cooper, a wheelwright then carpenter. They lived in Cawthorne, where the first four of six sons were baptised at All Saints' Church: Joseph, George, John, Thomas, Robert and Henry. They moved to 6 Silkstone by 1851 and their sons were all coal miners. Mary Cooper died in July 1869, the same year as her father, aged 60, and she was interred in All Saints' churchyard, Silkstone. Jonathan Cooper died early 1871, aged 63.

Harriet Haigh (1814–1894) married Thomas Banks, a weaver, on 25 September 1837 at All Saints' Church, Silkstone and they had five children: George, Ann, William Henry, Joseph and Charles. Harriet, a linen weaver like her husband, resided with their children at John Street, Barebones, where Thomas died on 3 November 1854, aged 37, of phthisis (tuberculosis or TB). He was interred in St George's churchyard and his name was included on his sons' headstone in Christchurch churchyard, Ardsley. In 1861, Harriet lived in Stairfoot with four children: Ann, a house servant, and three sons, coal mine labourers, two of whom were killed in colliery accidents. Harriet got married again in summer 1875 to John Church Dewing and they resided at 35 Duke Street. Harriet Dewing died in spring 1894, aged 81.

William Henry Banks (1843–1865) was baptised on 26 March 1843 at St George's Church and became a coal mine labourer. He was killed on 29 September 1865, aged 22, in an accident at Wombwell Main Colliery. Details were reported in several newspapers, the clearest being in the *Manchester Courier and Lancashire General Advertiser*.

> BREAKING OF A WIRE ROPE – An inquest was held on Tuesday at Wombwell, near Sheffield, on the body of a man named Banks, who met his death under rather peculiar circumstances, at the Wombwell Main Colliery. It appeared that the shaft, which is 220 yards deep, is worked by a wire rope, and this rope had been tested to stand a strain much more severe than would be imposed upon it in the ordinary work of the mine. The inspector of mines for the district was at the mine on the morning of the accident and examined the rope, and it appeared to be perfectly sound. In the afternoon a load of corves was attached to the end of the rope at the bottom of the shaft and the signal given to the deceased, who was banksman. The load had not been drawn more than a few yards before the rope snapped on the drum over the pit mouth. The broken end flew with great force across the

top of the shaft, struck the deceased on the back of the head, killing him instantly, and dragged him after it down the shaft. The sudden breakage was totally unaccounted for, but no blame seemed to be attached to anyone. The jury brought in a verdict of 'Accidental death'.

William was buried on 3 October 1865 in Christ Church churchyard and there is a substantial family headstone with the inscription:

THY WILL BE DONE
In Affectionate Remembrance

THE LATE
THOMAS BANKS
THE BELOVED HUSBAND OF HARRIET BANKS
WHO DIED NOVEMBER 3RD 1854
AGED 38 YEARS.

ALSO OF WILLIAM HENRY THEIR SON
WHO WAS KILLED AT WOMBWELL MAIN
COLLIERY
SEPT 29TH 1865,
AGED 22 YEARS.

BE YE THEREFORE READY ALSO: FOR THE SON OF
MAN CO-
METH AT AN HOUR WHEN YE THINK NOT S. LUKE
XII.40.

ALSO OF ELLEN THE WIFE OF GEORGE BANKS
WHO DIED APRIL 13TH 1866

George Banks (1838–1875), baptised on 11 February 1838 at St Mary's Church, was a linen weaver, aged 13, but subsequently worked in the local colliery. He left home when he married Ellen Headen on 11 November 1860 at Christ Church, Ardsley. They lived at 2 Stairfoot, Ardsley, and had five daughters: Sarah, Mary, Ann, Elizabeth and Ellen. Ellen Banks senior died on 13 April 1866, aged 23, and was buried in Christ Church

Banks family headstone, in front of the Micklethwaites' enclosed grave.

churchyard, in the same grave as George's brother William Henry; her name was inscribed at the bottom of the headstone. George got married again on 19 April 1867 at Christ Church to Sarah Jane Arnold and they lived in Mitchell Street, Swaithe. George had another six children with Sarah: Thomas, Hannah, William Henry, Eliza and Emma.

George Banks was killed on 6 December 1875, aged 38, in the Swaithe Main Colliery explosion (see chapter Information about Other Collieries page 46). Many of the 143 victims were so badly burnt that identification proved extremely difficult; George was only identified on 10 December. He was interred two days later in Christ Church churchyard. The Coroners Notebooks recorded details of the inquests on many of the victims, held 'At the house of Zillah Oxley the Masons Arms Inn Worsbrough' by Coroner Thomas Taylor.

> Charles Banks of Worsbrough Common Colly underground labourer on his oath says, the decd George Banks was my brother, 38 years old & a Coalminer. I saw his body at Swaith Main Colliery last Friday morning. He was burnt about his face neck & body. He was in the Free Gardeners Club & the Miners Association.
> *Charles Banks*

Sarah Jane Banks (1844–1921) was widowed at 31 and left to raise alone the surviving children of eleven fathered by George. She would have received some compensation and a pension from the Ancient Order of Free Gardeners Club and the Miners Association, as well as relief from the Subscription Fund for that disaster. In 1881, Sarah was living at 24 Highstone Low, Worsbrough, with seven children aged from 17 to 5: Ann, a domestic servant unemployed, Ellen, a dressmaker, and the five youngest, Thomas, Hannah, William, Emma and Eliza, were at school.

Sarah married again on 25 November 1889 at All Saints' Church, Silkstone, to Rowland Osborne, a colliery labourer, who was also widowed with children. Rowland had given evidence at the inquest for the Swaithe Main Colliery explosion on behalf of one of the victims, his brother-in-law James McCullough, a horse driver aged 17. They lived at 88 Cope Street then 26 Agnes Road with their combined families, and Rowland became an electrician's labourer. In 1911, Sarah and Rowland occupied four rooms at 6 Pinfold Hill. Sarah Jane Osborne died in 1921, aged 76 and Rowland died in 1925, aged 79, in Wakefield.

John Haigh (1819–1891) worked in the local colliery and became an 'engineer'. He got married on 6 July 1845 at All Saints' Church, Silkstone, to Ann Coldwell, aged 26. They had five children: Mary Ann, Emma, George, Sarah Jane and Walter. In 1851, John, a labourer, and Ann resided in Barebones with their three oldest children, Ann's widowed mother, Elizabeth Coldwell, and a lodger, George W. Burrows (see chapter for Burrows page 260). John, an engine tenter, and Ann moved to Sebastopol in Hoyland Nether by 1861 with five children, four were at school and George, aged 10, worked 'in rolling mill'. According to his brother Matthew's testimony to the inquest for the Oaks Colliery explosion in 1866, John volunteered to help with the rescue of any survivors, but mostly the recovery of bodies from the pit the next day. This experience undoubtedly prompted John to change his employment to beer-house keeper at the Rock Inn, Stubbin. By 1881, John and Ann managed an inn at Nether Field, where they had thirteen people staying: son Walter, his wife and two daughters, an adopted son and eight boarders, including two theatrical actors. John died early 1891, aged 71, and Ann died in 1900.

Oaks Colliery explosion 1866 in the *Illustrated London News*. (Courtesy of Barnsley Archives)

Matthew Haigh (c.1826–1899) was a miner when he married Ellen Row on 12 June 1848 at St Mary's Church; they had five children: Elijah, Walter, William, Ann, and Esther Ellen, but only Walter outlived his father. Matthew and Ellen resided at 11 Measbrough Dyke with his father until Charles' death in 1869.

Matthew gave evidence at the inquest into the Oaks Colliery explosion in 1866 (see chapter Information about Other Collieries page 46). On 7 January 1867, he was cross-examined and provided a detailed account:

> I have been night-deputy or fire man at the Oaks the last eight months. Altogether I have worked there four or five-and-twenty years. ...I went down the pit the night before the explosion. ... My district was on the north side of the engine plane, called the low end, the low drift, and Jones' jinny. I looked after the night men, and examined the workings for the day shift. I found gas in four different working places. In three places the gas was in the goaves. I warned the men by writing 'fire' on their chocks. I did not find more gas than usual, but less than I had found many times before. ... I put

the signal up for them to keep their lamps out of the goaves. I reported to John Robson the day-shift man, when I came out in the morning ... I cannot say what he did. There were two falls of the roof in my presence, and I reported them. When the explosion happened I had just got up. I made for the pit ... I went to get some lamps, and I went down about quarter to three, with Cartwright and Thomas Sugden. When we got to the bottom they handed us some bodies; some alive, but badly burnt: some dead. We came up about four times ... I then went ... to the stables, 400 yards from the pit bottom, to see if anything was on fire. I got there and found no fire, but everything dead on the way. ... By this time, from the fatigue and after-damp (which had almost stifled us), we were exhausted and had to return to the pit bottom. Then I came out, about seven o'clock I should say – it was quite dark and I was nearly insensible ... I went to bed but did not sleep. I rose at four on Thursday morning and went towards the pit. I went down with my brother and four other men, volunteers whom I did not know. I found many dead bodies ... I recognised Peter Day [and others]. They seemed asleep. They were not burnt at all – not even their hair or whiskers singed; some of them had fractures by the blast... We got the bodies away as fast as we could. I stayed there till all bodies were recovered that were in sight ... I found the air returning on us, and being sucked again from us ... three times. I knew this to be the effect of an explosion. I am one of the survivors of the last explosion 20 years ago. We then started for the bottom.... After I had been out eight or ten minutes there was an explosion – a very severe explosion. This was about five minutes to nine.

By 1871, Matthew had been promoted to colliery deputy steward and they had moved to Doncaster Road, where they remained for more than twenty years. All five children were with them in 1871: Elijah, a colliery labourer, Walter, a telegraph clerk, William, a colliery labourer, Ann, who died at 5 years old shortly after the Census was taken, and Esther Ellen. Matthew was a colliery checkweighman by 1881, when Walter, working for the civil service, had left home and was boarding in Leeds.

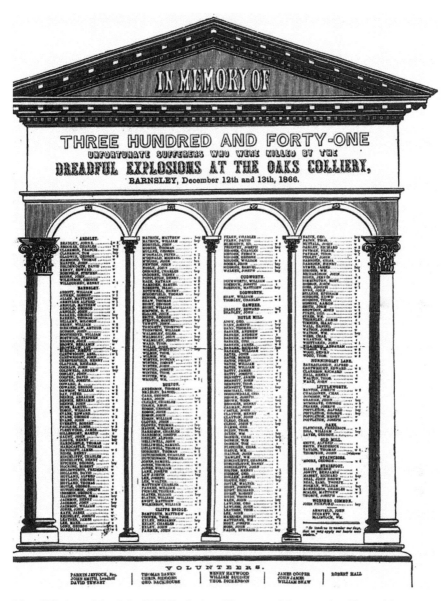

List of Victims of the Oaks 1866 Explosion. (Courtesy of the *Barnsley Chronicle*)

Ellen died in summer 1882, aged 54, and their youngest daughter Esther Ellen died two years later, aged 15. In 1891, Matthew was a corporation labourer with two sons at home: Elijah, a coal miner, and William, a widower of 32 and labourer in a stone quarry, with his 3-year-old son Charles.

Matthew, aged 68, was a porter in Measbrough Dyke when he got married again on 10 June 1894 at St Mary's Church to Ann Whitham, a 63-year-old widow of Richardson's Yard, who had two children. Two of his sons died around this time; Elijah in spring 1893, aged 38, and William early 1896, aged 37. Matthew died on 23 July 1899, aged 73, at 280 Doncaster Road. He had made a Will and left an estate worth £61,880 today based on RPI. Matthew made provision for his second wife Ann to receive an annuity of £26 'during her life if she shall so long continue my widow and chaste', payable in equal quarterly instalments from the Trust. He confirmed that the furniture and effects in their home had belonged to Ann before they got married and remained hers. Ann died late 1901, aged 72.

Matthew had specified that the residue of his estate, after payment of debts and funeral costs, was to be invested in a Trust, in 'government or real securities in England or in the preference or debenture stock of any Railway Company or in the shares of or otherwise with any Building Society or Savings Bank'. He left an allowance of 'four shillings per week in respect of the maintenance and clothing of my grandson Charles Haigh' until he reached the age of 14. The remainder of his principal and income were then to be shared equally between his grandsons: Charles and Matthew's son Walter.

The Interior of St Mary's church. (Courtesy of the Tasker Trust)

John Harper (1831–1847)

John Harper was baptised on 23 January 1831 at St Mary's Church, Worsbrough, the son of Michael and Hannah Harper. In 1841, he was a colliery labourer aged 10, residing in Worsbrough Common with his mother, two younger brothers, Charles, aged 3, and Thomas, aged 1, plus two lodgers. John was killed, aged 16, in the 1847 explosion and buried three days later in Christ Church churchyard, Ardsley.

<u>Michael Harper</u> (1799–1881) was baptised in 1799 at St Mary's Church, the fifth of eight children of James and Martha Harper. His five brothers were also colliery workers; John Harper lost two sons in different colliery accidents (see chapter for Riley page 194). Michael married Hannah Glover on 12 December 1824 at All Saints' Church, Silkstone, and they relocated to Worsbrough, where they remained, moving from Guest Houses to Wright's Yard then 49 High Street. All of Michael and Hannah's seven children were baptised at St Mary's Church: Anne, John, Reuben, James, Charles, Thomas and Mary. Three of them died in childhood and were interred in the churchyard: Reuben in 1834, aged 1 year, James in 1836, the same age, and Thomas in 1843, aged 3 years.

Michael was a colliery labourer in 1861 but a linen weaver by 1871, when he was too old to undertake heavy manual work. He and Hannah had lodgers to supplement their income until their daughter Mary got married and lived with them. Michael died in summer 1881, aged 83, and Hannah died in January 1891, aged 83; they were buried in St Thomas' churchyard, Worsbrough Dale.

John's Two Siblings

<u>Charles Harper</u> (1838–1890), baptised on 12 September 1838, found work as a brick maker then coke burner. He married Hannah Haigh in

summer 1860 and they had seven children: Harriet, George, Mary Ann, Catherine, Emily, John and Sarah. Charles and Hannah resided in Pantry Hill, Worsbrough, for at least sixteen years from when they got married. In 1861, two coal miners were boarders: Henry Winter (see chapter for Winter page 249) and Joseph Haigh. Hannah died in summer 1876, aged 37. Charles, left with five children under 10, got married again late 1879 to Hannah Wildsmith, who was a widow with three children. In 1881, Charles and Hannah, aged 46, resided at 6 Dillington Square, Worsbrough, with her two sons, both coal miners, and his six children. Charles died in summer 1890, aged 52. His second wife Hannah went to 11 Dumfries Road to live with her son John Wildsmith and family; she died there early 1900, aged 66.

George Harper (c.1864–1920) a coke burner, married Ann Sherbon late 1882 and they lived in Moss Square, where they had sixteen children, eight of whom died young. In 1911, George and Ada, aged 46, occupied four rooms at 23 Highstone Road, Worsbrough Common, with their children. Ada died in spring 1912, aged 48, and George died late 1920, aged 56.

John Harper (1870–1951) worked in a colliery and became an engineman. John got married to Annie Jackson in summer 1889 and their first home was with her parents in Charles Street, Worsbrough. They moved to Darfield Road, Cudworth, where they remained and had seven children, two of whom died in infancy. In 1911, John, a stationary engine driver at a colliery, and Annie, aged 41, occupied five rooms at 176 Barnsley Road with their five children, aged from 21 to 5 months. In 1939, John, retired, and Annie resided at 136 Barnsley Road with their son Leonard, a colliery wagon repairs labourer, and his wife Eleanor. Annie died in spring 1946, aged 75, and John died in December 1951, aged 81.

Mary Harper (1848–1927) got married on Christmas Day 1866 at St Mary and All Saints' Church in Chesterfield to George Firth, a coal miner. They had ten children but nine died in childhood. Mary, George and their only surviving daughter Agnes resided with her parents in Worsbrough Dale until they died. In 1891, they were staying at 41 High St, Worsbrough, with George's younger sister Annie, her husband Thomas

Wood, a grocer, and their four young children. George's widowed father John Firth was also there, a coal miner aged 68. After a period in Carlton they returned to Worsbrough Dale by 1911, when they occupied two rooms at No. 1 Smith's Yard, off George Street. George, aged 65, was still working as a coal miner hewer and Agnes, a 30-year-old charwoman, had an illegitimate daughter Rhoda, aged 1. George died in spring 1919, aged 73, and Mary Firth died in summer 1927, aged 79.

'Waiting to go down the Mine.

Postcard of miners. (Author's Collection)

George Hartley (1804–1847)

George Hartley was baptised, aged 2, on 17 March 1806 at All Saints' Church, Darton, the son of Charles Hartley, a carpenter; his mother's name is not known. George married Elizabeth Royston on 9 April 1832 at All Saints' Church, Darfield, and they had three children, who were baptised at St Mary's Church: Jane on 30 June 1833, Eliza on 9 August 1840 and the third unknown. George was killed in the 1847 explosion, aged 43, and was buried three days later in All Saints' churchyard, Darton, with three other victims.

The *Illustrated London News* reported that George Hartley had been working, along with William Ayre, on scaffolding in one of the two air shafts, carrying out repairs to damage caused by a fire in the pit on 24 December 1845, when he was killed. The explosion in the pit caused a rush of air which damaged the partition between the two air shafts resulting in timber,

Postcard of All Saints' church, Darton. (Author's Collection)

bricks and stones falling on the men; while George was killed on the spot, William was unhurt. Rescuers ensured that both were brought out quickly.

William Ayre gave evidence to the inquest, as reported in the *Leeds Intelligencer*:

> I heard the explosion in the pit; it was similar to a clap of thunder. I said to George, 'It's fired.' He said, 'I doubt it has.' Immediately after I said so, bricks and other matter fell down the shaft; when I found myself, I was laid upon the scaffold; the rubbish caught my head, by which I was insensible. I held fast by the rope. Hartley was laid down on the scaffold. I called out, 'George,' but he never spoke. I believe he was dead. The scaffolding was blown up with the explosion, but I think not far.

Several newspapers reported that George was a widower of Gawber with three children. Elizabeth Hartley had died in 1845, aged 33. As only two of their children, Jane and Eliza, were mentioned in the ledger, any third child must have died soon after his/her father.

The Two Daughters of George and Elizabeth

Jane and Eliza Hartley experienced a very traumatic childhood; they were orphaned young, then uprooted from their home and separated, to be brought up in different places by strangers. They were discussed at many meetings of the Colliers' Relief Fund Committee, the first two occasions regarding allowances. On 24 June 1847, they decided 'That the weekly Allowance of two shillings and six pence [worth £100] to each of the Orphan children of George Hartley ... be continued.' There is no mention as to where the children were living but it seems probable that they were in Barnsley Union Workhouse, records for which have not survived.

Jane Hartley (1833–1909), orphaned aged 14, was disabled and the Committee had difficulty finding suitable employment. On 4 May 1849, they negotiated with Joshua Mason,

> as to his Wife taking Jane Hartley for a Term of two years to teach her the Trade of a Bonnet-maker & to conclude with

him if it can be effected at in Cash for 5s per week including her board and that they be further authorised to procure her an outfit suitable for her proposed Position.

A note on the same date states:

it was agreed that Jane Hartley should go to him (that is to Mrs Mason) on Monday next on Trial for a month & if she should be approved of & likes the Business that he would take her for 2 years at 5s/- per week it being understood that she was to wash her own clothes.

On 30 November 1849, they ordered an outfit to be provided for Jane at a cost of £5 7s 4½d (worth £562 based on RPI) – a detailed inventory was recorded (included at the end of this chapter). The Committee agreed that 'at a future and suitable Time [she] be furnished with another Bonnet, a pair of Stays & a pair of Shoes or Boots', and they confirmed on 4 October 1850 that she had been given a pair of boots, her old pair were mended and five yards of Black Coburgh were supplied at a total cost of 17s 6d.

On 11 January 1850, they felt 'happy to say that the Guardians of the Poor for the Township of Hickleton, near Doncaster, are contributing towards her support, and have promised to continue to do so during that period.' On 27 December 1851, the Records stated:

The most difficult case with which the Committee for the ensuing year will have to contend is that of Jane Hartley one of the Orphan Children of George Hartley, she being a Girl of weak Intellect and somewhat of a Cripple was, altho' at the Time nearly 15 years of age considered to be an object of this Charity and ultimately placed with Mrs Mason as a Straw Hand Bonnet Maker where she has been for nearly 3 years but your Committee regret to say that her Employer now reports that she will never be able to earn her living in that line of Business. – During the Time she has thus been with Mrs Mason your Committee have made allowance on her behalf (independently of 3s/- per Week contributed by the Guardians of the Doncaster Union) amounting to £20. 17. 9.

[worth £17,200] and they would gladly recommend a further Trial of her powers if they could conscientiously say that they believe that it would tend to her ultimate Benefit but inasmuch as they cannot, they reluctantly advise that their Successors find themselves into immediate communication with the Clerk to the above Union as to her future Destination.

In 1851, Jane, aged 17, was a straw bonnet apprentice staying at May Day Green with Joshua Mason, a hairdresser, his wife Hannah, a bonnet maker, and their two children. Jane got married in spring 1857 to James Guest, an agricultural labourer ten years older, with whom she had three children, who were baptised at Christ Church: Elizabeth on 5 September 1858, Harry on 21 July 1867 and Herbert on 6 November 1870. The family moved from Parkers Houses to Hunningley Lane by 1871 and remained there. James died late 1874, aged 62, and Jane Guest died in spring 1909, aged 76.

Elizabeth Guest married Henry Houldsworth Cooper in 1883. They were inn keepers at Silkstone Common, where they had seven children, one of whom died young.

Harry Guest married in 1893; he moved away from Barnsley until he died in 1929, age 62.

Herbert Guest, a railwayman, married Sarah Ann Holt, a widow aged 35, in Wakefield Parish Church (Cathedral) on 26 November 1892. By 1939, he was a widower and retired railway engine driver, living in Pogmoor Road with a paid housekeeper.

Eliza Hartley (1840–1918) was orphaned aged 8. The Committee recorded on 25 January 1849 that they,

> have to announce the gratifying Fact that Mr Marshall of Birkhouse has in the most disinterested manner proposed to relieve their Successors from any further charge on account of Eliza Hartley one of the orphan Children of George Hartley who, though only 8 years of age, he has consented to take into his House, educate and provide for so long as

she shall conduct herself with propriety merely requesting
that she may be provided by your Committee with a suitable
out-fit on being confided to his care.

Provision of an outfit was approved and it was hoped it would be 'an
incitement to good conduct on the Part of all the junior objects of your
Charity.' The Committee agreed on 30 November 1849, 'That the sum
of £4. 5. 0 (worth £3,442) be paid to Mrs Mason (Mrs Marshall) for the
Maintenance for Eliza Hartley up to the 31st of Decr next- the end of
the present year.'

In 1851, Eliza was at school and lodging at Birk House, Ardsley, with
Timothy Marshall, aged 45, his wife Elizabeth and a domestic servant.
Timothy was proprietor of the Oaks Colliery and his generosity may
have been to help salve his conscience about the explosion that killed
Eliza's father and seventy-two others. Eliza had left them before 1861,
when she was a house servant for Sigsworth Simpson, a hosier, glover
etc, and his family at 2 Queen Street.

Eliza gave birth to a son, Wilfred, in 1866 and although she remained
unmarried, she appears to have done well for herself. She was a general
servant 'visitor' to James Hodgson, a commercial clerk, and his family at
129 Dodworth Road in 1881. She moved into 38 Church Street with her son
by 1891, when he was 24 years old and a maltster's clerk; they remained
there for over ten years. By 1911, Elizabeth and Wilfred occupied four
rooms at 23 Hopwood Street. Eliza Hartley died in February 1918, aged 77,
at New Lodge in Carlton; she was buried on the 28th in Carlton Cemetery.

Wilfred Crowther Hartley (1866–1950) was born on 28 June 1866; his
father is not known but the middle surname may be his. Wilfred married
Benigna Annie Hall in summer 1901 and they had three children: Donald
George, Kathleen Mary and Marion Eva. In 1911, Wilfred was a wine
& spirit merchant clerk, and Benigna, age 38, was sub-postmistress and
owned a provision shop at 23 Hopwood Street, which had four rooms of
accommodation for them and their three children. They had relocated
to Scarborough by 1939 and ran a boarding house with their unmarried
daughter Kathleen, at 4 Ramshill Road, where they remained. Wilfred
died in Scarborough in 1950, aged 84, and Benigna died there on
22 August 1951, aged 78. Begnina left a Will and probate was granted to
two children: Donald George, a local government officer, and Kathleen.
The estate was valued at £3,089 10s 9d (worth £97,760 based on RPI).

Provision of an Outfit for Jane Hartley

The outfit was provided at a cost of £5 7s 4½d

Inventory	Cost		
1 Bonnet –	Mrs Carnelly	4. 6.
1 Shawl	--- Do ---	3. 3.
2 Gowns & making	Mrs Mason	6. 0.
2 Flannel Petticoats	John Bashforth	10. 6
6 Aprons	Messrs Smith	3. 6. 1½
4 Shifts	Bill for Stockings	7 –
4 Night Caps	Thos. Barrows	10–
4 Pocket handkerchiefs		£5 – 7. 4 ½
2 Pockets		
1 Pair of Stays		
1 Pair of Boots		
1 Cloak		
4 Pairs of Stockings		
1 Box		
1 Bible		

And that she be at a future and suitable Time be furnished with another Bonnet, a pair of Stays & a pair of Shoes or Boots. –
　Additional items supplied:

A pair of Boots	10.6
Mending old pair	1.6
5 yards of Black Coburgh	55
	17–5

Postcard of female miners in Wigan. (Author's Collection)

Robert Hazle (Hessle) (1815–1847)

There are various spellings of the surname in records, but the ledger mainly uses Hessle and most genealogical records use Hazle, which is the version I have used.

Robert Hazle was born on 11 April 1815 and baptised on 7 May at St Mary's Church. He was the son of Thomas Hazle, a coal miner, and Anne (née Wyke), who had married there on 5 December 1813. Robert's two younger siblings were also baptised at St Mary's: Elizabeth in 1820 and Thomas in 1823. Robert would have started work in a colliery with his father by the age of 10. He was a collier when he got married on 6 September 1840 at St Mary's Church to Elizabeth Kirk. In 1841, Robert and Elizabeth were residing at Wortley Street with two daughters: Charlotte born in 1841 and Hannah in 1846. Robert was killed in the 1847 explosion, aged 31, and was interred three days later in one of the communal graves in St Mary's churchyard.

Illustration from the 1842 Royal Commission Report. (Courtesy of the National Coalmining Museum)

Elizabeth Hazle (c.1820–1901) was widowed, aged 25, and left with two young daughters to raise: Charlotte, aged 6, and Hannah, a few months old, who died in February 1848, aged 1, and was interred in St Mary's churchyard. Elizabeth was referred to in the ledger on four occasions. On 22 April 1848, the Committee decided to suspend payments until they could investigate unfavourable reports about her behaviour; they confirmed this on 4 May 1848, but agreed to continue paying the allowance for children provided that they continued to attend school.

Elizabeth was a power loom weaver in 1851, living at Nelson Street with two children: Charlotte, aged 9 at school, and Walter, aged 2. Joshua 'Reynard', a coal miner aged 23, was a visitor, but he became Elizabeth's partner and may have been Walter's father, because she married Joshua Rayner that year.

On 11 July 1851, the ledger recorded 'that the supply of Clothes to the following Parties is approved viz to Widow Hessle's Girl £1: 10.0.' (worth £165 based on RPI). In their report to the General Meeting on 27 December 1851, they confirmed that payments had been discontinued for 'Charlotte the Daughter of Robert Hessle, having attained the age of 10 years in November last.'

Elizabeth and Joshua lived at 27 Ash Row, Hoyle Mill, with their five children: Walter, James, Joshua, William and Hannah; all sons joined Joshua at the colliery starting as horse drivers then hurriers. Elizabeth suffered a triple tragedy in the Oaks Colliery explosion on 12 December 1866 when her husband and two sons were killed: Joshua Rayner was 40, Walter Hazle, aged 18, and James Rayner, aged 14.

James Rayner was named in the newspapers among the first victims to be removed from the pit and identified. The *Leeds Mercury* published a list of men from information gathered by the Oaks Branch of the South Yorkshire Miners' Association, who had visited families of members to identify who had died and their status, i.e. which were children, single or married, and whether they left any dependents. Joshua Rayner, leaving a widow and three children, James Rayner, a boy, and Walter 'Hoyle', single, were listed under Hoyle Mill. They were all interred in Christ Church churchyard in Ardsley.

Elizabeth was only 43 when she was widowed for a second time and left with her three youngest children to raise: Joshua, William and Hannah Rayner. By 1891 Elizabeth Rayner had moved to 'Stafford Colliery',

9 Tune Street, and died there in December 1901, aged 82, being buried in Barnsley Cemetery. She was outlived by only one of her eight children.

The Daughter of Robert and Elizabeth Hazle

Charlotte Hazle (1841–1885) was baptised on 29 September 1844, aged 3, at St Mary's Church. She would have been aware of her father's death followed by that of her baby sister. Charlotte got married, aged 17, in the summer of 1859 to Richard Wilson, a 23-year-old coal miner from Bradford. They moved from Ardsley to Wombwell Main and had five children: Robert, Alice, Walter, James and Arthur. The Wilson family had moved to 5 Summer Lane in Wombwell, by 1881, when the two older sons were working in the colliery with their father and the two younger sons were at school. Charlotte Wilson died there on 12 April 1885, aged 43, and was buried in Wombwell Cemetery. Richard got married again in the summer of 1886 to Ann Barnes, a widow. He died in 1913, aged 76.

Robert Wilson (1860–1923) was a coal miner hewer at Wombwell Main Colliery when he married Sarah Ogley in 1881. They continued to live in Wombwell, where they had eleven children, the surviving five were: Anne, Charlotte, Alice, John and Florrie. Robert died in 1923, aged 63, and Sarah died ten years later, aged 72.

Alice Wilson (1861–1892) married Benjamin Lawson, a coal miner from Penrith, in 1880 and they had four daughters: Margaret Ann, Mabel, who died late 1882 aged 1, Sarah Alice and Hannah. The family lived at 22 Park Row, where Benjamin died in 1888, aged 33. Alice Lawson died late 1892, aged 34.

Margaret Ann Lawson (c.1879–1921) was orphaned, aged 13, and became a domestic servant for William Totty, publican at the Tollhouse Inn in Monk Bretton. She married Robertson Priestley, a coal miner, at St Mary's Church on 26 December 1903 and they did not have any children. Margaret Priestley died at 36 Grace Street in 1921, aged 43.

Sarah Alice Lawson (1883–1955) became an orphan, aged 9, and moved with Hannah to 21 Park Row, the home of their widowed grandfather,

George Newsome, still working as a moulder's labourer in his seventies. She was a bobbin tester when she married William Marshall in 1902 and they had ten children: Nellie, Harry, Elsie, Frank, Arthur, Frederick, who died in infancy, Audrey, Jean M. and two others who died in childhood. In 1939, Sarah and William, a journeyman builder's bricklayer, were residing at 22 Albion Terrace, close to Hannah, with five children. William died late 1944, aged 62, and Sarah Marshall died early 1955, aged 71.

Hannah Lawson (1888–1976), orphaned at 4, married Hubert Goodman, a collier, in 1908 and they had three sons: Edward, who died early 1914, aged 5, Ernest and George. The family occupied four rooms at 28 Albion Terrace by 1911 and remained there until at least 1939; the sons worked in a colliery. Hubert died in 1959, aged 76, and Hannah Goodman died in spring 1976, aged 88

Walter Wilson (1867–1905) was a miner at Wombwell Main Colliery when he married Esther Hanson in summer 1886. They had four children: Charlotte, Arthur, Blanche and Elsie, and resided at 32 George Street. Esther died in 1897, aged 34, and Walter got married again in 1901 to Elizabeth Padgett, a widow. Walter and Elizabeth had one child, Clara, before Walter died in summer 1905, aged 37.

Elizabeth Wilson, widowed again, aged 41, had nine children with her first husband but five of these had died in childhood. The four survivors, Fred, John William and James Padgett, resided with her and daughter, Clara Wilson, in four rooms in Main Street, Wombwell. Elizabeth's sons all worked in the local colliery and two enlisted in the First World War.

John William Padgett (1895–1937) joined the 5th (Territorial) Battalion of the York and Lancaster Regiment on 19 May 1913, aged 18, but he was assessed as permanently unfit for war service on 16 May 1915 because of a painful congenital problem. He subsequently got married and had eight children before he died in 1937, aged 43.

James Padgett (1899–1949) attested on 4 February 1917, aged 18, as a 2nd Class Air Mechanic in the Royal Flying Corps Central Aircraft Repair Depot. He was discharged on 2 May 1917 as 'no longer physically fit for War Service', having 'spent almost his entire service in hospital' because of fits, probably caused by epilepsy. According to his medical assessment, James was 5ft 6½in tall, weighed 124 lbs, with a 36in girth; he had a fresh complexion, blue eyes and brown hair. His 'military character' was described as 'Good' and he earned a gratuity of £7 10s (worth £2,077). James died late 1949, aged 50.

Charlotte Wilson (1886–1966) married Albert Knight, a coal miner hewer, in spring 1907. They lived in Wombwell, moving from four rooms at 6 Myrtle Road to 90 Main Street by 1939. Only one of their four children survived infancy: Albert died in 1951, aged 67, and Charlotte Knight died in 1966, aged 70.

Arthur Wilson (1888–1959) was a coal miner hewer when he married Ellen Longley on 11 October 1909. By 1911, they occupied two rooms at No. 8 Sovereign Yard, Westgate, and they had seven children, two of whom died in infancy. Arthur attested on 29 August 1914 as a Private (Service Number: 11914) in the York and Lancaster Regiment but subsequently transferred to the Royal Naval Division. He was 5ft 5in tall, weighed 137 lbs, had girth 37½in, fresh complexion, grey eyes and brown hair; his home address was 28 Honeywell Street, Old Mill. In 1939, Arthur and Ellen were at 125 Colley Crescent with two children: Edith, a bus conductress, and Frank, occupation illegible. Arthur died in summer 1959, aged 71, and Ellen died two years later, at the same age.

Blanche Wilson (1892–1965) lived at 66 Huddersfield Road by 1911, when she was a general servant domestic for Matthias Kenworthy, a butcher, and his family. She had moved to Bank Farm, Monk Bretton, when she got married on 2 March 1916 to Samuel Cooper Fitzgerald, a widower and storekeeper of 35 Granville Street. They had four children, one of whom died in infancy. Samuel died in 1932, aged 42. By 1939, Blanche was at 58 Bridge Street with her three children: George, a cinema attendant, Eileen, a machinist cannister work, and Kenneth, a glasshand 'taker in'. Blanche Fitzgerald died in spring 1965, aged 72.

Clara Wilson (1901– ?) married Arthur R. Anderson, a coal miner hewer, in summer 1922 and they had three children. In 1939, they resided at 10 Pickup Crescent, Wombwell, with their children: Dorothy, Jean, a 'handwriter printing works', and Derrick A., a scholar. Arthur died early 1969, aged 68, and Clara seems to have died after 1983.

James Wilson (1869–1939) became a coal miner hewer and did not get married. He lodged with his brother Arthur at Horseshoe Croft, Wombwell, then with Walter's widow Elizabeth. James died early 1939, aged 69.

Arthur Wilson (1871–1927) was a coal miner hewer when he married Harriet Jepson in summer 1890. They had ten children, one of whom died young, and lived in Wentworth Road, Hoyland Nether, then Wombwell. By 1911, the family occupied five rooms at 308 Hough Lane, where they remained; their sons worked in a colliery. Arthur died late 1927, aged 56, and Harriet shared her home in Wombwell with several sons and their families until she died in 1944, aged 74.

The Children of Elizabeth Hezle and Joshua Rayner

Joshua Rayner (1857–1885) was baptised on 3 January 1858 at St Mary's Church then worked in a colliery and lived in Hoyle Mill. Joshua died on 2 July 1885, aged 27, of pneumonia.

William Rayner (c.1860–1885) was a miner living in Hoyle Mill when he married Mary Anne Jane Thorley on 20 June 1881 at Christ Church, Ardsley. William died on 11 July 1885, aged 25, of typhoid fever, from which he had suffered for nine days. Mary got married again in 1888 to Matthew Henry King, a police constable.

Hannah Rayner (1862–1945) got married at Christ Church, Ardsley, on 20 March 1881 to George Briggs, a colliery timekeeper. They moved to 3 Pit Yard Strafford, Dodworth, by 1891, when George was a colliery under manager. They had seven children, one of whom died in infancy. Their sons worked in a colliery while one daughter was a tailoress and Charlotte Elizabeth was a schoolteacher. George died early 1939, aged 78. Hannah, 'incapacitated', stayed at 11 Keresforth Hall Road with her married daughter Nellie, whose husband, Herbert H. Danby, was an elementary schoolteacher and special constable to help with the Second World War effort. Hannah Briggs died early 1945, age 82.

George Hinchcliffe (c.1819–1847)

George Hinchcliffe was a colliery labourer, aged 20, in 1841, when he was one of four lodgers at Common Side Houses in Ardsley, the home of Matthew Bedford, an agricultural labourer, and family. One lodger was a stonemason and the other two were coal miners, including William Scales (see chapter for Scales page 212).

George was residing in Hoyle Mill when he was killed in the 1847 explosion, aged 28; he was buried three days later in Christ Church churchyard in Ardsley.

Illustration from the 1842 Royal Commission Report. (Courtesy of the National Coalmining Museum)

John Hitchen (c.1834–1847)

John Hitchen resided in Worsbrough Common in 1841 with his parents, William, a miner aged 38, and Mary, a weaver the same age, as well as two sisters: Sarah, aged 11, and 6-month-old Hannah. John was killed, aged 13, in the 1847 explosion and interred three days later in St Mary's churchyard in Worsbrough, 'By Coroner's order for burial'.

<u>William and Mary Hitchen</u> had another daughter Martha soon after John died. William died in summer 1849, aged 48, and his widow worked as a weaver to help support their family. In 1851, Mary lived in Wilkinson

Postcard of St Mary's church, Worsbrough. (Author's Collection)

Houses, Worsbrough, with her two daughters, both at school: Hannah, aged 10 and Martha, aged 4.

James Hitchen, a weaver, was interviewed for the Royal Commission; he may have been related to John.

> There is not a shop in Barnsley where there is above four children working together. I've been a weaver here for 24 years. The children will begin in the morning at seven on an average, and they work generally till nine or ten at night; they are not well fed. I can answer for it mine own don't, and it is the case with many others. They get but middling of schooling, but it is chiefly on Sundays. The collier children are stronger, better fed, and healthier, but that trade is not so good as it was; but take 100 collier-boys and 100 weaver-boys, and the collier-boys will be the strongest and healthiest.

Ledger entry about seeking donations. (© Barnsley Archives)

Aaron Hobson (1820–1847)

Aaron Hobson was baptised on 20 February 1820 at St Mary's Church, Worsbrough, the son of George and Mary Hobson. In 1841, he was a 20-year-old miner, residing at Highstone, Worsbrough, with his parents, George, a miner aged 55, and Mary, aged 50, as well as his three younger siblings: Mary Ann, aged 15, Stuart, aged 10, and Zillah, aged 5. Aaron was killed, aged 26, in the 1847 explosion and interred three days later in St Mary's churchyard, Worsbrough, 'By Coroner's order for burial'.

George Hobson (c.1785–1856) was baptised on 10 April 1785 in Rawmarsh, the son of Joseph and Elizabeth Hobson. He married Mary Howarth on 19 December 1809 in York; they probably had older children who had left home by 1841 Census. In 1851, George, still working as a coal miner at 66, remained at Highstone with Mary, who was blind. Their two youngest children, Stuart and Zillah, lived with them as well as their granddaughter, Margaret Ogden. George died early 1856, aged 71, and Mary died in summer 1860, aged 73.

Aaron's Three Siblings

Mary Ann Hobson (c.1822–1902) married Samuel Ogden late 1841 and they settled in Worsbrough, moving from Jonas Taylor Houses to 3 Taylor Row, where they remained for the rest of their lives. They had twelve children: Margaret, Mary Ann, George, who died in 1863 aged 17, Elizabeth, who died in 1853 aged 5, Jane, Sarah, Zilla, Charles, William, John, Elizabeth, who died in 1867 aged 7, and Ellen. Samuel, who was born in Lancashire, worked as a hand loom weaver then linen bleacher; his widowed mother Mary Ogden senior, receiving parochial relief, was staying with them in 1851. Their daughters worked as weavers in a factory and their sons worked in a colliery. Samuel, who was a 'fancy weaver' at 75, died two years later. Mary Ogden continued to live with her unmarried son William, a coal miner, until she died in spring 1902, aged 80.

Stuart Hobson (1826–1893) was baptised on 19 November 1826 in Worsbrough and he became a coal miner. He got married to Mary Ann Bencliff on 24 January 1848 in Darfield, but she died soon afterwards. Stuart got married again to Margaret Ellis in spring 1859. They remained in Worsbrough, residing at Highstone Fould then 17 Dillington Square, and had seven children: George, Emily, Mary, Aaron, Joshua, Allen and Annie. Margaret died late 1885, aged 54. In 1891, Stuart lived at 21 Back Howard Street with four children, aged from 20 to 11: Aaron, Joshua, a glass blower apprentice, Allen and Annie, both at school. Stuart died in spring 1893, aged 66.

Aaron Hobson (1871–1935) was baptised on 24 December 1871 in Worsbrough and he was named after his uncle. He became a glass blower and glass bottle maker; he did not get married. In 1901, Aaron lived at 21 Dillington Square with his brother Allen; a young couple were boarders. Aaron was convicted for debt in March 1906 at Barnsley Court and imprisoned at HMP Wakefield for twenty-one days for his first offence as unable to pay £1 17s 9d (worth £759); he was 5ft 1½in tall with brown hair. By 1911, he was staying with his niece, Lily Greenhoff, a variety artist, her husband George, a coal miner hewer aged 24, and their two young sons in four rooms at No 7 Howard Street, Worsbrough Common. Aaron Hobson died in February 1935, aged 65, at 80 Gawber Road; he was interred on the 26th in Barnsley Cemetery.

Zillah Hobson (c.1836– ?) got married in spring 1859 to William Sharrock and they had two children: Ralph in spring 1860 and Mary Ann, who died in spring 1863, aged 1. In 1861, Zillah and William, aged 36, born in Wigan and a coal miner, resided in Worsbrough Common with Ralph. William died late 1863, aged 39, and Zillah had to work as a domestic servant to support herself and their young son. She moved to Elsecar by 1871 with Ralph, working for William Allott, a widower and miner, his son and their lodger.

Richard Hodgson (1815–1847)

Richard Hodgson was baptised on 5 April 1820, aged 5, at St Mary's Church, the son of John, a weaver, and Mary Hodgson. Richard, a miner, got married on 19 May 1839 at All Saints' Church, Silkstone, to Harriet, daughter of John Cartwright, a mason of Sheffield. In 1841, Richard was residing at Eastfield, Thurgoland, with Harriet, aged 20, and their baby son, George, who had been baptised on 27 September 1840 at All Saints' Church, Silkstone. They subsequently moved to Hoyle Mill and had two more children. Richard was killed in the Oaks Colliery explosion on 5 March 1847, aged 32. He was buried on the 8th at Christ Church churchyard in Ardsley.

Postcard of Christ Church, Ardsley. (Author's Collection)

Harriet Hodgson (c.1821–1891) was widowed at 26 and left with three children, according to contemporary newspapers: infant Eliza's death was registered early 1848 and she could have been born just before or after her father was killed, George died early 1849, aged 9 years, but the third is unknown. Harriet would have been dependent on relief to support a family. She got married again in 1851 to widower Joseph Oxley, who had several children. The ledger confirmed on 27 December 1851 that payments had been discontinued for 'the Widow of Richard Hodgson, on her Marriage to Joseph Oxley of Pogmoor on the 7th September last.'

In 1861, Harriet Oxley, a staymaker aged 40, was living in Pogmoor with Joseph, a coal miner aged 53, and his daughter Mary Ann, a staymaker aged 18. Harriet and Joseph continued to live in Pogmoor for more than twenty years, moving to 5 Greaves Street by 1891, when Joseph, a coal miner until at least 75 years old, had retired. Harriet died late 1891, aged 78, and Joseph died early 1899, aged 91.

The Interior of Christ Church, Ardsley. (Courtesy of the Tasker Trust)

Abraham Holland (c.1815–1847)

Abraham Holland got married on 22 January 1837 at All Saints' Church in Darton to Sarah Milner. In 1841, he was a coal miner, residing at 'Back of Cheapside', Silkstone, with Sarah, aged 20, and two children: George, aged 3, and 1-year-old Ann, who died in 1847. They had another three children: Eliza, baptised on 21 August 1842 at St Mary's Church, Thomas, baptised there on 28 August 1844 but died in infancy, and Abraham Thomas. Abraham was killed, aged 32, in the 1847 explosion and was buried in one of the communal graves in St Mary's churchyard three days later.

Sarah Holland (c.1817– ?) was baptised on Christmas Day 1817 in St Mary's Church in Kippax; she was the daughter of Charles, a waterman, and Anne Milner of Ollerton. Sarah was widowed at the age of 26 and left with four young children to raise, being either about to give birth to their youngest or nursing a new baby at the time of her husband's death. She was dependent on relief from the Subscription Fund.

Sarah's oldest daughter Ann died soon after her father, aged 7, and the committee agreed at their meeting on 3 September 1847 to pay 10 shillings (worth £46 based on RPI) to Sarah towards the funeral expenses of her daughter. Sarah would have lost the weekly allowance for Ann. In 1851, Sarah was a shopkeeper at Nelson Street, with three children, who were all at school: George, aged 13, Eliza, aged 8, and Abraham, aged 6. Sarah got married again to George Gawthorpe, a corn miller, and moved to Birstall, near Batley, where she worked in the woollen industry.

Abraham and Sarah's Two Sons

George Holland (c.1838–1911) was baptised on 26 March 1838 at St Mary's Church. He became a painter and lodged in Halifax before moving to Bradford. He got married on 29 March 1862 at St Peter's Church (Bradford Cathedral) to Mary Normington, a 20-year-old weaver. George and Mary moved house within Bradford several times and Mary worked as a worsted reeler in a mill to help support their children, who were also employed in the wool and worsted industry. The four survivors of thirteen children had left home; those named on Censuses were: Arthur (1862–1936) a violinist, Elizabeth born in 1864, Anne in 1867, Sarah Ann (1870–1873), Lillie born in 1877 and Fred in 1881. In 1911, George, a painter, and Mary, still working as a worsted reeler at 67, occupied three rooms at 53 Back Wood Street, Bradford, where George died that summer, aged 73. Mary died in the summer of 1913, aged 69.

Abraham Thomas Holland (1847–1882) was baptised on 27 June 1847 at St George's Church. Abraham was convicted of three offences as 'Rogue and Vagabond'; for the first two he was sentenced to fourteen days and two month. For his third offence, however, Abraham was convicted at Sheffield Petty Sessions on 16 February 1860 to two months in Wakefield House of Correction, followed by five years in a Reformatory; he was admitted on 14 April 1860, aged 15, to Calder Farm Institution in Mirfield, which had opened late 1855. The records describe him as 4ft 7in tall, fresh complexion, brown hair, hazel eyes with a scar on his right eyebrow. He had been employed as a collier. Abraham's general educational ability was fair; he could read and write a little. The regime would have been tough, but he would have received a better education than in the community, regular meals and assistance with finding employment.

It was probably after serving this sentence that he started using the name Thomas; he moved to Bradford to be near to his brother. Thomas Abraham Holland, a painter of 110a Abbey Street, Bradford, got married at St Peter's Church (Bradford Cathedral) on 26 July 1873. Martha Ellen Firth, an 18-year-old spinner of 82 Abbey Street, Bradford, was the daughter of Thomas Firth, an overlooker in a worsted mill. It was not long before Thomas and Martha separated.

Unable to afford a divorce, Martha went to Manningham by 1881 to lodge with her parents and three siblings, who all worked in a worsted mill. Martha was accompanied by her 11-month-old daughter, Selina Green Holland, and her partner, Jonathan Green, with whom she had another illegitimate daughter. Thomas was convicted again on 13 July 1882 of being a rogue and vagabond in Bradford; he was sentenced to two calendar months with hard labour in HM Prison Bradford. Records describe him as a painter aged 37, born in Barnsley, 5ft 4in tall, with grey hair and 'large scar bottom of back'.

Thomas Abraham Holland died late 1882, aged 38, in York. Martha and Jonathan, who worked as a worsted reeler and dyer, got married on 6 May 1883 at St Peter's and they had another three children. Jonathan had died by 1901; Martha Ellen Green died in summer 1936, aged 81.

Pinfold Steps and Shambles Street. (Courtesy of the Tasker Trust)

John Hough (1817–1847)

John Hough was baptised on 20 July 1817 at All Saints' Church, Cawthorne, the son of William and Elizabeth Hough. He married Christiana Simmons there on 16 April 1838. John and Christiana's first child William was born three months before they got married. They had five more children: Benjamin, who died in infancy in May 1840 and was buried in Cawthorne, Harriet, who was baptised at St Mary's Church on 21 August 1842 but died early 1843, Elizabeth, a second son named Benjamin, baptised at St Mary's on 20 July 1845, and John, born in summer 1847.

In 1841, John, a coal miner, his wife Christiana, aged 22 and their two children: William, aged 3, and 3-month-old Harriet, were residing in Wilson Street with her parents, Samuel Simmons, a linen weaver, and Esther, as well as her five younger siblings. John was killed, aged 30, in the 1847 explosion and was interred in one of the communal graves in St Mary's churchyard three days later; the burial register recorded that he resided in Hoyle Mill.

Christiana Hough (1819–1859), baptised on 31 January 1819 at St Mary's Church, was widowed, aged 27, and left with four young children to support. She would have been dependent on weekly relief from the Subscription Fund and on 11 July 1851, the Committee approved 'the supply of Clothes … to Widow Hough's Boy £1. 2. 9' (worth £125 based on RPI). In 1851, Christiana was a lodging house-keeper in Albert Street with her four children and four lodgers, two railway labourers and their wives. Christiana got married again on 25 April 1852 at St Mary's Church to Richard Robinson, who was ten years younger and a miner. Christiana Robinson died in Pontefract late 1859, aged 39.

John and Christiana's Three Children

William Hough (1838–1903) was born on 10 February 1838 and baptised on 22 April 1838 at All Saints' Church, Cawthorne. He became a miner and got married on 30 May 1859 at St George's Church to Ellen Brown, aged 19. In 1861, William, Ellen and their son John, aged 1, were lodging with his cousin Samuel, a coal miner, and family at 10 Doncaster and Saltersbrook Turnpike Road. William and Ellen had two more sons, John and George Herbert, before relocating by 1871 to Denison Square in Methley, Leeds, where they had another two sons, Benjamin and Dennis. Their five sons became coal miners. In 1891, John, aged 31, was living next door with his wife Sarah and their three children. William, who had not been working for at least two years, died at home in 1903, aged 64, and was interred in St Oswald's churchyard in Methley on 6 October 1903.

Elizabeth Hough (1843–1891) was baptised at St Mary's Church on 4 June 1843. She became a linen weaver and moved to Holbeck, Leeds. In 1861, she was boarding with Edward Bellhouse, a cloth dresser, and his family at 68 Nicholson Street before getting married to Charles Scott, a woollen warp dresser. They continued to live in the Leeds area, where they had four children: Irwin, Emily, Alfred and Harry. They moved from 17 Woolwich Street in Holbeck to 23 Weldon Place in Hunslet by 1881 and Elizabeth Scott died there early 1891, aged 47.

John Hough (c.1847– ?) worked as a coal miner and got married on 29 April 1872 at St Peter's Church (Minster), Leeds, to Fanny Fletcher, aged 21, of Wilson Street. By 1881, John and Fanny were living in Denison Yard, Methley, with their four sons, aged from 8 to 2, the older three at school: Tom, Sam, Walter and Fred. The family had moved around according to the places of birth, from Methley, where Fanny had been born, to Barnsley, to Methley again then Rotherham and back to Methley, where they settled. Tom died in 1886, aged 13, and he was interred on 5 October in St Oswald's churchyard. When their fifth son was born in 1888, he was named Tom Gelder. John was convicted of several offences. On 1 November 1895, he was imprisoned in HMP Wakefield for twenty-eight days for 'wife desertion' because he was unable to pay the fine of £3 9s 6d (worth £1,555). John was a collier from Barnsley, able to read, 5ft 4½in tall with brown hair and eyes, and he had a heart tattoo inside his left forearm; this was his fourth offence. On 8 June 1896, he was convicted at Pontefract for debt and served twenty-one days rather than pay 19s 5d. All four of John and Fanny's children got married and had families; Walter worked as a gasman, Sam a railway worker at Newton Colliery, Fred a coal miner hewer, and Tom a fitter.

The Wire Trellis Inn in Gas Nook. (Courtesy of the Tasker Trust)

John Jessop (1829–1847)

John Jessop was born on 24 February 1829 and baptised, at the age of 9 years, on 24 October 1838 at St George's Church; he was the only son of Thomas Jessop, a weaver, and Sarah Jessop, who died young. Thomas got married again on 24 August 1837 at All Saints' Church in Silkstone to Jane Scruton, a weaver, who was a widow with three children, the daughter of Barnett Winterbottom, a weaver. In 1841, Thomas, a 35-year-old mason, and Jane, aged 30, resided in Copper Street with his son John, aged 11, and Jane's three young sons surname Scruton: William, Thomas and Benjamin.

John was killed, aged 17, in the 1847 explosion; the *Illustrated London News* reported that John was brought out alive on Saturday 6 March but died soon afterwards. He was interred two days later in the communal graves in St Mary's churchyard.

<u>Thomas Jessop</u> (c.1806–1850) was the son of Thomas, a labourer. The Prerogative & Exchequer Courts of York Probate Index for May 1850 recorded that 'Jessop Jane (Wife of Thomas Jessop) of Barnsley', was left £100 when he died without a Will (worth £82,330).

Postcard of
St Mary's
church.
(© Barnsley
Archives)

James Kelly (c.1803–1847)

James Kelly was in his 40s, married and living in Hoyle Mill when he was killed in the 1847 explosion and interred three day later in Christ Church churchyard, Ardsley. The *Leeds Intelligencer* provided details of the inquest. Mr Wilson, one of the proprietors involved in recovering the bodies, explained:

> The air was very foul indeed in the board gates… There were many bodies laid all along the board gate. I saw James Kelly; he had been killed by the blast…. All the colliers that were found in the south level were killed by the choke damp.

James' widow was eligible for relief from the Subscription Fund but the ledger recorded that, at their meeting on 27 December 1851, payments had been discontinued for 'Widow Kelley, who died on the 21st of March last'. Mary Kelly died on 21 March 1851, aged 59.

Church Street, Ardsley. (Courtesy of the Tasker Trust)

William Kirk (c.1826–1847)

William Kirk was 21 years old and residing in Wilson's Piece when he was killed in the 1847 explosion; he was interred three days later in one of the communal graves in St Mary's churchyard.

Illustration in the 1842 Royal Commission Report. (Courtesy of National Coalmining Museum)

James Lees (c.1830–1847)

James Lees was baptised on 22 August 1830 at St Mary's Church, the son of Benjamin Lees, a weaver, and Sarah. It seems that both of James' parents died before the 1841 Census, when James Lees, aged 11, and his sisters, Ann, aged 13, and Mary, aged 7, were living at Old Toll Bar House with their aunt Martha (née Lees), aged 40, and her husband John Moss, a publican of the same age. James was killed in the 1847 explosion, aged 17, and he was interred three days later in Christ Church churchyard, Ardsley, as James Lee of Hoyle Mill.

The Colliers' Relief Fund Committee agreed at their meeting on 24 June 1847 'That the Revd A.G. Micklethwaite be allowed to draw upon the Committee for any Sum not exceeding two pounds for the Relief (as he may see occasion) of the Aunt and Sisters of <u>James Lee</u>'.

<u>Mary Lees</u>, a weaver aged 16, was at Hoyle Mill in 1851 with her aunt Martha and uncle John Moss, a weaver. They moved to Kendray Row, Ardsley, by 1861, where they managed a grocer's shop. Ann and Mary both got married.

Kendray Hospital with the Oaks Colliery in the distance. (© Barnsley Archives)

Lindley (Linley) Brothers: Isaac (c.1817–1847), Samuel (c.1818–1847) And Matthew (1824–1847)

<u>Matthew Lindley</u> senior (1789–1851) was baptised on 23 August 1789 at Wentworth Church, the son of John Lindley and Elizabeth (née Scholey). He married Selina Birks on 8 December 1814 at Rotherham Minster. After Selina died, Matthew got married again on 16 May 1836 at All Saints' Church, Darton, to Ann Nicholson, a widow from Wortley. In 1841, Matthew, a coal miner, was residing at 'As Barr'(close to Red Brook), Gawber, with Ann, aged 55, and their four children aged from 22 to 14: Sam, John, Matthew and Ann.

Matthew Lindley, gave evidence to the Children's Employment Commission in 1841:

> I am nearly 52 years old. I am a collier in Messrs. Day and Twibell's pit. Children are sometimes brought to pits at the age of six years and are taken out of their beds at four o'clock and between that and five throughout the year. They leave the pits between four and five in the afternoon, making on an average 12 hours' work. They have a little milk or a little coffee and a bit of bread in the morning before they go to the pit, and they will take nothing with them but a bit of bread and perhaps a little tea, but oftener dry bread than anything else. Their parents cannot often get them more. They do not have meat. The parents do not get wages enough to provide meat for the children. When they come out of the pit at night, they may have a little meat or milk porridge, but a bit of dry bread and a sup of milk is the usual supper. The boys do look healthy, it is true, but it is

159

because they are young. The work they get to do is not hard as far as trapping is concerned, but hurrying is very slavish work, and I have known boys go to work all the 12 hours without more than a bit of dry bread to eat. The boys are sometimes very cruelly used by the elder ones, they get beaten too often. Their education is much neglected. Nineteen out of twenty of the boys in pits cannot write. One half cannot read, and they cannot generally answer common questions when asked. The morals of the pit children are uncommonly bad for want of cultivation. They are both given to cursing and swearing for want of better tutorage; they are also Sabbath-breakers, and the young men are as bad; they mislead the young ones. I was talking to the lads to-day about their wickedness in swearing and cursing when we might at any moment be destroyed by sulphur. There is a great deal of it in our pit. Where I work it is more clear of sulphur than where you went to-day.

I think nine hours quite long enough for coal-pits to be working, including an hour for meals; and men ought to have sufficient wages; a man ought to have 4s a-day clear of the hurriers' wages, out of which he would have to buy gunpowder and candles, and this would cost between 4s and 5s per fortnight. The younger men work longer at the end of the fortnight and less at the beginning, but not the elder men. It would be better for the health of the children, better for their morals, better for their education, better for the Government and for the country, that children should be prevented from working till they were 11 years old; but I think it would be hard on many parents unless wages rose. I think that it is true that children doing men's work lowers wages. I wish also that the Government would expel all girls and females from mines. I can give proof that they are very immoral, and I am certain that the girls are worse than the men in point of morals, and use far more indecent language. It unbecomes them in every way; there is not one in ten of them that know how to cut a shirt out or make one, and they learn neither to knit nor sew; and I believe also that they are themselves a cause of lowering

[Putting, in Mid and East Lothian.]

Illustration from the 1842 Royal Commission Report. (Courtesy of the National Coalmining Museum)

wages for the men. They ought to go out to service. I think that as there is so much cursing in pits there ought to be a law fining the men for every oath used, for this would deter the children from following their example. I have known myself of a case where a married man and a girl who hurried for him had sexual intercourse often in the bank where he worked.

Matthew was living in Gawber when he died in 1851, aged 61, and he was interred on 11 November in All Saints' churchyard, Darton.

As I have been unable to find details about the partners or children of Samuel and Matthew, their short stories are first.

Samuel Lindley (1818–1847), baptised on 27 December 1818 at Wentworth Church, got married on 8 August 1842 at All Saints' Church, Darton, to Ann Hampson, a widow and the daughter of Joseph Whittaker, a basket maker. According to newspaper reports they had three children. (Forty children with surname Lindley were born between 1842 and 1847 in Ecclesfield).

Matthew Lindley (1824–1847), baptised on 14 March 1824 at All Saints' Church, Silkstone, was not married but had a child with Ann Jackson. Ann was baptised on 3 May 1829 at St Mary's Church, daughter of Thomas, a weaver, and Elizabeth Jackson. (Fifteen children with surname Jackson were born in 1845 and 1846, seventeen with surname Lin(d)ley). The Colliers' Relief Committee decided at their meeting on 24 June 1847 'That under the peculiar circumstances of the case Ann Jackson be from

Postcard of All Saints' church, Darton. (Author's Collection)

henceforth treated as the Widow of <u>Matthew Lindley</u> (27) and allowed two shillings (worth £80) weekly for herself and one shilling for her child.'

Samuel and Matthew were killed together in the Oaks Colliery explosion on 5 March 1847; Samuel was 29 years old and Matthew was 23. They were both interred in All Saints' churchyard, Darton, on 8 March 1847, along with their brother Isaac and another miner.

Isaac Lindley (c.1817–1847) was a miner when he married Jane Wooffenden, aged 22, on 26 June 1838 by Licence at St George's Church. In 1841, they were residing in Gawber with their son Sam, who died in summer 1842, aged 3; they had a lodger. Isaac and Jane subsequently had two daughters: Selina and Mary. Isaac was killed, aged 30, in the 1847 explosion and he was interred three days later in All Saints' churchyard, Darton, with his brothers Samuel and Matthew.

<u>Jane Lindley</u> (1816–1889) was baptised on 14 July 1816 at All Saints' Church, the daughter of Edward, a blacksmith, and Ann Wooffenden of Gawber. Jane was widowed, aged 30, and left with two young daughters to raise alone. In 1851, Jane was a pauper living with them in Gawber; she would have been dependent on relief from the Subscription Fund, although it seems to have been insufficient.

162

Jane got married again in summer 1854 to Henry Lander, a miner aged 38 from Stoke and she lost her entitlement to relief. She had three more children: Henry, Ann and Thomas. Jane a stay maker, was at 56 Pickering Row, Gawber, by 1861 with Henry, a pit furnace man, and all five children. Henry was a colliery banksman in 1871 and they resided at Engine Fold, Barugh, with three children. Henry had become a 'hawker drapery' by 1881, when he and Jane were at Barugh Bridge with a grandson. Henry died there late 1883, aged 70. Jane Lander died in August 1889, aged 74, and she was buried in All Saints' churchyard.

The Two Daughters of Isaac and Jane Lindley

Selina Lindley (1843–1870) was baptised on 9 July 1843 at All Saints. She worked as a cotton weaver before getting married on 9 March 1863 at St Thomas' Church, Gawber, to Joshua Turner, a boat builder aged 20. They lived in Barugh where they had five children: Mary Elizabeth, Joseph, Ernest, Annie Gertrude, who died in spring 1869, aged 1, and Laura Beatrice, who died early 1870, under 6 months old, and was interred on 16 February 1870 in All Saints' churchyard. There are many burials of children in All Saints' parish registers, which looks like some epidemic, such as cholera, typhoid or smallpox. Tragically both Selina and Joshua died soon after Laura and they were all buried together; Selina on 1 March 1870, aged 27, then Joshua on 13 March, aged 26. Three young children were orphaned.

Mary Elizabeth Turner (1863–1944), orphaned aged 6; she and Joseph went to live with their Turner grandparents and uncle in Barugh, next door but one to where Ernest was staying. Mary married Charles Shaw, a colliery labourer, on 3 July 1882 at All Saints Church, Silkstone, and they had nine children. They moved to five rooms at 27 Blucher Street by 1901 and remained there for some time. In 1939, 'Elizabeth' resided at 11 Columbia Street with Charles, a retired beer barrel washer, their married daughter Harriet Cooper, aged 43, and her two children. Charles died in spring 1940, aged 82, and Mary Shaw died early 1944, aged 80.

Joseph Turner (1865–1914) was baptised on 31 December 1865 at All Saints' Church and orphaned aged 5. He was brought up by his Turner grandparents and became a coal miner. Joseph got married on 6 April 1896 at St George's Church to Harriet Cherryholme, aged 20. They had six children, three of whom had died by 1911, when they occupied three rooms at 31 Nelson Street. Joseph died late 1914, aged 49.

Ernest Turner (1867–1928), orphaned aged 3, he was raised by his married uncle Holling, a colliery deputy, in Barugh. Ernest became a blacksmith and married Ada Dawson on 28 July 1884 at All Saints' Church. He was convicted for debt on 23 April 1894 at Barnsley County Court and served twenty-eight days in HM Prison Wakefield as unable to payment the fine of £1 9s 6d (worth £669). Ernest was convicted of another two similar offences on 15 March 1907 and 2 October 1907. By 1911 they occupied four rooms at Upper Carr Green, Mapplewell. Ernest died early 1928, aged 62.

Mary Lindley (1844–1918) was baptised on 8 February 1846 at All Saints' Church. She worked as a cotton winder before she got married on 21 March 1864 at St Thomas' Church to Joseph Brown, a miner aged 21. They had eleven children. Mary and Joseph, a hewer, had moved from Barugh by 1891 to five rooms at 52 Carlton Terrace, where they remained for the rest of their lives. In 1911, four of their children were at home: Ada, aged 30, Arthur a 'stationary engine-man (colliery below)', Mary Elizabeth, a teacher aged 25, and Alice, aged 22. Joseph died in summer 1916, aged 73, and Mary Brown died in January 1918, aged 72; they were buried in the same grave in Carlton Cemetery.

The Three Children of Jane Lindley and Henry Lander

Henry Lander (1855–1930) was a hewer and he got married early 1875 to Harriet Ives, with whom he had two daughters in Barugh: Ada and Jane Ann. Harriet died early 1898, aged 42. Both daughters got married and had families; one grandson was employed in a chemical works and another as a railway tunnel engineman. Henry died late 1930, aged 75.

Ann Lander (1857–1925) got married on 24 April 1876 at All Saints' Church to Jabez Richardson, a miner aged 20. They had a son, John Henry, early 1877 but the family were separated by 1881. Ann, recorded as unmarried, was a domestic servant at Haigh Hall in Kexborough; her husband Jabez was elsewhere, and their son John Henry was staying with Ann's parents. It was extremely difficult then to obtain a divorce and for a woman to support herself. Ann became the common-law wife of George Dawson, a miner, using his surname. They had two daughters, Ellen and Eliza, and resided in Barugh then Low Ackworth. John Henry Richardson, a hewer, married Clara Parkin on 24 May 1896 at St Mary's Church, Wombwell. Ann Richardson ('Dawson') died late 1925, aged 68.

Jabez Richardson (1856–1919) led a very troubled life; his health problems would have been exacerbated by responsibility for a wife and child. As a collier of Darfield, aged 23, he was convicted at Barnsley Court of his first offence on 27 February 1879 and sentenced to a period of imprisonment at HMP Wakefield for neglect of his family; he was 5ft 7¾in tall with brown hair. Jabez was discharged on 13 March and it was noted that he had been in the Coldstream Guards for eighteen months but discharged as an invalid. In 1881, Jabez, a coal miner aged 24, was a pauper patient 'lunatic' at South Yorkshire County Lunatic Asylum in Wadsley. (This subsequently became Middlewood Hospital and is now a gated housing development in Sheffield). He was one of 541 male patients, with a wide range of occupations, and more than 500 female patients; there were 117 resident staff. Jabez was transferred from Wadsley Asylum before 1901 and may have been in the West Riding Asylum for Pauper Lunatics, Stanley Royd, in Wakefield, before being moved to Storthes Hall Asylum in Kirkburton, Huddersfield, which opened in 1904. He died there in 1919, aged 62, and was buried on 20 March 1919 in St Thomas' churchyard in Thurstonland, where patients were usually interred in communal, unmarked graves.

Thomas Lander (1858–1904) was baptised on 24 April 1859 at St Thomas' Church. He worked in a colliery and got married in 1880 to Sarah Harper. In 1881, Thomas, Sarah, aged 24, and their baby daughter were living close to his brother Henry and family in Barugh, where they remained. Thomas and Sarah had four children by 1891: Jane Ann, Frances, Mary and Edward. Sarah died late 1899, aged 43. Thomas Lander died early 1904, aged 44. Their two youngest orphaned children went to stay with their uncle Henry.

John Littlewood (c.1824–1847)

John Littlewood was residing in Hoyle Mill when he was killed in the 1847 explosion, aged 23. He was interred three days later in one of the communal graves in St Mary's churchyard. According to contemporary newspaper reports, he left a widow and two children, but they were not mentioned in the ledger.

Hoyle Mill general view. (Courtesy of the Tasker Trust)

George Matthewman (1818–1847)

George Matthewman was baptised on 8 November 1818 at All Saints' Church, Darton, son of Francis and Mary Matthewman of Gawber. Francis, son of George and Ann Matthewman, was born on 4 May 1786 and baptised on the 6th at St Mary's Church. He became a weaver and got married to Mary Foweather on 18 January 1808 at All Saints' Church, Silkstone. Mary, born on 9 September 1774, was the daughter of Thomas Foweather, a glassmaker of Gawber. They had four children: Ann, who was baptised on 14 July 1816 in Darton and died in spring 1842, aged 26, George, Huldah and Isaac. Huldah and Isaac were baptised at one week old, but 'entered into the church' in Darton together on 14 July 1833.

George was a coal miner when he got married on 17 February 1839 at All Saints' Church to Mary Shirt, aged 21. They had four children: John, Ellen, Ann and Francis. In 1841, George, Mary and their infant son were staying at Gawber Height with his parents and siblings. He was killed, aged 28, in the 1847 explosion and interred three days later in St George's Churchyard.

Mary Matthewman senior (1774–1865) lived with her children after Francis died in 1850, aged 64; he was buried on 11 December in St George's churchyard. She joined her widowed son Isaac in Nelson Street, then stayed with daughter Huldah at 2 Court, 2 Sackville Street. Mary died in 1865, aged 90, and she was interred on 2 July in St Thomas' Churchyard, Gawber.

George's Two Siblings

Huldah Matthewman (1824–1896) married John Hardcastle, a weaver, on 13 April 1845 at All Saints' Church, Silkstone. They lived at different addresses in Barnsley and had seven children: Ann, Hannah, Mary,

167

Sarah, Thomas, Clara and George. John was a 'rifle volunteer range marker' by 1871, and Huldah was a 'linen factory operative winder', like her married daughter Sarah, who was staying there. John died late 1889, aged 67, and Sarah was also widowed around this time, left with two young sons. Huldah Hardcastle died in spring 1896, aged 72.

Isaac Matthewman (1826–1851), a miner, married Ann Hardy in spring 1844 and their only son was born in 1846: John Campbell Matthewman was baptised on 1 December 1848 at St Mary's Church, soon after his mother's death, aged 22. In 1851, Isaac was living in Nelson Street with his son and widowed mother. Isaac died soon after the Census, aged 25, making his son an orphan, aged 5.

George's Widow

Mary Matthewman junior (1817–1892) was baptised on 12 October 1817 at All Saints' Church, Silkstone, daughter of Benjamin, a maltster and gardener of Nabs Wood, and Ellen (née Shirt), who had nine children. Her mother died when Mary was young, and her father got married again on 4 May 1823.

Postcard of All Saints' church, Silkstone. (Author's Collection)

All Saints' church, Silkstone. (Author's image)

Mary, a cotton winder before she married George, was widowed aged 29, and left with four children to raise alone. She was dependent on relief from the Colliers' Relief Committee. The ledger recorded that on 22 April 1848 her allowance was suspended while unfavourable reports about her behaviour were investigated. This was confirmed on 4 May 1848, but payments were reinstated for children provided that they attended school regularly.

Mary gave birth to an illegitimate daughter, Elizabeth, in summer 1848, and subsequently got married again on 7 October 1849 in Darfield to Boaz Haigh. Her eldest son John was mentioned in the minutes on 28 December 1850 as having 'attained the age of 10 years in 1850', at which age his allowance ceased as he was expected to work. The Ledger recorded that on 11 July 1851, 'the supply of Clothes to the following Parties is approved viz to Widow Matthewman's Boy £1. 1. 9' (worth £120 based on RPI).

In 1851, Mary Haigh and her second husband Boaz, a weaver of linen cloth aged 36, were living in Ardsley with her six children. Four with George Matthewman were at school, aged 10 to 5: John, Ellen, Ann and Francis, Elizabeth, aged 2 plus their 6-month-old daughter Amanda Haigh. Mary and Boaz moved to 11 Pitt Street and had three more children: Susanna, Benjamin and Arthur, before Boaz died late 1865, aged 51.

Mary was widowed for a second time, aged 48, with four children under 15. In 1871, she resided at 43 Park Road with various children and grandchildren. Mary moved to 29 Pindar Oaks Street by 1881 with Arthur, a coal miner, and her daughter Ellen and family. Mary, living on her own means, and Arthur subsequently moved in with Ellen and William Barraclough at 19 Commercial Street, where Mary Haigh died in April 1892, aged 74. She was buried in Barnsley Cemetery.

The Four Children of George and Mary Matthewman

John Thomas Matthewman (1838–1900) was apprenticed to an iron founder from the age of 10 until he qualified. He was an iron moulder residing at Melton Place when he got married on 26 May 1860 at St George's Church to Annie Nelson, aged 19, of New Street, daughter of Horatio Nelson, a weaver. They had six children: Evangeline, Clara, who died summer 1875, aged 10, Ann Elizabeth, Ada, John and Lilian.

John and Annie moved with their family from Back Joseph Street to 19 Summer Street then 63 Summer Lane, where Annie died late 1890, aged 50. John continued to live with his children until they had all got married and started families of their own; three moved away from Barnsley, to Mansfield, Huddersfield and Rotherham. John died in April 1900, aged 60, at 26 King Street and he was buried in the same grave as his wife in Barnsley Cemetery.

Ellen Matthewman (1840–1916), baptised on 9 June 1842 at St Mary's, became a linen weaver. She got married in summer 1866 to her brother-in-law, William Barraclough, who went on to do various jobs in a colliery. They had six children: Henry, Ann, Frederick, Bertram – who died early 1885, aged 6 – Tom and Francis (Frank). In 1871, Ellen, William, aged 29, and their two oldest children resided with her widowed mother at 43 Park Road; they all moved into 29 Pindar Oaks Street by 1881. By 1891, William was working as a linen weaver and the family lived at 19 Commercial Street. All their children got married and had families; the men working in the local collieries or factories. He became a warehouseman and linen factory hand when they had moved to Emmanuel Street. After William died in January 1905, aged 63, Ellen joined a married daughter at 30 Corporation Street. Ellen Barraclough died there in July 1916, aged 74, and she was buried with her husband in Barnsley Cemetery.

Francis (Frank) Barraclough (1883– ?) married Ellen Atherton in summer 1907 and they had one daughter, Evelyn, before Ellen died in 1910, aged 25, possibly in childbirth as baby Amelia Barraclough died around the same time. Frank and Evelyn moved into his parents-in-laws' large house at 20 Grove Street; Thomas Atherton was a caretaker for the Borough Council and Sarah managed the home for their eight surviving children out of seventeen. Frank enlisted as a private in the Royal Army Ordnance Corps, having got married again in spring 1916 to Sarah Harrison. In 1939, Francis, a foreman in a bobbin factory, and Sarah resided at 33 Lang Crescent with his daughter Evelyn.

Ann Matthewman (1843–1868), baptised on 31 October 1843 at St George's Church, married Henry Blomeley, a miner, on 22 April 1867 at St Mary's. She died in spring 1868, aged 24. Henry got married again in 1870 at St Mary's to Sarah Bamforth, who had one son before she died by 1881. Henry and his son moved into a shared property at 22 Union Street then lodged in Doncaster Road with his brother-in-law Frank and family. He was employed in a bottle works by 1901 and had moved next door. Henry died in 1906, aged 66.

Francis (Frank) Matthewman (1846–1903), was a linen dresser when he got married in summer 1865 to his sister-in-law Harriet Barraclough. They moved into Doncaster Road, with her widowed father and remained there for the rest of their lives. Frank and Harriet had two children and Harriet died in April 1891, aged 44. Their married daughter and family lived with Frank until he died in December 1903, aged 57; he was buried on 3 January 1904 in Barnsley Cemetery.

Mary's Illegitimate Daughter and Four Children with Boaz Haigh

Elizabeth Matthewman (1848–1913) married Edwin Wildsmith, a sawyer, on 11 February 1871 at St John the Baptist Church. Their home for most of their lives was 52 Commercial Street and they did not have any children. Eliza Wildsmith died in summer 1913, aged 66, and Edwin was a widower for twenty-one years.

Amanda Haigh (1850–1874) was a linen weaver until she married James Todd, a coal miner, on 19 June 1871 at St John the Baptist's Church. They had a son but Amanda died early 1874, aged 23. James got married again in 1876 to Catherine Adams.

Susannah Haigh (1852–1927) got married in summer 1876 to Robert Greenwood, who had his own greengrocery business. They moved from 70 Commercial Street to 4 Corporation Street then four rooms at 142 Sheffield Road and had seven children, three of whom died young. Susannah died early 1927, aged 74. Robert retired and moved to lodgings at 100 Park Road, where he died in 1941, aged 88.

Benjamin Haigh junior (1856–1932) worked in a glass works then as an engine tenter when he married Emily Beaumont on 2 April 1877 at

St Mary's. They moved from 6 Taylor's Yard to 1 Foundry Street as their family grew and Emily worked as a linen weaver early on. They had fourteen children but lost eight of them in childhood. Benjamin became a house painter by 1901, when they resided at 5 Rockingham Street, and their three sons were apprentices. He was a school caretaker for the Council by 1911, occupying five rooms at 52 Princess Street with Emily as his assistant and four adult children, who worked as two tailoresses, an iron moulder and a plasterer. Emily died in 1927, aged 71, and Benjamin died early 1932, aged 76.

Arthur Haigh (1858–1929), worked in a colliery and resided with his mother until she died in 1892. In 1901, Arthur, a 'colliery roadman', was living at 142 Cemetery Road with his widowed niece Mary Haigh, housekeeper, and her baby daughter. Arthur died in summer 1929, aged 71.

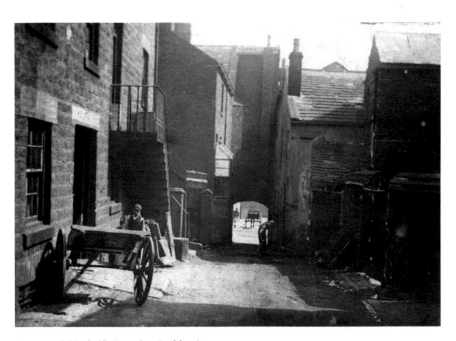

Lancaster's Yard. (© Barnsley Archives)

Abraham Matthews (1799–1847) and His Son Vincent Matthews (c.1832–1847)

Abraham Matthews was baptised on 19 May 1799 at St Mary's Church in Mirfield, near Dewsbury, the son of Abraham and Sarah Matthews. Abraham junior got married on 8 April 1822 at All Saints' Church in Wakefield (Cathedral) to Sarah Mitchell. Abraham worked as a miner and they lived in the Wakefield area, in Horbury then Emley, before relocating to Ardsley. In 1841, Abraham was living at the 'Oaks Colliery' in Ardsley with Sarah, aged 45, and their seven children: John, Abraham, Sarah, Mary, George, Vincent and Andrew. No occupations were recorded for the older children, but John and Abraham junior would have joined their father by then.

Vincent Matthews was baptised on 25 November 1832 at St Michael's Church, Emley, and he became a miner like his father and brothers.

Abraham and Vincent were both killed in the 1847 explosion; Abraham, aged 48, and Vincent, aged 15. Vincent was buried three days later in Christ Church churchyard, Ardsley; the interment for his father, whose body could not be recovered until later, was in the same churchyard on 19 March.

The *Illustrated London News* reported: 'On Tuesday morning the pit was very full of sulphur, and in the evening it was impossible to descend. At that time there remained in the pit three individuals,' including Abraham Matthews and William Walton, who had been working close to each other and were suspected as having caused the explosion. It took time to recover their bodies because they were buried in the fall of rock caused by the explosion. Abraham had been working near to the old breaks but he was exonerated by the discovery that William had taken

Illustration from the 1842 Royal Commission Report. (Courtesy of the National Coalmining Museum)

a candle into them. Abraham's was the last body to be recovered and it was brought out on 16 March, the closing day of the Inquest.

Sarah Matthews (c.1793–1878) was born in Horbury but baptised on 21 February 1793 at St John the Baptist's Church, Penistone, daughter of George Mitchell. She was widowed aged 51 and left with six children to bring up alone. It must have been particularly painful for Sarah to have to wait so long for her husband's body to be recovered for burial and for him to be blamed initially for the explosion.

The Committee referred to the Matthews family on two occasions. On 24 June 1847, they agreed an amount 'towards defraying the Expenses of Administration to the Effects of her late Husband ten pounds [worth £8,030] to the Widow of Abraham Matthews … and that an eye be kept upon her youngest Son [Andrew]. On 15 February 1848 they agreed,

175

'That the further Sum of 18s be paid to the Widow of <u>Abraham Matthews</u>, the Balance of the Costs of Administration to her late Husband's Effects.'

By 1861, she was residing at 33 Summer Lane with her married daughter, Mary Wood, and granddaughter Edith. Sarah Matthews died there on 12 November 1878, aged 85, and she was buried on the 14th in Barnsley Cemetery. Sarah had made a Will and her executors were her son-in-law, George England, a builder, and Charles Newman, a 'gentleman and solicitor', the son of Edward Newman, secretary of the Colliers' Relief Committee. Sarah's personal estate was valued at less than £200, but what she left was shared equally between her surviving sons and daughter: Abraham, George Mitchell and Sarah Ann.

The Children of Abraham and Sarah Matthews; Vincent's Siblings

It proved difficult to find records, especially for the eldest and youngest sons. <u>John Matthews</u> was baptised on 17 August 1823 at St Peter and St Leonard's Church, Horbury. <u>Andrew Matthews</u> was baptised on 3 June 1836 at St Michael's Church, Emley.

<u>Abraham Matthews</u> (1826– ?) was born in Horbury and baptised on 26 March 1826 at St Peter and St Leonard's Church. He joined his father as a colliery worker and was an engine tenter when he married Hannah Chew on 18 September 1849 at St Mary's Church, Barnsley. In 1851, Abraham, Hannah, aged 24, and their 8-month-old son John were staying with her widowed father John Chew, a 70-year-old farmer of six acres, in Huddersfield Bradford Road, Wike, Bradford, next to the Toll Gate. They had moved to Paradise Place, Hunslet, Leeds by 1861, when they had three sons: John, aged 11, Edward, aged 8, and George, aged 4.

<u>Sarah Ann Matthews</u> (c.1827–1903) was baptised on 4 November 1827 at St Michael's Church, Emley, while her parents were living at Bank Furnace. Sarah was working as a milliner in 1851 for Jane Raywood, a widow and annuitant aged 65, of Sheffield Road, Barnsley; one of Jane's two daughters was a milliner and she also employed a milliner apprentice and a domestic servant. Sarah got married on 4 April 1858 at St George's Church to George England, a widower with children. Sarah and George had four children

together: John, Amy, Helena and Louis. In 1861, Sarah and George, a joiner aged 38, resided in West Bretton with George's two children and their son John, aged 2; they employed a domestic servant. By 1871, they had relocated to 6 Summer Lane, where George employed several men and boys in his joinery and building business, until he died on 25 June 1895, aged 72. George left effects of £4,741 16s 8d (worth £551,800 based on RPI).

Sarah was living on her own means at 41 Victoria Crescent by 1901 with her two daughters: Amy, a school mistress aged 32, and Helena, a music teacher of piano, aged 28. Sarah Ann England died there on 14 November 1903, aged 76, and she was buried on the 22nd in the same grave as her husband in Barnsley Cemetery. Probate was granted to two friends, a draper and a tallow-chandler. She left them £5 each for dealing with her estate, paying any debts and her funeral costs, in addition to selling items. The remainder of her estate, the total value of which was £2,551 10s 5d (worth £276,000 based on RPI), was left in trust to be shared equally between her children and stepchildren, surname England: William Goodworth, John Mathews, Mary Elizabeth, Amy and Helena.

Mary Ann Matthews (c.1829–1895) was born at Bank Furnace and baptised on 9 August 1829 at St Michael's. She got married on 14 August 1859 at St Mary's Church in Barnsley to Alfred Wood, a fitter aged 26, son of James Wood, a woodman. They had one daughter, Edith Matthews Wood, who was born in December 1860 and baptised at St Mary's on 17 May 1861, when Mary, a milliner, and baby Edith were staying at 7 Summer Lane with her widowed mother. Alfred died late 1870, aged 35, and her mother died in 1878.

Mary, employed as a warehouse seamstress and tailoress, moved to one of the Courts in Old Town with Edith, who also worked as a tailoress. Mary Ann Wood died on 11 December 1895, aged 65, and was buried in Barnsley Cemetery. Mary had made a Will about three weeks before her death, in which she nominated as executors her nephew, John Matthews England, a schoolmaster, and a county court clerk. She left £37 13s 10d (worth £4,386 based on RPI) which was to be invested to provide money for the maintenance of Edith. Any remainder after her daughter's death was to be shared equally between Mary's nieces and nephews.

Edith Matthews Wood was boarding at 12 Church Field with Anne Briggs and her daughter by 1901. She died at 27 Back High Street in February 1904, aged 42; and was interred in her own grave in Barnsley Cemetery.

<u>George Mitchell Matthews</u> (1831– ?) was born at Bank and baptised on 24 April 1831 at St Michael's Church. He became a coal miner and got married. George and Elizabeth, aged 21, were living in Ratt Row, Stainborough, by 1861.

Above and below: Colliers Row. (front and rear) (Courtesy of the Tasker Trust)

178

Robert McLear (c.1828–1847)

Robert McLear was killed, aged 19, in the 1847 explosion and buried in one of the communal graves in St Mary's churchyard three days later. The Subscription Fund Committee initially paid relief to his widowed mother but they decided at their meeting on 4 May 1849, 'that the Pay to the following Parties be henceforth discontinued altogether they being merely Widows who lost Children upon whom it is considered they did not much depend viz- to Widows … McLear etc'.

May Day Green. (Courtesy of the Tasker Trust)

179

Daniel Mellor (c.1828–1847)

Daniel Mellor was 14 years old in 1841, when he resided in George Street with his parents, Thomas and Martha, plus his older brother William, aged 16; they were all linen weavers. William lost his family within a five-year period: his mother died in 1844, aged 56; Daniel, who had become a miner, was killed, aged 19, in the 1847 explosion, being buried three days later in one of the communal graves in St Mary's churchyard; his father died in 1849, aged 72.

William appears to have married Catherine, who was Irish, and they had two daughters: Martha, baptised on 1 May 1849 at St George's Church, and Harriet, born in Oldham. William worked on a power loom, for linen in Barnsley and for cotton in Oldham, where Catherine was a charwoman and Martha, aged 12, was a cotton minder.

Ledger summary at the end of 1848. (© Barnsley Archives)

George Parker (c.1833–1847)

George Parker was baptised on 20 October 1833 at St Mary's Church, the son of William and Mary Parker. His father died before 1841, when George was residing at Blucher Street with his mother, aged 30, who had independent means. George was killed, aged 13, in the 1847 explosion and was interred three days later in St George's churchyard.

Mary Parker was initially awarded relief but the Committee decided at their meeting on 4 May 1849, 'that the Pay to the following Parties be henceforth discontinued altogether they being merely Widows who lost Children upon whom it is considered they did not much depend viz- to Widows … Parker etc'. In 1851, Mary was a washerwoman, living in Albert Street with her daughter Fanny, aged 6.

Fanny Parker (1844– ?) was at 1 Cheapside in 1861, working as one of two general servants for widow Elizabeth Denton, a keeper of spirit vaults, and her family. Fanny got married on 10 March 1862 at Christ Church, Ardsley, to Ephraim Sellers, a coal miner and son of Ephraim and Nancy Sellers of Hoyle Mill. Ephraim Sellers senior was killed on 13 December 1866, aged 63, in the Oaks Colliery Explosion; he was listed as one of the trammers and daymen.

Illustration from the 1842 Royal Commission Report. (Courtesy of the National Coalmining Museum)

John Peach (1829–1847)

John Peach was baptised on 20 September 1829 at St Mary's Church, where his father William had been baptised on 14 September 1789, the son of Edward and Mary 'Peech'. His mother, Mary (née Tottershall), had married William on 12 September 1825 at All Saints' Church, Silkstone. This was William's second marriage as he had a daughter Martha with his first wife Isabella. William and Mary had four children: William, baptised on 8 October 1826 at St Mary's but died in infancy, John, William, named after his deceased brother, and Jane.

In 1841, John was living in a shared property in Oxford Square, Silkstone, with his parents, William, a weaver aged 50, and Mary, as well as his two siblings: William, aged 10, and Jane, aged 4. Their mother Mary died early 1845, aged 46. John, who began work as a hurrier in the Oaks Colliery when he was 10 years old, was killed in the 1847 explosion, aged 17. He was interred three days later in one of the communal graves in St Mary's churchyard. His father, twice widowed, continued to work as a hand loom linen weaver until his 80s; William resided with his married daughter Martha until he died in summer 1872, aged 86.

Illustration from the 1842 Royal Commission Report. (Courtesy of the National Coalmining Museum)

John's Half-Sister and Two Siblings

Martha Peach (1819–1888) was baptised on 24 June 1824, aged 5, at St Mary's Church, the daughter of William and Isabella Peach. She got married to Joseph Reynolds, an engine tenter, with whom she had six children: George, Isabella, Richard, Eliza, Mary Ann and Elizabeth. In 1851, Martha, a weaver, and Joseph, an engineer aged 30, were living at Grimsby Cottage in Dodworth Old Road with three children. Martha's widowed father William, a labourer aged 60, and her two half-siblings: William and Jane, were lodging with them. The Reynolds family were at 9 Oak Street in 1861, sharing the property with her father, Jane and her daughter. By 1871, they were at 2 Oak Street, where Joseph died in 1887, aged 69, and Martha Reynolds died in spring 1888, aged 69.

William Peach (1831– ?) was baptised on 1 April 1832 at St Mary's, son of William and Mary. He worked in the Oaks Colliery from a young age and was named in the contemporary newspapers as one of the survivors of the 1847 explosion, living at Wilson's Piece. He got married early 1865 to Martha Field, who was one of four illegitimate daughters of Nancy Field. In 1871, William, a coal miner, resided at 5 Court, 1 Racecommon Road, with Martha, aged 27, her illegitimate daughter Elizabeth Ann, baptised on 27 December 1868, aged 4, at St George's Church as 'Elizabeth Ann Peach Cate Field', and Martha's sister, Christiana Field, aged 24. Martha died early 1879, aged 36. William was lodging at 8 Sackville Street with Hannah Coward and her family in 1881, but he had his own room in a shared property at 17 Silver Street by 1891, when he worked as a rag and bone gatherer.

Jane Peach (1837– ?) was born on 9 April 1837 and baptised on 28 October 1838 at St George's Church. She was working as a linen dresser, aged 14, and had an illegitimate daughter, Sarah Ann, in 1857. She lived with her parents until she got married in spring 1864 to Thomas Malking, a coal miner, with whom she had two more children. In 1871, Jane and Thomas, aged 30, resided at 16 Oak Street with three children: Sarah Ann, a linen winder aged 17, John, aged 6, and 1-year-old Mary Ann; they also had a boarder.

John Riley (c.1837–1847)

John Riley was 4 years old in 1841, when he resided in Dawson Walk with his parents, both born in Ireland: Bernard, a weaver aged 45, and Mary, aged 40, as well as his six siblings aged from 15 to 2: Caroline, Ellen, James, Mary, Margaret and Michael. John was killed, aged 10, in the 1847 explosion. The *Illustrated London News* reported that his body was only brought out of the mine on Monday night, three days later. John Riley was buried on 10 March in St Paul's churchyard in Monk Bretton.

Bernard Riley (c.1791–1868) was born in Ireland but, by 1851, he was a weaver of linen cloth, residing in Ardsley with his wife Mary and their three children, the two oldest working as weavers. They would have been among the million Irish forced to emigrate during the cruel

St Paul's church, Monk Bretton. (Author's Collection)

St Paul's church, Monk Bretton.

'Potato Famine' or 'Great Hunger' of 1845 to 1852, in which about a million people died of starvation. The family were Roman Catholic, but baptisms and marriages took place in the Church of England because that was the Established Church. They looked after Caroline's 6-year-old daughter, Sarah Walton, and also had a lodger. Bernard and Mary lived at 4 Watson Fold, Ardsley, by 1861 and were looking after their grandson Henry. Bernard died in spring 1868, aged 73, and Mary died late 1869, aged 65.

John's Six Siblings

<u>Caroline Riley</u> married William Walton (see chapter for Walton page 241).

<u>Ellen Riley</u> (c.1826–1902) had an illegitimate son Henry in 1844. She got married on 14 May 1848 at Christ Church, Ardsley, to William Charlesworth, illegitimate son of Ann Charlesworth. They had eight children: George, Joseph, Mary, William, Sophia, Michael, Walter and Sarah. In 1851, Ellen and William, a coal miner aged 46, resided in Ardsley with three children. William's widowed mother Ann, aged 74, 'receiving parish relief formerly wife of ag lab', was staying with them as well as several lodgers. They shared accommodation with her brother James and his family at 35 Wilson Street in 1861 until after William's death early 1862, aged 58.

Ellen, who subsequently had three children baptised at St John the Baptist's Church, moved sometime after 1868 to one of the Courts in Joseph Street then Wellington Street, where she worked as a linen weaver. She was supported by her coal miner sons, Joseph and Michael, until they left home. Ellen Charlesworth, aged 64, got married again on 19 October 1890 at St John's Church to William Carr, a widowed agricultural labourer aged 68, of Heelis Street. They moved to Dodworth, 6 Green then 17 Lambert Fold, where Ellen Carr died early 1902, aged 75. William died late 1903, aged 82.

Most of Ellen and William Charlesworth's children got married and had families of their own. Many of the men worked in collieries but they appeared to suffer financial hardship and three siblings committed thefts for which they were imprisoned, while two were punished for their bad behaviour when drunk.

Joseph Charlesworth (1851–1902), a collier of Ardsley, 5ft 7¾in tall with dark brown hair and marks on his left arm and hand, was convicted twice. In 1885 he assaulted a constable, for which he served his sentence of one month in HM Prison Wakefield, then in 1887, he served twenty-eight days with hard labour for being drunk and riotous because unable to pay the alternative fine of £1 17s 3d (worth £937). Joseph died in spring 1902, aged 52, in Wakefield.

Sophia Charlesworth (1856– ?) married John Henry White and was convicted three times; she was 5ft 3½in tall with dark brown hair and worked as a mill hand. Her first offence was in June 1891, when she served fourteen days for being 'drunk and riotous' because unable to pay the fine of £1 1s 9d (worth £524). On Christmas Eve 1896, she was convicted for assaulting a female but paid the £1 6s 9d fine (worth £593) rather than serve another twenty-eight days; in December 1904, she served fourteen days for stealing a blouse rather than pay £2 10s fine (worth £1,006).

Michael Charlesworth (1860–1942) was baptised on 9 November 1868, aged 8, at St John the Baptist's Church, at the same time as Walter and Sarah. He was a coal miner and got married in spring 1883 to Jane Ann Fletcher, with whom he had eleven children, five of whom died young. They moved from Wombwell to Crofton then Glasshoughton by 1911 and both spent time in prison for a series of offences. Jane died in summer 1918, aged 54, and Michael, who was still working as a coal miner underground in 1939, died early 1942, aged 81, in Castleford.

Michael, who was 5ft 7in tall with brown hair, could become violent after getting drunk on a Saturday night. He was sentenced to fourteen days' imprisonment with hard labour in HMP Wakefield for being drunk and disorderly in 1894, unable to pay the alternative fine of £1 0s 3d (worth £460). A report in the *Sheffield Independent* in 1895 provided a detailed description of another incident:

> A brutal case of assault by a miner whilst in a drunken state came before the Barnsley bench yesterday. Michael Charlesworth, miner, Barnsley, was charged with having assaulted his sister Sarah Allott, married woman, on the 25th inst. – Defendant said he was drunk and knew nothing

about the charge – The woman, who appeared in court with a black eye, said on the night named the defendant was 'larving' his wife in their house adjoining. She went outside and the defendant's wife had run into their house for protection. She remonstrated with him for coming there 'every Saturday night' creating a noise. He rushed upstairs to follow his wife and she went for the police. He then turned upon her, dealing her several blows to the shoulders and face, giving her a black eye and rendering her almost senseless. Her husband succeeded in pulling him away, when he turned upon him. They struggled on the floor together, and he bit her husband on the muscle of his arm – Complainant's husband and a neighbour corroborated, the husband adding they did not want to lay two informations against the man. The Chairman (Mr Brady) remarked drunkenness was no excuse. There were seven convictions against him, and they would treat the assault on the woman as an aggravated one and he would have to go to gaol for one month.

Michael's wife Jane, who was about 5ft 3in tall with auburn hair and a scar on her forehead, worked as a fletcher (fitting feathers into arrows), laundress and charwoman, but was a persistent offender, being convicted thirteen times for theft. Her first offence was in 1876, aged 12, for stealing 15 shillings (worth £382) for which she was sentenced to fourteen days with hard labour in HM Prison Wakefield. Most of her convictions were for stealing 'wearing apparel': coats, vests, women's boots, a jacket, a suit, skirt, trousers and sheets and her sentences varied up to six months with two fines of 30 shillings. Her latest conviction was in November 1911, when she was bound over for £5 (worth £2,000) until she was sentenced; she served time in Leeds prison for the theft of clothing in Pontefract.

James Riley (c.1829–1880) was a coal miner and got married on 19 March 1861 at St John the Baptist's Church to Maria Wake, aged 37; they were both living in Joseph Street. Maria had two illegitimate sons: Joseph and James Wake. The family shared a home with his sister Ellen before relocating to Top Row, Church Street, Ardsley, by 1871, when

Maria's sons were working as coal miners. After James died in summer 1880, aged 51, Maria was a charwoman. Her son James moved in with her along with his wife Eliza and their only surviving child, George. George Wake was orphaned aged 6, after his mother's death in 1884, aged 24, followed by his father's in 1886, aged 29. He was brought up by his grandmother and supported her when he started work in a colliery. Maria Riley died late 1902, aged 79.

Mary Ann Riley (c.1832– ?) got married on 16 April 1848 at All Saints' Church, Darfield, to Charles Harper, a colliery labourer aged 26 (see chapter for Harper page 137). Mary and Charles had at least seven children: John, William, Elizabeth, Priscilla, Emily, Mary Ellen and Clara. Both of their families suffered deaths in several colliery disasters.

Amos Harper (c.1812–1849), Charles' oldest brother, was killed in the explosion at Darley Main Colliery on 24 January 1849, aged 37, when his widow Sarah was expecting their seventh child.

In 1861, Mary and Charles resided at 3 Garlic Square, Ardsley, with four children, aged from 10 to 2 and all at school: John, William, Elizabeth, and Priscilla.

John Harper (1851–1866) was baptised on 12 January 1851 at Christ Church, Ardsley. He was a hurrier when he was killed, aged 16, in the Oaks Colliery explosion on 13 December 1866. It would have been distressing for his parents that his body could not be recovered for burial at that time. It was almost two years later, on 9 November 1868, when his body was brought out of the pit along with five others. John was given a proper burial at last in Christ Church churchyard on 12 November, with another victim. The *Barnsley Chronicle* reported:

> On Monday afternoon last the explorers were successful in recovering six more bodies from the first board of the No. 2 firing and the new level. The whole of the bodies were shortly afterwards brought to bank and placed in the dead house where they were identified ... The bodies were in a better state than those which were recovered on the 26th October. They were chiefly identified by their clothes and boots, but were in a good state of preservation,

considering that they have been entombed for nearly two years… The bodies, in most cases, were removed to the homes of their relatives and friends and were interred in the cemetery on Thursday afternoon. The total number of bodies recovered since the explosion is 63, of which 11 have been recovered in the month of October. It may be interesting to some of our readers to know that the shafts at the New Oaks pit, at Ardsley, have reached a depth of sixty-four yards. At the present time preparations are been made for 'tubbing' the shafts, by which means it is expected a good deal of water will be got rid of, and the sinkers will then be able to prosecute their labours better than has already been the case.

The Harper family moved to 50 Boundary Street by 1871, when son William, aged 18, was employed as a colliery hurrier.

Charles Harper (c.1821–1878) died in Beckett Hospital and Dispensary on 16 November 1878, aged 58, following an accident at Edmunds Main Colliery, Worsbrough, the previous day; he was interred on the 19th in Barnsley Cemetery. Details of the inquest, opened at the hospital but adjourned to the Coach and Horses Inn so that a witness from the colliery and the inspector of mines could attend, were recorded in the Wakefield Charities Coroners Notebooks and reported in local newspapers. The jury's verdict was that Charles had been accidentally crushed, but they agreed that his own actions had contributed to his death.

> Mary Harper of Greenwood Square, Barnsley, Widow sw says, Dec'd was 58 years old & a Colliery labourer & my husband. He has been working at Edmunds Main Colliery for the last 11 or 12 months. He left me at home about 5 o'clock yesterday morning. I next saw him about 2 o'clock in the afternoon as he was being brought down Sheffield Road. He was then insensible. I followed him to hospital.
>
> Hannah Lee of the Hospital, Matron, sw says, Dec'd was brought here about ½ past 1 o'clock yesterday afternoon. He was conscious & said that he had been crushed between

Lithograph of names on memorial to victims of the Oaks 1866 explosion.
(© Barnsley Archives)

two wagons on the Pit top but he did not give any explanation. His wife did not see him alive here. He complained of pain in his right shoulder & body. There was not any fracture of the bones. Dec'd vomited everything which he took. He never rallied and <u>he died</u> about ½ past 11 o'clock this morning. *Hannah Lee*

<u>Peter Kelly</u> of Dale, Worsbro, Coal Screener at Edmunds Main Colliery sw says, I have known dec'd about 15 months, by his working as a labourer. On Friday the 15th inst. about noon he went to fetch an empty wagon to put it under the screens. He had a brake stick. The incline is about ½ inch to the yard. The forenoon was wet. He took a wagon from others which he did not sprag. He took the wagon about 4 yards & then went behind the wagon & put his breast against the buffer & pushed the wagon towards the screen. The other wagons came after him & caught him between the buffers. He fell & I & others picked him up. There were sprags lying on the ground near the wagons. Dec'd was taken to the Workshop & then removed in an Ambulance.

In 1881, Mary was living at No 12 Oak Street with her two youngest daughters, Mary, a rag sorter aged 15, and Clara, aged 12 attending school; they also had two boarders.

<u>Margaret Riley</u> (c.1835–1903) was a linen weaver until she got married in summer 1854 to her brother-in-law, Thomas Harper (see chapter for Harper page 137). They had seven children: Charles, Benjamin, James, Mary Ellen, John, Eliza and Laura. Thomas was a coal miner into his 50s then worked in a glass bottle works. They moved from Brick Terrace, Ardsley, near her married nephew John Harper, to Bridge Street, Stairfoot, by 1881. They were residing at 4 Pindar Oak Terrace, Ardsley, by 1891, with two children, John, a glass bottle maker aged 22, and Laura, aged 14, their 5-year-old granddaughter, Florence Harper, as well as four boarders. Thomas died early 1900, aged 68, and Margaret went to live with Laura, a dressmaker, her husband John W. Wilkinson, a house painter aged 27, and their 7-month-old daughter Dorothy, at 19 Beech Street. Margaret Harper died there late 1903, aged 69.

<u>Michael Riley</u> (c.1839–1865) was an iron stone miner in 1861, when he was boarding with Isaac Sutcliffe and his family at 25 William Street, Ormesby, near Middlesbrough. Michael died late 1865, aged 26, in Barnsley.

Above: Postcard of the Beckett Hospital and Dispensary. (Author's Collection)

Right: Miners parade. (Courtesy of the Tasker Trust)

193

William Roe (c.1806–1847) and His Three Sons: William (1826–1847), John (1832–1847) and Luke (1835–1847)

The Roe family suffered the largest loss of life in the Oaks Colliery explosion on 5 March 1847 with four members being killed. They were particularly challenging to research because of the various spellings of their surname: Roe, Wroe, Rowe, Row, Roa. The family originated in

St John's Terrace and Wright Street. (© Barnsley Archives)

Derbyshire, relocated to Barnsley for a short period then returned to Derbyshire after the colliery disaster.

Roe (and variants) is an uncommon surname in the parish registers for St Martin of Tours' Church in Alfreton, where the land was rich with iron and coal. The family lived in Somercotes, where most men worked as colliers.

William Roe (c.1806–1847) was a collier when he got married on 20 August 1827 at St Martin's Church to Rebecca Taylor, aged 23; they had seven children. (The two families were intertwined: her brother Thomas got married on 5 April 1828 to Mary Ann Roe; Joseph Taylor and Mary Roe married on 3 March 1835).

William and Rebecca lived in Somercotes, Alfreton, where five children were born: William in 1826, Sally (Sarah Ann) baptised on 23 September 1828, John on 29 July 1832, Luke on 6 April 1835, and Mariane (Mary Ann) on 10 July 1837. They moved to Barnsley, where their two youngest were born: Elizabeth in 1843 in Blacker Hill, and Matthew in 1846 in Cudworth. By summer 1837, William was working as a stockinger (a knitter, weaver or dealer in stockings).

William and his eldest son William were not on the 1841 Census with the rest of their family and I think they were seeking work and accommodation in Yorkshire. Rebecca and four children were living at Cotes Park, Alfreton, with her parents, John Taylor, still working as a coal miner at 80, and Sarah, aged 67. The family resided in Cudworth by 1846 and the men had obtained work in the Oaks Colliery. This was to prove disastrous as the explosion on 5 March 1847 killed the father and three sons: William, aged 41, William junior, aged 21, John, aged 15, and Luke, aged 11. They were all interred in the communal graves in St Mary's churchyard on the 8th.

The *Illustrated London News* reported: 'On Tuesday morning the pit was very full of sulphur, and in the evening it was impossible to descend. At that time there remained in the pit three individuals, Abraham Matthews, John 'Wroe', and William Walton.' John was brought out of the pit alive but died of his severe burns and bruising.

Rebecca Roe (c.1804–1881) was widowed aged 43; devastated by her loss and concerned for her surviving children: Sarah Ann, Mary Ann, Elizabeth and Matthew. She would have struggled to support her family alone, even with relief from the Subscription Fund.

Rebecca returned to Alfreton with her children to avoid the threat of being admitted to Barnsley Union Workhouse, but she suffered another three deaths there. Her mother, Sarah Taylor, died in November 1847, aged 73, and was buried in the churchyard; her daughter Sarah Ann died early 1848, aged 19, closely followed by Rebecca's father, John Taylor, aged 86, who was interred with his wife on 23 May 1848.

Rebecca was admitted to the Belper Union Workhouse before dinner on Tuesday 27 June 1848 with three children, aged from 11 to 2 years: Mary Ann, Elizabeth and Matthew. Each of them was allocated a different 'Class for Diet' and given a reference number, which was affixed to their uniform issued on admission. The local receiving officer had made the order for admission because Rebecca was a widow and Alfreton Parish were responsible for paupers in their area; she may have been evicted from her parents' home when her father died. The family were discharged on Monday 5 July 1848 by the Board, but no reason was provided.

The nine days in the workhouse must have seemed long and hard. Rebecca would have been separated from her children, who were segregated by gender, and they endured a strict regime with a basic diet. Rebecca would have worked in the kitchen, laundry or unpicking old rope, which was purchased by Belper Union from the local collieries.

The ledger referred to Rebecca and her children several times, without using their first names. On 4 May 1849, they ordered that the eldest children of 'William Wroe be continued at School til a further order be made on the subject.' On 11 January 1850, they recorded that, 'Your Committee still continue to hear favourable accounts from The Revd J.R. Errington of Alfreton of the conduct of Widow Wroe and of the progress at School of her Children – this is the only Widow and Family which your Committee do not see periodically'.

In 1851, Rebecca, a framework knitter aged 48, was living in Alfreton with her three children, the two youngest attending school; George Holmes, a framework knitter aged 35, was there. It seems that George was more than a lodger, according to a report to the Subscription Committee meeting on 27 December 1851:

> Your Committee very much deplore the Circumstances of this case – up to the month of June last they had every reason to suppose that she was conducting herself in a highly satisfactory manner, but on a complaint made by her

that the Guardians of the Belper Union had discontinued to relieve her, solely on the ground of her being a Recipient of your Bounty, a searching Inquiry was instituted as to the Truth of her Statement when it was ascertained that she was cohabiting with a Collier of very bad Character and setting at defiance the Remonstrances and Advice not only of the Guardians but of the Incumbent of Alfreton where she is residing and what renders this case the more distressing is that she has taken her Children from School and thus put it out of the power of your Committee to render even to them any assistance so long as they remain under her influence

Further Inquiries have been made respecting her during the present month and the Correspondent of your Committee after lamenting her continued open depravity adds that 'having seen them at their meals they fare <u>suspiciously</u> better than their Neighbours' -

The Revd R. J. Ozanne the Incumbent of Alfreton has still in hand £2. 15. 0 [worth £2,291] part of the last remittance to him on account of this Family which he promises to expend for the Benefit of the Children if an opportunity present itself so to do without giving encouragement to the mother.

Rebecca, a 'stocking frame worker', was living in Nesbit Row, Alfreton, by 1861 with her children, Elizabeth, Matthew and Mary Ann, with her husband and daughter. Five other people were staying with them, two visitors, her brother, Joseph Taylor, an excavator aged 54, with his son Walter W. Taylor, a coal miner aged 13, and three lodgers: George Holmes, William Stones and John Harper, a coal miner aged 18. Rebecca, still working at 67, had moved by 1871 to Station Road, Ripley, Derbyshire; her daughters Mary Ann Stones and Elizabeth Harper were staying there. Rebecca Roe died early 1881, aged 77.

The Three Surviving Children of William and Rebecca Roe

<u>Mary Ann Roe</u> (c.1837– ?) got married in 1858 in Alfreton to William Stones, a coal miner aged 27, who had lodged with Mary's mother. They had four children: Ann Maria, Rebecca Elizabeth (known as Elizabeth),

William and Mary Ann. William senior died in summer 1865, aged 31, and, widowed at 28, Mary worked as a charwoman to support her family. By 1871, she had moved to her mother's home in Ripley with her children. Mary got married again early 1877 in Barnsley district to George Orly Marshall, a brickmaker from Lincolnshire aged 45. They resided in Hoyland Nether with their son, John, born there in 1873. In 1881, Elizabeth Stones was a domestic servant aged 18, William Stones, a labourer aged 12, and John Marshall, aged 8. Mary Ann junior was married and living elsewhere. By 1891, Mary and George were at 31 Hawshaw Terrace, Hoyland Nether, with sons, William, a brickmaker like his stepfather, and John, a coal miner, as well as Mary's grandson, George R. Stones, aged 9.

Ann Maria Stones (1860–1888 USA) was baptised on 30 July 1860 at St Mary's Church. In 1881, she was a domestic servant for her aunt Elizabeth in Platts Common. Moses Major, a coal miner aged 21, was boarding next door with his brother Benjamin and family; William Burrows, a miner aged 27, was also there. Ann married Moses in spring 1885 and they had a daughter, Mary Ellen in 1886. They subsequently emigrated to USA; Moses reached New York on 23 September 1887 followed by Ann and Mary on 27 December, sailing from Liverpool. Ann died there in 1888. Mary got married to Robert Sherwin on 17 July 1905 in USA; they had eight children. Mary Ellen Sherwin died there in 1969, aged 83.

Moses Major (1860–1943 USA) was convicted for 'Bastardy' on 18 August 1884 and served one month in HM Prison Wakefield rather than pay the fine of £2 3s (worth £1,087). He was a collier aged 23, born in Wigan, Wesleyan, 5ft 4½in tall with dark brown hair and a blue dot on his left arm.

After Ann died, Moses got married again on 3 July 1891 to Sarah Ann Taylor, from England; they had two daughters, Emily and Elizabeth. He died on 28 May 1943, aged 83, in Pennsylvania and was interred in Monongahela Cemetery.

Rebecca Elizabeth Stones (1862– ?) resided with her brother William in 1891 at 18 Foundry Street, with her illegitimate daughter Millicent, aged 4, born in Wortley. She got married on 12 July 1891 at St George's Church to Walter William Wilson, a railway servant aged 29; they both resided at 18 Foundry Street.

Taylor's Row. (© Barnsley Archives)

<u>William Stones</u> (1869–1940) was a railway guard in 1891, sharing his home with Rebecca. He married Annie Elizabeth Hayes, aged 20, late 1892 and they had eight children: Thomas Edwin, Ethel, Gladys, Lily, Cyril and three whom died young. They resided in Hoyland then Wath-on-Dearne before moving to Eastwood, Rotherham, by 1901, when William was a coal miner hewer. They returned to Wath and occupied six rooms at 46 Doncaster Road in 1911; William was an insurance agent assistant supervisor and son Thomas, aged 16, a colliery lamp cleaner. William, pensioner incapacitated, and Annie resided at 32 Armitage Road, Doncaster, in 1939. William died the following year, aged 70.

<u>John Marshall</u> (1873– ?) John married Frances, aged 20, in spring 1892 and they had six children, including: George William, Elizabeth, Harold, May and Gwendolin. They occupied six rooms at 13 North Street, Goldthorpe by 1911, when John was a 'colliery platelayer' and George a labourer, both above ground; they had a boarder.

<u>Elizabeth Roe</u> (1843–1924) Elizabeth married John Harper, a coal miner aged 20, in spring 1864 in Belper, Derbyshire; they met when John lodged

with her mother. Their first home was at 5 Hawshaw Terrace, Platts Common, where Elizabeth's niece Ann was a domestic servant. They lived in Bethel Street, Hoyland in 1891, with their only daughter Emma, who died early 1884, aged 2. By 1901, they occupied five rooms at 62 Market Street, Hoyland, where they remained, with various Shaw relations and Ada Harper, aged 19. John, retired by 1911, when they had a lodger, died in 1913, aged 69. Elizabeth Harper died in spring 1924, aged 82.

Matthew Roe (1846– ?) was a coal miner and he married Eliza Booth, aged 18 born in Ripley, early 1867 in Belper. Their first home was in Nottingham Road, Ripley, and son William was a baby. By 1881, Matthew was unemployed and they had three children, William, Mary and John, at 6 Northcote Terrace, Nottingham, next door to his niece Ann Maria. Matthew, a coal miner, was lodging with Thomas Tetley and family in 1 Colliery Row, Alfreton, by 1891. Mary married Jacob Hilker and emigrated to USA; she died a widow on 26 February 1949, aged 73, of a heart attack at home in Pennsylvania.

Postcards of St Martin's church, Alfreton. (Author's Collection)

William Rushforth (c.1828–1847)

William Rushforth was baptised on 17 June 1827 at St Mary's Church, the son of Henry Rushforth, a calenderer, and Elizabeth. William was killed, aged 19, in the 1847 explosion and interred three days later in one of the communal graves in St Mary's churchyard.

Elizabeth was a widow and would have been dependent on relief. The ledger recorded that on 3 September 1847 'the sum of 10/- was ordered to be paid to Mother to enable her to redeem her Clothes from Pledge' (worth £402).

Illustration from the 1842 Royal Commission Report. (courtesy of the National Coalmining Museum)

William Scales (1821–1847)

William Scales was born on 21 December 1821 in Dodworth to Joseph Scales, an agricultural labourer born c.1786, and Mary (née Ruddlestone). They married on 27 August 1810 in Worsbrough and had nine children. William was baptised, aged 9, on 18 September 1831 at All Saints' Church, Silkstone, with six siblings: Christopher, Elizabeth, Mary, Harriet, Joseph and Sarah; they had two older siblings: Ann, baptised in Worsbrough, and George, baptised at All Saints in 1813. Mary and baby Sarah died soon after the baptism of their seven children in 1831.

Joseph, a widower with eight children to support, got married again on 21 February 1834 at St Mary's Church to Mary Wheatley, a widow ten years younger. By 1841, Joseph and Mary, aged 35, shared their home with her daughter, Charlotte Wheatley, aged 16, his son Joseph, aged 14, their 2-year-old daughter Eliza and a lodger.

William, a coal miner aged 20, was lodging at Common Side Houses, Ardsley, in 1841, at the home of Matthew Bedford and family (see chapter for Bedford page 60). The three other lodgers were: a stonemason, Moses Roystone, and two coal miners: John Gunneshall and George Hinchcliffe, aged 20 (see chapter for Hinchcliffe page 152). William married Jane Bedford, whom he had got to know as a lodger, at All Saints' Church, Darfield, on 5 June 1843. They had two children: Matthew in 1843 and Mary Ann in 1845.

William was killed in the Oaks Colliery explosion on 5 March 1847, aged 32. He was buried on the 8th at Christ Church churchyard, Ardsley.

Joseph died in 1849, aged 69, in Dodworth and was interred on 23 February in All Saints' churchyard, Silkstone.

Jane Scales (c.1824–1880) was widowed, aged 23, with two young children and would have been dependent on relief from the Subscription

Fund. Jane was referred to in the ledger on 22 April 1848 – 'in consequence of Reports unfavourable', all allowances were suspended for several named widows prior to further investigation, then it was resolved that,

> their conduct rendered themselves so truly undeserving of sympathy [Allowance] be wholly withdrawn but that the Payments be continued to their Children on its being proved to the Committee that they regularly attend some School – that the fortnight's pay to the Children which was witheld on the 22nd Ult. be paid up to-morrow.

By 1851, Jane, 'pauper assistant', had moved with her two young children, both attending school, into the Almshouses in Ardsley with her widowed mother Margaret Bedford, aged 61, on parochial relief. Five single men were lodging with them in this small home. The report to the General Meeting on 27 December 1851 confirmed that payments had been discontinued to the 'Widow of William Scales on her marriage to Harry [Henry] Wilby of Mirfield, a railway labourer.' Jane had got married again on 9 June 1851.

Jane was expecting her fourth child by Harry when her mother died late 1860, aged 77. By the following spring, she was residing at Commonside, Ardsley, with Harry, a colliery labourer aged 39, and her six children: Matthew and Mary Scales and four with the surname Wilby: Sarah Ellen, baptised on 2 May 1852 at Christ Church, William, Henry, baptised on 31 January 1858, and Ann (Annie), who died in 1862, aged 1. Their fifth child, Tom, was born in summer 1864.

Jane and Harry's two surviving sons, William Wilby (1855–1936) and Tom Wilby (1864–1927) were both coal miners, married and remained in Ardsley. William married twice, having four children with his first wife, who died young, and two sons with Jemima Fleetwood (née Leach). He became a gas stoker in the glass bottle works, where his sons joined him. Tom had eight children with Hannah Elizabeth (née Taylor).

Henry Wilby (c.1822–1866) was the son of William Wilby, a clothier, and Sarah (née Parker), who were living in Whitley Wood when he was baptised on 7 April 1822 at St Mary's Church, Mirfield. He was killed by the huge explosion at the Oaks Colliery on 12 December 1866, aged 46.

He was brought out alive but subsequently died of his severe injuries 'at five o'clock on Tuesday night', 18 December, according to the *Barnsley Chronicle*. Henry was buried in Christ Church churchyard on the 23rd.

Jane was not only widowed for a second time, aged 44, but also lost her oldest son and son-in-law in the same disaster.

Jane got married for a third time on 21 June 1868 at Ardsley Church to George Kenyon, a tailor nine years her junior. About a year later, her son Henry Wilby died, aged 11; Sarah Ellen may also have died before 1871. Jane and George lived next to the Black Bull Inn, Stairfoot, with her youngest son Tom, aged 7 and at school.

Jane Kenyon died on 1 June 1880, aged 55, at Cliff Bridge, Monk Bretton, and she was interred on the 13th in St Paul's churchyard there. George Kenyon, who got married again on 9 December 1880 to Alice Royston, died in spring 1901, aged 66.

The Two Children of William and Jane Scales

Matthew Scales (1843–1866) was baptised on 23 November 1843 at Christ Church, Ardsley. He worked at the Oaks Colliery like his father and he was killed, aged 23, by the explosion on 12 December 1866. The *Sheffield Daily Telegraph* reported that he was one of eighteen men brought out of the pit alive, but that he had died afterwards of his injuries. According to the *Barnsley Chronicle*, he died 'at half past eleven on Tuesday night', the 18th, six hours after his stepfather. Matthew was interred eleven days after the accident in Christ Church churchyard.

Mary Ann Scales (1845–1889) was baptised on 26 January 1846 at Christ Church. She got married in spring 1864 to John Everett, a colliery labourer, and they had one son, John Henry, late 1865.

John Everett died on 13 December 1866, aged 29, on the second day of explosions at the Oaks Colliery. The *Sheffield Daily Telegraph* reported: 'One of the poor fellows was identified by means of his watch, which, when found, was still going, and on the inside of the case of which was inscribed, "John Everett, Union-row".' John was interred in a communal grave at Christ Church.

Mary was widowed aged 21, with a young son to look after. She got married again on 7 November 1867 at All Saints' Church, Wakefield,

The Oaks Colliery Explosion 1866 in the *Illustrated London News*. (Courtesy of Barnsley Archives)

(Cathedral) to Manwaring Webster, a butcher of Westgate. They resided at 4 Low Street, Monk Bretton, by 1871, when Manwaring, aged 29, was a coal miner. He had been elected as 'coal miners check weighman' by 1881, having moved to 9 Crookes Street with Mary, her half-brother Tom Wilby, aged 16, and four children: John Henry Everett, aged 15, and their three, surname Webster: Alice Ann, Kate and James William. Their daughter Ada was born in 1883.

Mary Webster died in March 1889, aged 43, at Pinfold Hill, Ardsley; she was buried on the 14th in Barnsley Cemetery. Her widowed husband moved into Kenyons Buildings, Ardsley, with their five children; he died there on 21 November 1896, aged 55. He was intestate but left £173 10s 11d (worth £77,680).

John Henry Everett (1865–1948) was a coal miner when he married Elizabeth Scott on 17 January 1893 at Christ Church. They had two children: Thomas Scott Everett early 1894 and Mary in summer 1896. John, a 'road roller engine for district council', Elizabeth, aged 41, and daughter Mary occupied three rooms at 33 Church Street, Ardsley, by 1911 and remained there. Their son Thomas, a drapery shop assistant aged 17,

205

was with his grandparents, Thomas Scott, 'a beer house keeper Clarksons limited' aged 70, and Ann, aged 66, in eight rooms at 37 Church Street; their unmarried daughter Harriet Ann was assistant innkeeper. Elizabeth Everett died late 1944, aged 75, and John died early 1948, aged 82.

Alice Ann Webster (1871–1942) was the family housekeeper after her mother died in 1889, She got married on 13 May 1894 at Christ Church to Stephen Garland Taylor, a coal miner aged 24; they had two children. In 1901, Alice's sister Ada was living with them in four rooms at 23 Doncaster Road, where they remained until Alice Ann Taylor died early 1942, aged 70.

Kate Webster (1876–1961) was baptised on 12 May 1878, aged 2, at St Paul's Church, Monk Bretton. She left home by 1901 to be housemaid for a physician and surgeon in Holmfirth, then a wool merchant in Harrogate, and a retired worsted spinner in Skipton, where Ada also worked as a domestic servant. When they retired, Kate and Ada lived together at 548 Doncaster Road, Ardsley, where Kate died on 13 February 1961, aged 84, leaving her sister an amount worth £44,480 today.

James William Webster (1879–1949) was baptised on 3 August at St Paul's Church. In 1939, James, 'loco-driver LNER', was living at Rockleigh, Brierley Road, Hemsworth, with Mary A. Featherstone, aged 28, and a child. James died in 1949, aged 70.

Ada Webster (1882–1973) was a housekeeper by 1939 in Skipton, where Kate was housemaid. She retired with her sister to 548 Doncaster Road, Ardsley, where Ada died on 9 June 1973, aged 91, leaving £801 (worth £14,560).

William Scales' Seven Surviving Siblings

Ann Scales (c.1811–1871) was a linen weaver when she married Edward Clegg on 25 November 1832 at All Saints' Church. They had one son John in 1833 and lived in Dodworth. Ann Clegg died in 1871, aged 64, at 13 Jackson Square, and was buried on 1 August in St John the Baptist's churchyard.

George Scales (1813–1862) became a coal miner and got married c.1840 to Elizabeth, with whom he had seven children: William, Matthew, Elizabeth, Mason, Joseph, Priscilla and Jabez. The family lived in Dodworth and all sons worked in the colliery. George died at Lees Fold in 1862, aged 45, and was buried on 19 January at St John the Baptist's churchyard.

Christopher Scales (1815–1891), born on Christmas Day, was a collier when he got married on 8 June 1838 at St Mary's Church in Prestwich, Lancashire, to Sophia Smith. They had nine children, the first two in Lancashire, the others in Barnsley: Thomas, George, Sarah, Elizabeth, Levi, Mary, Maria, Matthew and Alfred. The family lived in Oxford Square then the Courts in New Street, where Christopher and Sophia died within a month of each other early 1891. They were buried in the same grave in Barnsley Cemetery.

Elizabeth Scales (1819–1864) got married at All Saints on 4 April 1852 to Edwin Wainwright, an engine tenter of East Gable. They lived at 76 Hemingfield in Wombwell, where they had four children: Ann, Thomas, William and Hannah. Elizabeth Wainwright died early 1864, aged 44. Edwin got married again in 1875; he died early 1899, aged 71.

Mary Scales (1824–1877) was a weaver when she married Joseph Winter, a coal miner, on 25 April 1842 at All Saints. Mary and Joseph had six children: Dinah, Ann, Sarah, Thomas, Emma and Allen. They resided in Dodworth, Bottom, Green then Rotten Row. Mary Winter died in 1877, aged 53, and was buried on 3 May at St John the Baptist's churchyard.

Harriet Scales (1826–1854) was a domestic servant in Stairfoot for Ellen Ostcliffe, a farmer and publican aged 30. Harriet Scales died early 1854, aged 27.

Joseph Scales (1828–1887) became a miner and married Ann Clarey on 13 September 1847 at St Mary's Church. They had six children: William, George, Mary, Alfred, Annis and Walter. They moved from Croft Ends to Brightside Bierlow, Sheffield. Ann died in 1863, aged 33 and Joseph returned to Court 5, New Street, Barnsley. Joseph died at No 10 Court, Providence Street, in spring 1887, aged 60, and he was buried in Barnsley Cemetery.

George Sedgwick (1833–1847)

George Sedgwick was born on 18 October 1833 and baptised on 24 October 1838, aged 5, at St George's Church, at the same time as his sister Sarah. Their parents, George and Sarah Sedgwick, had an older child named Rachel. George Sedgewick senior died early 1840, aged 51. In 1841, George resided in Common Side Houses, Ardsley, with his widowed mother, aged 40 and of independent means, his sisters, Rachel, aged 13, and 3-year-old Sarah, plus lodger John Woodcock (see chapter for Woodcock page 254). George was killed, aged 13, in the 1847 explosion and was buried three days later in Christ Church churchyard, Ardsley.

Sarah Sedgwick (c.1801–1850) was awarded some relief from the Colliers' Relief Fund when George died because she had been dependent on his wages. However, at their meeting on 4 May 1849, the committee decided 'that the Pay to the following Parties be henceforth discontinued altogether they being merely Widows who lost Children upon whom it is considered they did not much depend viz- to Widows ... Sedgwick etc.' Sarah died in spring 1850, aged 43. Her younger daughter Sarah was orphaned, aged 9, and may have been admitted to the Barnsley Union Workhouse.

George's Older Sister

Rachel Sedgwick (c.1828–1885) married William Crank, a weaver, on 2 May 1850 at St Mary's Church; they had five children: Hannah, Ellen, who died in 1851 aged 1, John, Mary and Agnes. Rachel had moved from Crofts End to Osmotherley in Lancashire by 1861, with William, an iron ore miner, and children; their oldest daughter Hannah, aged 12, was a winder of cotton. William died young and Rachel had to work as a linen winder. In 1871, they lived at Rosshead, Ulverston, where John was an iron ore miner aged 17. Rachel and daughter Agnes returned to Barnsley by 1881 and lodged with William Walker, a blacksmith, and his family at Court 3 Nelson Street 1. Rachel Crank died in spring 1885, aged 58

Hannah Crank (1848– ?) was born in Monk Bretton and accompanied her parents to Lancashire. She got married on 13 November 1871 at St Mary's Church, Lancaster, to William Greenbank, a labourer and son of a farmer. Hannah and William relocated to Barnsley soon afterwards and William died there early 1876, aged 28. In 1881, Hannah, a housemaid, was one of four domestic servants – the others being housekeeper, waitress and kitchen-maid – for Samuel Joshua Cooper, a colliery owner aged 50, and his wife Fanny, aged 42, at Mount Vernon in Worsbrough Common. (Joshua was a generous benefactor to Barnsley; among his donations were the Cooper Art Gallery and the Oaks Colliery Memorial to the rescuers in 1866).

John Crank (1853–1924) was born in Monk Bretton and baptised, aged 4, on 31 May 1857 at St Mary's Church, Ulverston. By 1881 he was an iron miner and married to Mary Ann. They resided at Farm Close, Osmotherley, where they had ten children: Elizabeth, Mary, Agnes, Hannah, William, Robert, Rachel, Maggie, John and Minnie. The family returned to Barnsley by 1901 to occupy three rooms at 8 Ward Green, Worsbrough, where they remained and John became a coal miner hewer. Mary Ann died early 1907, aged 53. In 1911, John, out of work, resided with his daughter Maggie, a housekeeper aged 25, her illegitimate 2-year-old daughter Rachel, and his son John, a coal miner hewer aged 22. John died late 1924, aged 70.

Mary Crank (1858–1943) was born in Ulverston and got married on 14 December 1879 at St Mary's Church, Barnsley, to George Henry Wood, a miner aged 22, of Worsbrough Dale. They had six children: Hannah Rachel, Sarah, William Henry, Eliza, Edith Mary and Beatrice H. Mary and George, a cotton winder, moved to Ashton under Lyne, Lancashire, by 1881, but returned to Worsbrough by 1891, when George worked as a miner again; they remained at 8 Lob Wood for the rest of their lives. Hannah had her own dressmaking business until she left home, and William worked as a colliery joiner then colliery stationary engineman. George died late 1934, aged 77. In 1939, Mary, aged 80, shared her home with her married daughter Beatrice, aged 36, her husband Albert Guest, a joiner/carpenter with a role during the Second World War in the Rescue, Demolition and Repair Team. Mary Wood died in spring 1943, aged 84.

Agnes Crank (1864–1932) was born in Ulverston and baptised on 31 March 1864 at the Bible Christian Church in Barrow. She lived with her mother until Rachel died in 1885, then boarded at 2 Eastbrook Lane, Bradford, with John A. Kenworthy, a tapster, and his wife. Agnes died early 1932, aged 68, in Bradford.

The blacksmith's shop, Ardsley. (Courtesy of the Tasker Trust)

Edward Stanfield (c.1825–1847)

Edward Stanfield was a coal miner in 1841, when he resided in Park Row with his widowed mother Sarah, aged 46, of independent means, and his brother Charles, a linen weaver aged 22. Edward was killed, aged 22, in the 1847 explosion and was buried three days later in one of the communal graves in St Mary's churchyard.

Sarah Stanfield was initially awarded relief but the Committee decided at their meeting on 4 May 1849 'that the Pay to the following Parties be henceforth discontinued altogether they being merely Widows who lost Children upon whom it is considered they did not much depend viz- to Widows … Stanfield etc'. In 1851, Sarah and Charles, both linen weavers, lived in Primrose Hill. They had moved to 4 Pontefract Road by 1861, where Charles died in 1875, aged 57. Sarah Stanfield continued until the impressive age of 90, dying in 1884.

Illustration from the 1842 Royal Commission Report. (Courtesy of the National Coalmining Museum)

Thomas Steel (c.1777–1852) and Three Sons:
George Thomas Steel (1815–1847), Charles Steel (1820–1847) and Joseph Steel (1822–1847)

Thomas Steel (c.1797–1852) was a farmer residing in Burton (Monk Bretton) with his wife Mary until at least 1817. Their four sons were baptised at St Mary's Church: **George Thomas**, born on 2 March 1815 when one month old; **Henry** on 19 October 1817, **Charles** on 6 February 1820 and **Joseph** on 4 August 1822.

By 1841, Thomas, a widower and colliery labourer, lived at Old Bleach Croft King Well, Worsbrough, with three of his sons, all coal miners: George, aged 26, Henry, with his wife Hannah, and Charles, aged 20. Edward Burrows was a lodger (see chapter for Burrows page 260).

George Thomas, Charles and Joseph were killed together in the 1847 explosion, respectively aged 31, 27 and 24; they were interred three days later in the communal graves at St Mary's churchyard.

Thomas, aged 50, was injured in the disaster and he was paid an allowance for nearly two years by the Colliers' Relief Committee; they stopped payments at the end of 1848 but provided no explanation. Thomas, a labourer, was living in Shambles Street by 1851, with son Henry and family, as well as Edward Burrows. Thomas died in summer 1852, aged 55.

Joseph Steel (1822–1847) was a collier in 1841, when he was lodging at King Well, Worsbrough, with Benjamin Harrison and family. He married Martha Musgrave on 31 January 1842 at All Saints' Church, Silkstone. Joseph and Martha had two children: Mary Ellen in 1844 and William Thomas in 1846.

Postcard of St Mary's church. (© Barnsley Archives)

Martha Steel (c.1822–1867) was widowed, aged 24, and left with two young children, being dependent on relief from the Subscription Fund. She was referred to twice in the minutes, on 22 April and 4 May 1848, when her allowances were stopped because of behaviour disapproved of by the Committee, who continued to make payments for children provided they were satisfied they attended school regularly.

Martha got married again in summer 1848 to John Wilson, a miner aged 27. In 1851, they resided in Ardsley with her two children at school, and their first two of four children; John's brother Benjamin, a coal miner aged 18, was lodging with them.

John Wilson (c.1820–1860), a 'coal getter', was killed on 15 February 1860, aged 40, in an explosion of gas at the Old Silkstone (Higham) Colliery. Thirteen men and boys lost their lives, eleven underground, 'charred and scarcely recognisable', and two died of their injuries after

213

being brought to the surface. John and Martha's son Joseph, a pony driver aged 11, who worked with his father using a candle rather than a safety lamp, was a victim along with John's brother Henry, a hewer aged 38, who died of internal injuries on 26 February leaving a widow and three children. A nephew appears to have survived his severe injuries. The jury's verdict at the inquest was: 'We are of the opinion that the explosion is purely accidental; at the same time we earnestly recommend the Messrs Charlesworth to make a more general use of safety lamps.'

A night or two previous, John had returned home from the colliery 'much depressed in spirits', and told his wife he feared something was about to occur to either himself or his brother Henry,

> but he hoped if anything occurred to him he should be brought home dead, as he should not want to lie on a sick bed. After making this remark he embraced his son, and wished him to be a good lad, and do whatever he could for his mother and him. His wish was gratified, for in a few hours afterwards the lifeless bodies of both himself and his son were brought into the house. His brother Henry and nephew, who live close by, were also conveyed to their homes seriously injured.

John and Joseph were interred together in St Thomas' churchyard, Gawber.

Martha Wilson, widowed again, aged 38, had six children, aged from 16 to 2, by 1861: Mary, a pit mill worker, William, a coal hurrier, Ann, Hannah, at school, Henry, at school and Benjamin. Martha would have struggled to support her family without any assistance. Martha died on 23 February 1867, aged 44, at Higham Common, Barugh, and she was interred at St Thomas' Church, Gawber. An inquest was held, the tragic details of which survive in the Coroners' Notebooks.

> At the house of Joseph Darlington the Miners Arms Inn Higham (Barugh)
>
> on Tuesday the 26th day of February 1867 on view of the body of
>
> <u>Martha Wilson</u> decd

St Thomas' church, Gawber.

<u>Ann Wilson</u> of Higham Scalepicker at Messrs Charlesworth's Higham Common Pit sw. says, Decd was my Mother. <u>She was 44 years old & the widow of John Wilson a Coalminer.</u> He died 7 years ago. I have lived with my Mother. She said she had palpitation of the heart about a fortnight before Xmas. She was a Charwoman but has not worked since Xmas. She has attended to the house since that time. Last Friday she was out & said she was much better than she had been for many a week. Last Saturday morning soon after 12 o'clock she called me up & asked me to give her some brandy. I got some out of a pot & she drank part of it & she said she was better. I went to bed again. She did not call me up again. I got up about 8 o'clock & found her in bed. She complained of pain & sent me for Mr Rowley of Silkstone. He came soon after me but decd was then dead.

<u>Karen</u> the wife of Thomas Rylah of Higham Common Coalminer sw. says We have lived in the same row as decd for the last 13 years. About half past 2 o'clock last Saturday afternoon her daughter Ann came for me & I went after her into their house & there found Mrs Wilson in bed

unconscious. She died in less than ten minutes after I got in. I had not seen her since the Thursday preceding.

(*Signature*)

Ann the wife of Joseph Dawson of Higham Common Coalminer sw. says, I have known decd upwards of 12 years. She began to be poorly on 13th Dec last after she heard of the Oaks explosion. I saw her last Wednesday. Her son Henry fetched me about 2 o'clock last Saturday. I found her upstairs. She said 'Ann I'm going to die' & then 'Give me some brandy.' Her daughter Ann then came in & fetched Mrs Rylah. Decd could not swallow & died in a few minutes.

Thomas Wainwright of Barnsley Surgeon sw. says, I have this morning made a post mortem examination of decd's body – there were no external marks. The brain was quite healthy – the lungs and heart were healthy – the Liver, Spleen, Kidneys & pancreas were all healthy. The uterus healthy & containing an 8 months female child with placenta firmly attached. The stomach's outer coating was healthy. The mucous membrane especially of the large curvature was very much inflamed. There were about 3oz of greenish yellow fluid with pungent odour to the smell. I am of opinion that the cause of death was gastritis of several days duration induced by some vegetable poison probably Savine. Symptoms of labour had commenced. [Savine is a Eurasian juniper plant, an extract from which was formerly used to induce an abortion].

Thos Wainwright (*Signature*)

Mary the wife of Joseph Darlington sw. says, I have not seen decd for many weeks past. Nobody has come for her or in her name until last Saturday soon after dinner when her son Henry came for 6 pen'orth of brandy. He brought half a crown & I gave him change.

Verdict poisoned herself.
   'Paid'.

The *Sheffield Daily Telegraph* reported, under the headline 'SUICIDE OF A MARRIED WOMAN BY POISON', that Martha 'had been in a depressed state of mind for some time', and the jury returned a verdict that 'the deceased died from inflammation of the stomach from taking poison, probably savin.'

The Two Children of Joseph and Martha Steel

Mary Ellen Steel (1843–1916) was baptised at St Mary's Church on 3 November 1844. She was a domestic servant at Pinder Oaks, Worsbrough, in 1861 for the Newman family, whose two young children, Agnes and Philip, were under the care of the housekeeper. Mary married John Bradley Morris on 21 July 1864 at All Saints' Church, Darton; she was a servant at Birthwaite Hall, and he was a widower and coal miner, aged 30. They had ten children, six of whom died by 1911. By 1871, Mary and John resided at 8 Fountains Row, Darton, with three children, Elizabeth, Edwin and baby Mary Edith. By 1881 John was a colliery deputy, Edwin, a colliery labourer, and they had two more daughters: Ellen, and baby Annie. They had moved by 1891 into seven rooms at 37 Church Street in Barnsley town centre, where they remained. John was a glass and china dealer, Ellen a shop assistant and their youngest child was Walter Percival. In 1901, Mary managed her own newsagents, John had retired, and their three unmarried daughters, Mary, Ellen and Annie, worked at the down quilt factory (McLintocks) while Walter was a 'sorting clerk and telegraphist'. In 1911, Mary junior had her own dressmaking business. Walter, overseer of the *Telegraph* newspaper, was married with two young children and living in Manchester. John died in summer 1915, aged 81, Mary Ellen Morris died early 1916, aged 73.

William Thomas Steel (1846–1899) was baptised on 4 March 1846 at Christ Church, Ardsley. He was a miner and got married late 1870 in Chesterfield to Mary Bradshaw, aged 25, who had two illegitimate daughters born in Bedfordshire: Elizabeth and Sarah Hannah. They resided at Court 2 Number 8 Westgate in 1871 and moved to 2 Tanyard, West Melton, Rotherham, by 1891, when they had five children together, aged from 16 to 4: Joseph, Fanny, Priscilla, Lilian and William Thomas (Tom). Both sons became hewers. William died early 1899, aged 52, in

Rotherham. Mary moved from West Street to five rooms in Sandymount Road, Wath-upon-Dearne, where she died early 1929, aged 84.

Sarah Hannah Bradshaw (1870–1923) used the surname Steel when she got married on 20 January 1889 at St Mary's Church to Tom Stainthorpe, a coal miner aged 27. They had one son, Herbert, in spring 1889 and he shared their homes at 9 Greys Holdings, Victoria Road, then five rooms at 103 Avenue Road, Sandy Mount, Wath-upon-Dearne until 1911. Sarah Hannah Stainthorpe died in summer 1923, aged 53, in Rotherham.

Herbert Stainthorpe (1889–1917) was baptised on 9 June 1889 at Wath Parish Church and he became a colliery labourer. He married Frances Brownsword early 1910 in Doncaster and they had three daughters:

First World War silk postcard for the York and Lancaster Regiment. (Author's Collection)

Ivy, Olive and Edna. Herbert enlisted at Wath as a Private in the 1/5th (Territorial Force) Battalion of the York and Lancaster Regiment. His battalion were on the front line in east Belgium, between Nieuwpoort and the sea. Herbert was killed in action on 9 August 1917, aged 28, and buried in Ramskapelle Road Military Cemetery. He was owed £5 17s 8d when he died and this was eventually paid to his widow early in 1918. Frances subsequently received a War Gratuity of £7 (worth £1,189) for the loss of her husband in addition to his Victory and British War medals and the Memorial Plaque and Scroll.

Joseph Steel (1875–1955) was a coal miner hewer when he got married on 2 July 1905 at St Mary's Church to Susannah Hardcastle, a domestic servant aged 23. They moved to five rooms at 92 Sandymount, Wath, next door to his brother William; they remained there and had three children: Norah, Joseph and Harry. In 1939, Joseph was a 'colliery screen worker (surface)', as was their son Joseph, who was also a 'colliery air raid precautions (ARP) worker' during the Second World War. Joseph died in spring 1955, aged 80, and Susannah died in summer 1961, aged 77.

Fanny Steel (1878–1924) was baptised on 29 December 1878 at Wath Parish Church. She went into domestic service and, in 1901, was a general servant for Alfred Mann at 2 Heathfield Place, Skircoat, Halifax, just three doors away from her sister Priscilla. Fanny got married on 30 September 1905 at St John the Baptist's Church, Halifax, to Harry Greenwood, a carter aged 26. They did not have any children and remained in Halifax. In 1911, Harry worked for a brewery and they occupied two rooms at 32 Grant Street, Commercial Road. Fanny Greenwood died in 1924, aged 46, and was buried on 6 February 1924 in the Non-Conformist section at Calderdale Cemetery.

Priscilla Steel (1881–1940) was baptised on 5 June 1881 at Wath Church. Priscilla was a general servant in 1901 for Herbert C. Mounsey, a 'worsted spinning company secretary', and his family at 5 Heathfield Place, Skircoat. She got married on 8 August 1904 in Wath Church to Hanson Gleadhill Wadsworth, a slater and plasterer. In 1911, they occupied three rooms at 12 Grove Street, South Gibbet Street, Halifax, where they remained for the rest of their lives and had both sons: Thomas Harold and Jack.

Hanson Gleadhill Wadsworth (c.1883–1945) enlisted on 12 December 1915; he was 32 years old, 5ft10in tall, weighed 208lbs, had a 44in chest, good physical development and was a Wesleyan, according to the medical carried out at South Camp in Ripon. Hanson served as a Private in the Royal Garrison Artillery until he was demobilised on 2 March 1919; he was awarded the Victory and British War Medals.

In 1939, son Jack, a machine tool fitter, was at home. Thomas, a baker and confectioner as well as a volunteer for the Auxiliary Fire Service during the war, had got married in 1936 and they resided at 28 Bowman Terrace, Halifax; his wife, Violet (née Kendal) was a worsted worker and volunteer First Aid Air Raid Precautions (ARP). Priscilla Wadsworth died early 1940, aged 59, and Hanson died on 30 December 1945, aged 66, in Halifax Royal Infirmary. Thomas died on Christmas Eve 1948, aged 36, in Halifax General Hospital.

Lilian Steel (1884–1950) was baptised on 12 October 1884 at Wath Church. She was a general servant by 1911 in seven rooms at Wheatley Cottage, Grange Estate, Ilkley, where the owner was away from home. Lilian got married early 1916 to Titus Edward Lomas, a 'cartman for a grocery establishment' aged 36, with whom she had a daughter, Mary Margaret.

Titus Edward Lomas (c.1879–1950) enlisted on 1 September 1914, two days after his 35th birthday and soon after the outbreak of the First World War; he was 5ft 8in tall, weighed 126 lbs, had a 35in chest and very good vision. Titus was promoted to Lance Corporal and served in the Duke of Wellington's (West Riding) Regiment then in the Labour Corps. As he went to France on 15 July 1915, he was eligible for three medals: Victory, British War and the 1915 Star. Titus received multiple gunshot wounds to his face, body, right arm and both legs on 2 March 1916 resulting in his return to the UK, where he spent nine weeks in Edinburgh War Hospital. He suffered from some continued lameness and pain in his right leg from loss of muscle and tissue as well as effects of gas poisoning, but he was assessed as less than 20 per cent disabled.

In 1939, Lilian, a cleaner of municipal offices, and Titus, a fish, fruit and game salesman, resided at 'Whinburn' Leeds Road, Ilkley. Lilian Lomas of Stamore, Green Lane, Skipsea, died on 20 June 1950, aged 65, at the Alfred Bean Hospital in Driffield. Titus died at Stamore five months later, aged 70.

Mary Margaret Lomas got married in summer 1938 and had two sons: Anthony Peter and Michael S. Her husband, Frederick William Dainty, served as a Flying Officer (Pilot) in 58 Squadron of the Royal Air Force Volunteer Reserve during the Second World War. He died in service on 11 November 1944, aged 29, and was buried in Ilkley Cemetery. Frederick would have known his wife was pregnant, but he died before Michael was born.

William Thomas Steel (1887–1980) was baptised on 31 July at Wath Church. He was a 'colliery lamp cleaner on the surface' aged 14, then a hewer. William got married in summer 1919 to Marion Oldham, aged 30, with whom he had four children: John T., Edward, Dorothy and Harold. They lived at 94 Sandymount Road, Wath-upon-Dearne. William looked after his children alone in 1939 because Marion had been admitted to the West Riding Mental Hospital in Wadsley. (This opened as South Yorkshire Lunatic Asylum, later changed its name to Middlewood Hospital and is now a gated housing development). Marion died in spring 1960, aged 71, and William died early 1980 at the impressive age of 93.

The Brother of George Thomas, Charles and Joseph

Henry Steel (1817–1875), who worked in Oaks Colliery, married Hannah c.1843 and they had one son, Thomas Mark. Hannah died early 1858, aged 40, and Henry got married again on 6 July 1858 at St Mary's Church to Jane Burrows, aged 25 (see chapter for Burrows page 260). By 1861, Henry, a coal miner and publican, resided at the Prince of Wales Inn, 18 Spa Terrace, with Jane, Thomas, a coal miner, and her illegitimate daughter Mary Ann, who had been baptised at St George's Church in 1855. They moved to another pub at 16 Peel Square by 1871, when their daughter Ada was born. Henry died there on 20 January 1875, aged 57, and he was buried in Barnsley Cemetery. Jane got married again in 1878 to Willoughby Scorah, a widower and miner aged 45, who died in 1897. Jane Scorah died early 1902, aged 68.

Thomas Mark Steel (1844–1880) was baptised on 16 June 1844 at St Mary's Church and he became a coal miner. Thomas got married there on 16 April 1865 to Priscilla Brook, who had two daughters: Anne E. and

Hannah. They had four children together: George, Frederick, who was baptised on Christmas Day 1868 at St Mary's, Elinda and Thomas. They all resided at 43 Old Mill Lane by 1871. Thomas died at 8 Honeywell Street in spring 1880, aged 36, and was buried in Barnsley Cemetery. Priscilla got married again in 1885 to James Padget, a widower and miner; they lived at 5 Clifton Street with various children. George and Frederick became glass blowers, Elinda, a tailoress, and Thomas a miner. Priscilla Padget died in 1903, aged 62.

Ada Steel (1870–1940) was baptised at St Mary's on 20 August 1871. She married Tom Robinson a stonemason, on 10 November 1889 at All Saints' Church, Silkstone; they were neighbours in Gelder Row. They relocated to Burnley by 1901 and had eight children, two of whom died young: Harry, Arthur, Alfred, 'Jennet', 'Margarete' and Tom. They occupied four rooms at 13 Higher Water Street by 1911, when 18-year-old Harry was an aerated water carter. Tom became a coal miner. Ada Robinson, a widow, died late 1940, aged 69, in Burnley

Whitsuntide procession in Church Street, Ardsley. (Courtesy of the Tasker Trust)

Joseph Turton (1811–1847) and His Son James Turton (1834–1847)

Joseph Turton was born on 3 June 1811 and baptised on 27 December at St Mary's Church, the son of James, a linen weaver, and Elizabeth Turton. Joseph got married on 31 March 1834 at All Saints' Church, Darfield, to Martha Green, aged 18, and they had three children: James, Elizabeth and Charles. James was born in 1834 and baptised at St Mary's on 30 June 1837, aged 3, with his baby sister Elizabeth; their father was a bleacher in the linen industry. By 1841, Joseph, a collier, and Martha, were living in Pall Mall with their three children: James, aged 6, Elizabeth, aged 5, and 3-month-old Charles. James would have started work in the same colliery as his father when aged 10.

Joseph, aged 36, and James, aged 13, were both killed in the 1847 explosion and they were buried in one of the communal graves at St Mary's churchyard.

Martha Turton (1815–1888) was baptised on 13 July 1815 at St Mary's, daughter of Mary and Joseph Green, a linen weaver. She was widowed, aged 32, and left with two young children needing allowances awarded by the Colliers' Relief Committee. The family were referred to twice in the ledger. On 4 May 1849, they 'Ordered that eldest Child [Elizabeth] be continued at School till a further order be made on the subject.' On 27 December 1851, they confirmed that 'The Widow of Joseph Turton on her Marriage to George Ledger of Mapplewell Nailmaker on the 23rd of November last. And Charles the Son of Joseph Turton, on his attaining the age of 10 years on the 13th of June last' had been removed from the list of recipients of relief.

Martha, a steam loom weaver, resided in New Street with Charles; Elizabeth was a domestic servant. She got married again on 23 November

Housing in Silkstone. (© Barnsley Archives)

1851 at St Mary's Church to George Ledger, aged 45, and they lived at Carr Green, Mapplewell, where George died early 1869, aged 64. Martha continued to keep house for three boarders until she moved in with George's widowed brother David, a nailmaker aged 64, in Mapplewell by 1881. Martha Ledger died there late 1888, aged 66.

Two Children of Joseph and Martha Turton

Elizabeth Turton (c.1837–1929) was baptised on 4 May 1837 at St Mary's. She was a general servant for Henry Field, a bootmaker, and his family at Westgate in Rotherham by 1851. Elizabeth got married on 20 February 1853 at All Saints' Church, Darton, to Jonas Wood, a miner aged 20, of Gawber. They had twelve children: Jemima, George, Charles, Elizabeth, Martha, Joseph, Albert, William, Sarah Ann, Herbert and two unidentified who died in infancy.

Jonas continued to work as a coal miner and they changed addresses within Barnsley as their family increased. In 1871, they resided at No 21 Court,

9 New Street, with Jemima, a mule hand aged 17, while George was a coal miner, aged 15. They were at 16 Baker Street by 1881, when Martha was a linen weaver aged 13. Elizabeth and Jonas resided in Church Street, Barugh, by 1891 with five children, aged from 27 to 11: Charles, an iron moulder's labourer, Joseph, Albert, a coal miner, Sarah Ann and Herbert, at school as well as their 2-month old granddaughter, Ethel Wood.

They subsequently moved to 'New Scarbro' in Wombwell, residing at 85 Elliott's Terrace by 1901, when Jonas had retired and Herbert was a coal miner hewer. Their grandson James Sykes, a hewer aged 26, was there with his wife Harriet, aged 20, and their 1-month-old son John. By 1911, Jonas, aged 78 and in receipt of the new old age pension, occupied two rooms with Elizabeth, aged 74, at 95 East View, New Scarborough, Wombwell, where they remained. Jonas Wood died in January 1915, aged 82, and he was buried in Wombwell Cemetery. Elizabeth Wood died on 30 November 1929, at the impressive age of 94, at Elliott's Terrace and she was buried on 4 December in the same grave as her husband.

Charles Turton (1841–1898) was baptised on 24 April 1842 at St George's Church. He was a miner like his father and got married on 8 June 1862 at All Saints' Church, Darton, to Ann Lindley, aged 23, of Broach Royd Head. Charles and Ann had eight children: Hannah, Mary Ann, Joseph, James, Charles, John William, Austin and Ephraim. In 1871, they were living in Darton with four children and a boarder; Ann was a nailmaker. They moved to Spring Gardens in Mapplewell by 1881 then to Greenside in Staincross by 1891, when five sons aged from 21 to 11 were at home, four working as coal miners: James, Charles, John William, Austin and Ephraim, at school. Charles Turton died in 1898, aged 56, and he was interred on 3 March 1898 in All Saints' churchyard. Ann died in summer 1899, aged 61.

Most of their children lived reasonably long lives, except for Charles and Austin.

Charles Turton (1871–1903) was privately baptised on 10 September 1872 at All Saints' Church. He was a coal miner when he got married there on 3 September 1891 to Margaret Jane Ibberson, aged 21, of Mapplewell. Their only daughter, Mary Ann, was born early 1901, when they resided at Staincross Road, Darton. Charles died in 1903, aged 31, and he was interred in All Saints' churchyard. His widow Margaret got married again in 1906 to Samuel Turner.

<u>Austin Turton</u> (1876–1916) a coal miner, got married on 5 April 1900 at All Saints' to Emily Oxley, aged 26, daughter of George Oxley, a greengrocer of Mapplewell. They had two children: Frederick in 1907 and another child, who died in infancy. They moved from New Street, Mapplewell, to three rooms at No 2 Smithy Wood.

Austin enlisted as a Private in the 14th (Second Barnsley) Battalion of the York and Lancaster Regiment. They served in Egypt for the first few months of 1916 but transferred to the Western Front to participate in the Battles of the Somme. He was missing from 1 July 1916, which was reported in the *Barnsley Chronicle* on 9 September: Austin, who 'formerly worked at North Gawber Pit', was 'seen to climb the parapet', but not heard from since; 'His wife and children would be pleased if any of his pals could give any news of him.' They published a photograph of him as 'Missing' the following week. Austin was assumed killed in action on 1 July 1916, aged 39, and this was only confirmed months later. Emily put a notice in the *Barnsley Chronicle* on 21 April 1917 inviting people to attend a Memorial Service in the Wesleyan Reform Church in Staincross the next day.

Above left: Austin Turton. (© *Barnsley Chronicle*)

Above right: The Tiger & Rose emblem of the York & Lancaster Regiment

He bade no one his last farewell,
He waved his hand to none:
His spirit flew before we knew,
That he from us had gone.

Sleep on, dear husband, as the days go by,
We cannot see the grave where you lie:
For the waters of the ocean keep us apart,
But your smiling face shall shine in our hearts.

His brothers and sisters also paid him tribute:

To duty firm, and conscience true,
However tried and pressed:
In God's clear sight, high work we do,
If we but do our best.

Austin's body was not found, or not identified, and his name is on the Thiepval Memorial to the Missing in France. He was awarded posthumously two medals, Victory and British War, which were sent to his widow Emily Turton of 9 Smithy Wood, Smithies. The pay owed to him of £2 16s 11d was sent to Emily and his son on 31 July 1917 and, on 27 October 1919, they were sent a War Gratuity of £3 10s (worth £595). Austin's Service Records have not survived to provide more personal details.

John Wainwright (1835–1847)

John Wainwright was baptised on 12 August 1835 at St Mary's Church, the son of George and Mary Wainwright. George, a widower and weaver, had remarried on 12 July 1833 at St George's Church to Mary Wheat, a widow with a daughter Ann, baptised on 23 September 1832 at St Mary's. George and Mary had four children together: John, Elizabeth, Emma and Mary, baptised on 8 June 1845 at St Mary's Church, Worsbrough. In 1841, they were both aged 40 and living with their four children plus two lodgers at Upper Lewdin, Worsbrough. John was killed on 5 March 1847, aged 11, in the 1847 explosion and buried three days later in one of the four communal graves in St Mary's churchyard.

In 1851, the family resided at Mr Newman Houses in Worsbrough: George, a 'labouringman', Mary, a linen weaver, and three daughters, the older two at school: Elizabeth, Emma and Mary. Ann Wheat, aged 18, and her new husband James Davey, a labourer aged 22, were also staying there before moving to Mansfield. George died late 1852, aged 52, and his widow Mary died on 7 November 1872, aged 73; they were both interred in St John the Baptist churchyard, Penistone.

John's Two Sisters

Emma Wainwright (1840–1859) was baptised on 31 May 1840 at St Mary's. Although she was the third of the four children her story needs to be told first. Emma got married, aged 16, to Joseph Wood, aged 20. Emma Wood died late 1859, aged 19, after recently giving birth to their daughter Emma. Joseph would have needed to continue to work as a coal miner to support them and a parent or sibling would have raised Emma.

Emma Wood (1859–1919) got married on 18 June 1878 at St Mary's to George Wilson, a linen warehouseman aged 18. They had ten children, two of whom had died by 1911; the surviving children were: Mary Ann, William, Joseph, Tom, John, George, Henry and Elizabeth Hannah. By 1881, Emma, a cotton spinner, George and their three children lived at 20 Oak Street, next door to George's older brother William Wilson, a coal miner, and family. They had moved to 26 Keresforth Road by 1891, when Emma was a linen winder and they had seven children. In 1901, George and Emma had six children and were living at 96 Castlereagh Street: Joseph, a coal miner aged 20, Thomas, a metal worker aged 18, John, a blacksmith aged 16, and three at school aged from 12 to 9: George, Henry and Hannah. George and Emma occupied four rooms at 65 Racecommon Road in 1911 with their three youngest children: George, a fettler in metal, Harry, a plasterer, and Elizabeth Hannah, 'a clothier's machinist ready-made clothing'. George died in summer 1912, aged 53, and Emma Wilson died early 1919, aged 59.

Elizabeth Wainwright (1838–1904) resided in 1861 at Hampshire Row, Worsbrough, with her widowed brother-in-law Joseph and his daughter Emma. Elizabeth had a son, Joseph, late 1862 and she got married in summer 1863 to Joseph Wood, her son's father. Elizabeth and Joseph had three more children: Thomas, Hannah, who died aged 2 in summer 1871, and James, who was baptised on 16 April 1876 at St Thomas' Church, Worsbrough Dale, and buried in the churchyard on 12 January 1900, aged 24. They remained in Worsbrough, moving from 18 Hudson Buildings to 9 Holly Gate, and their sons worked in a colliery. Elizabeth Wood died late 1904, aged 66, and Joseph, who was a coal miner hewer until at least 75 years old, went to stay with his son and family. Having moved to 24 Lower Thomas Street after his son and daughter-in-law predeceased him, Joseph Wood died in summer 1918, aged 82.

Joseph Wainwright/Wood (1862–1917) used the surname Wood when he married Emily Topham, aged 23, in summer 1883 and they had ten children, the three survivors being Emily, Margaret Ann and Edith, who worked in a bobbin factory. Joseph, a coal miner, and Emily continued to reside in Worsbrough, moving from 17 Highstone Road to 9 Howard Street before they occupied three rooms at 7 Peel Street. Emily Wood died in December 1916, aged 56, at 26 Cresswell Street, Pogmoor, and she was buried in Barnsley Cemetery. Joseph died in November 1917, aged 57, in Beckett Hospital and was interred on 1 December in Barnsley Cemetery.

<u>Thomas Wood</u> (1864–1940) was a horse driver by the age of 16. He married Margaret White, aged 20, on 12 November 1887 at St Thomas' Church, Worsbrough Dale, and they had fourteen children but six died young. The family moved to 23 Heelis Street, Barnsley, before they moved into five rooms at 38 Summer Street by 1911, remaining there for the rest of their lives. All eight surviving children, aged from 23 to 1, shared their home: Joseph, John, George, Martha, James, Margaret, Harry and Mary (the three oldest sons were coal miner hewers); they also employed a domestic servant. In 1939, Thomas, retired and was living with Margaret and their son Harry, who had never worked. Thomas died in February 1940, aged 76, in St Helen's Hospital, which was originally the workhouse infirmary on the site of the present-day Barnsley Hospital, and he was buried on 4 March in Barnsley Cemetery. Margaret Wood died early 1947, aged 83, and she was interred in the same grave as her husband.

The Gospel Hall on Heelis Street. (Courtesy of the Tasker Trust)

Barnsley General Hospital c1975 incorporating the Workhouse. (© Barnsley Archives)

William Walton (1820–1847)

William Walton was baptised on 24 August 1823 at St Mary's Church, son of Joseph and Mary Walton, who had five children: Joseph, Christopher, William, Martha, who was baptised on 26 August 1826 at St Mary's, and Edward, who died late 1841, aged 13. In 1841, Joseph, a joiner aged 50, and Mary, the same age, were living in Baker Street with all five children; the three oldest were coal miners.

William got married on 27 December 1841 at All Saints' Church, Silkstone, to Caroline Riley, aged 17, and they had three children, all baptised at St Mary's: Thomas on 22 January 1843, Sarah Elizabeth on 6 October 1844, and William on 27 December 1846. William senior was killed, aged 27, in the 1847 explosion and buried ten days later at Christ Church churchyard in Ardsley.

According to the *Illustrated London News*: 'On Tuesday morning the pit was very full of sulphur, and in the evening it was impossible to descend. At that time there remained in the pit three individuals, including William Walton.' Sheffield and Leeds newspapers reported that Joseph Littlewood, a fireman at the Oak Pit, had found William using a candle instead of a lamp about a year previously and reported it; William was threatened with being laid off but had pleaded to continue. They confirmed that William's body was discovered on Monday morning 15 March 'on the north side of the workings beneath a massive piece of rock, which required seven men to remove it. There is no doubt that Walton was the cause of the sad calamity.'

William's body was found in an old part of the mine, in old breaks, where he ought not to have been, along with Abraham Matthews, James Whiteley and his two sons (see chapters for Matthews page 184 and Whiteley page 246). At the inquest on 16 March, Joseph Littlewood provided details of the workings and locations of the last bodies to be recovered. He testified that he had inspected the mine before men began

Above and below: Illustrations from the 1842 Royal Commission Report. (Courtesy of the National Coalmining Museum)

their work on the day of the accident and confirmed that it was safe; he had cautioned them about not going into the old breaks and had specifically told William not to take his candle into them. The coroner, in summing up the evidence for the jury, stated: 'there is no doubt, in my mind, that Walton was the cause of it, by going into one of the breaks with a candle.'

Caroline Walton (c.1824–1871) was widowed, aged 23, with three young children to support. Her grief was compounded by the loss of her brother, John Riley (see chapter for Riley page 194), in the same disaster and the knowledge that her husband had been responsible for the huge loss of life and destruction of the colliery. She would have been dependent on relief from the Subscription Fund.

The Committee decided at their meetings on 22 April 1848 and 4 May to stop payments because of behaviour of which they disapproved; they agreed to continue allowances for children provided that they attended school regularly. Caroline, a linen weaver, got married again on 27 May 1849 at All Saints' Church, Darfield, to Mark Smith, an agricultural labourer aged 21. In 1851, they were living in Stairfoot with her two sons and their daughter Elizabeth Ann Smith, who was baptised on 13 October 1850 at Christ Church, Ardsley. Mark died in spring 1853, aged 25, and Caroline was widowed again with four children. Elizabeth died late 1854, aged 4. Caroline and sons Thomas and William lodged at Haywoods House, Harrison Row, Ardsley, with widower George Ellis.

Another tragedy occurred when Thomas Walton, a coal miner labourer, was killed in the Oaks Colliery explosion on 13 December 1866, aged 24; he was interred three days later in Christ Church churchyard, Ardsley. William worked with his older brother and, although he is not on the list of victims, it seems that he might also have been killed. Caroline Smith died in summer 1871, aged 47.

William and Caroline Walton's Daughter

Sarah Elizabeth Walton (1844–1915) was baptised at St Mary's Church. By 1861, she was working as a house servant for John Mirfin, innkeeper at 16 May Day Green. Sarah resided at 28 Kingstone Place when she got married in 1865 to John Hepworth, a warehouseman aged 28. They had sixteen children: Emily, Sarah Elizabeth, Mary, Tom, Clara,

Ada, Gertrude, Frank, John, twins: Joseph and Benjamin, Arthur, Lydia, George Henry and Doris; four of these and one unknown died young. By 1871, they resided at 4 Park Road with two daughters, but relocated to Middlesbrough in 1874. They moved to Brompton then, by 1880, Lockwood, Huddersfield, where they remained at different addresses. In 1881 John was a pedlar drapery, aged 44, and they had seven children. John became a grocer by 1891 and they had eleven children, aged from 21 to 9 months; five employed, two in the worsted industry, a hairdresser, a dressmaker and an errand boy, while four were at school. John and four children worked in a worsted mill in 1901. John, a jobbing gardener aged 73, and Sarah shared four rooms by 1911 with their three youngest children, worsted mill workers, and a couple who were visiting. Sarah Elizabeth Hepworth died in 1915, aged 69, and John died in 1927, aged 85.

William's Two Brothers

Joseph Walton (c.1816–1901) was a coal miner when he got married; they had two daughters, but his wife died young. In 1851, Joseph, an agricultural labourer, and his two infants, Mary and Martha, were staying with his parents. After his father died in 1855, Joseph, Mary and Martha continued to reside with his widowed mother. Joseph's daughters both died young and were buried in Barnsley Cemetery, Martha in February 1864, aged 13, and Mary in December 1869, aged 22. His mother died in 1870. Joseph was admitted to Barnsley Union Workhouse by 1901 and died there in December; he was interred on the 23rd in Barnsley Cemetery. (Samuel Johnson Crawshaw, aged 41, was master and his wife Emily Mary, aged 44, was matron with eleven other resident staff for a total of 209 Paupers, 118 males and 91 females).

Christopher Walton (c.1821–1893) worked in a colliery and married Ann Helliwell in spring 1847 in Bolsterstone, near Stocksbridge. They had six children: Henry, Joseph, John, William, Thomas and Mary. In 1851, Christopher, an agricultural labourer, and Ann, aged 25, resided at Allen Croft, Bolsterstone, where they remained at different addresses as their family increased. They settled in Holly Bush Lane by 1871, when

Christopher was a coal miner again. Their sons were general labourers and coal miners. Christopher died late 1893, aged 72. By 1901, Ann, aged 76, was a Pauper Inmate in the Barnsley Union Workhouse and Infirmary, where she died early 1911, aged 85.

Postcard of Barnsley Cemetery. (Author's Collection)

Barnsley General Hospital 1977 incorporating the Workhouse. (© Barnsley Archives)

James Whiteley (1803–1847) and His Two Sons: William (c.1830–1847) & George Whiteley (c.1832–1847)

James Whiteley was born on 4 October 1803 and baptised on the 21st at St Mary's Church. He was a collier when he got married on 23 December 1827 at All Saints' Church in Silkstone to Elizabeth Simpson. They had three sons, who were baptised at St Mary's Church: William on 25 February 1830, George on 21 October 1832, and Joseph c.1834.

In 1841, James, a coal miner aged 36, was living in George Street, Silkstone, with his wife Elizabeth, aged 30, and their three sons. William and George worked at the Oaks Colliery with their father. All three were killed in the 1847 explosion, aged respectively 42, 18 and 15.

According to the *London Daily News,* their bodies were brought out of the pit on 8 March. The coroner and jury assembled at the White Bear Public House, Ardsley, to view the bodies the next morning; but the inquest was adjourned for a week. Newspapers described George and William as 'two fine youths'. The final inquest explained that James and his sons were working in close proximity to William Walton and Abraham Matthews; one son was working with his father while the other son was working with Walton. They all used candles rather than lamps.

They were buried together in one of the four communal graves in St Mary's churchyard. James, William and George have a small poignant headstone, which survives on South Lawn, Churchfields, at the base of a tree that has been cut down. It appears to have been 'home-made' and is inscribed: 'J. Whiteley / And 2 sons Who / Whas killed / 1847'.

Illustration from the 1842 Royal Commission Report. (Courtesy of the National Coalmining Museum)

Headstone for James, William and George.

<u>Elizabeth Whiteley</u> (c.1811–1848) was widowed, aged 36, and left with her youngest son to raise alone. She would have been dependent on support from the Colliers' Relief Fund. Elizabeth died in 1848 and was buried on 3 July 1848 in St Mary's churchyard.

At their meeting on 11 January 1850, the Committee confirmed that 'from the Day of the death of the Widow of James Whiteley they placed her surviving Child on the Orphan's List and have allowed for his support 2s/6d per Week instead of 1s/-' (worth £102).

<u>Joseph Whiteley</u> (c.1834– ?) was orphaned, aged 11, and he may have been admitted to Barnsley Union Workhouse, from where he would have been sent out to work until he could be independent. In 1861, Joseph was a coal miner, residing at 6 Court, Wood Street, with his 'wife' Ann, a dressmaker aged 32, and their daughter Eva Wood Whiteley, aged 6. Ann was separated from her husband, unable to afford a divorce, and only able to marry again after he died. Joseph married Ann Wood (née Buckley) on 20 April 1869 at St Mary's Church. By 1871, Joseph, a chimney sweep, and Ann resided at 92 Sheffield Road with their daughter and two lodgers.

<u>Eva Wood Whiteley</u> (1854–1910) was born in Holmfirth and she married coal miner George Bentley in 1873; they did not have any children. Eva and George boarded at 9 Wright's Terrace, then moved by 1991 to 39 Pindar Oaks Street, where his widowed mother joined them. Eva Bentley died early 1910, aged 56. George died in 1935, aged 82.

Postcard of Sheffield Road. (Author's Collection)

Ezra Winter (1819–1847)

Richard Winter (1753–1835) was baptised on 22 July 1753, son of Thomas Winter of Dodworth. Richard married Sarah Shaw in 1780 and they had eleven children. Richard died in 1835, aged 82. Three of Richard and Sarah's sons, baptised at All Saints' Church, Silkstone, had descendants who worked in the Oaks Colliery: Thomas (1782–1853), John (1786–before 1841), and Benjamin (1789–1869). Six Winters were killed in the explosion on 12 December 1866 (see chapter Information about Other Collieries page 46) – there are other relations with different surnames.

Thomas's son William lost five of his seven sons in 1866: John, aged 32, Thomas, aged 27, Duncombe (Duncan) aged 25, Joseph, aged 20, and William, aged 17. John lost one of his three sons in 1847. Benjamin lost Henry, the youngest of his five children aged 24, in 1866.

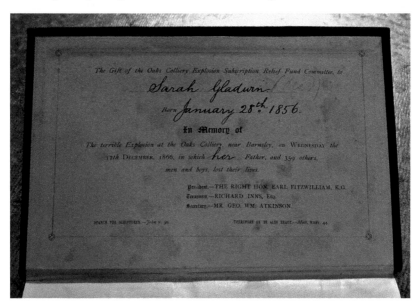

Inscription in the Oaks 1866 Bible. (Courtesy of NUM)

EZRA was baptised on 15 August 1819 at St Mary's Church, Worsbrough, son of John Winter, a collier aged 33, and Charlotte née Rodgers, aged 28, who had married on 11 February 1811 at the same church. John died before 1841, when Charlotte resided in a shared property at Hill Side Dale with three sons, all coal miners: Ezra, aged 20, Andrew and Henry, both aged 15.

Ezra got married on 6 June 1842 at All Saints' Church, Darfield, to Sarah Glover, aged 19; she had been, baptised there on 13 July 1823, one of three daughters of James and Elizabeth Glover. They had two children: Henry and Arthur, who was baptised on 3 May 1846 at All Saints'. Sarah died in 1847, aged 23, and was buried on 11 January in the churchyard. Ezra, who would have needed help looking after his young sons while he worked long hours in the colliery, was killed about two months later, aged 27, in the 1847 explosion. He joined his wife in All Saints' Churchyard.

Ezra and Sarah's sons were referred to twice in the Ledger: on 24 June 1847, the Committee agreed, 'That the weekly Allowance of two shillings and six pence (worth £100) to each of the Orphan children of … Ezra Winter be continued.' This decision was confirmed on 22 January 1848.

Arthur Winter died in 1849, aged 3, and was interred on 26 March in St Mary's Churchyard, Worsbrough.

The Surviving Son of Ezra and Sarah Winter

Henry Winter (1844–1913), baptised on 7 January 1844 at Worsbrough Church, went to live with his widowed grandmother, Charlotte Winter, who was receiving parish relief, and uncle Henry, a miner. After Charlotte died in 1860, aged 73, he boarded with Charles Harper in Pantry Hill, Worsbrough (see chapter for Harper page 137).

Henry, a coal miner hewer, married Ann Booth in 1866, but she died in November 1889, aged 34. In 1881, he was lodging at 21 High Street, Worsbrough, with Susan Christopher, housekeeper, who had several other coal miner lodgers. Henry got married again late 1889 to Alice Mary Fleetwood, daughter of Richard Fleetwood, a stonemason. They lived at 2 Taylor Row, where they had four children: Sarah Elizabeth, who was baptised on 9 February 1892 at St Mary's Church but died in summer 1893, aged 1, Leonard in 1896, Elsie, baptised on 1 September

1897 at St Peter's Church, and Walter, baptised there on 26 June 1901. In 1911, Henry and Alice, aged 46, occupied three rooms at 5 Taylor Row with three children: Leonard, a 'coal miner pony boy' aged 16; Elsie, a bobbin maker aged 13; and Walter, aged 9, attending school. Alice's older brother Richard Fleetwood, a 'fitter iron foundry', was staying with them. Henry Winter died early 1913, aged 69, and Alice got married again. Two of their children died in 1917, Elsie, aged 19, and Leonard.

Leonard Winter (1896–1917) worked in a colliery before serving in the First World War. He enlisted as a Private in the 1st Battalion of the King's Own Scottish Borderers, but his service records have not survived to provide personal details. He was killed in action at Cambrai, France, on 30 November 1917, aged 23, and his name is on the memorial in the war cemetery at Louverval. The Army owed Leonard £4 17s 1d pay (worth £1,344) and he qualified for a war gratuity of £3; these amounts were paid to his mother one year and eighteen months after his death respectively. Alice received his inscribed medals, Victory and British War, as well as the Memorial Plaque and Scroll.

Walter Winter (1901–1973) was a labourer of 16 Taylor Row, when he married Elsie Padgett, aged 18 of the same address, on 27 October 1923 at St Peter's Church. They had five children between 1924 and 1940: Elsie, Walter, Doreen, Betty and Jean. In 1939, Walter, a brewery lorry driver, and Elsie resided at 46 Keresforth Hill Road with three children under 15 years: Elsie dipped filaments for electric globes, while Walter and Doreen attended school. Elsie died in summer 1967, aged 62, and Walter died in summer 1973, aged 72.

Ezra's Two Brothers

Andrew Winter (c.1823–1888) was baptised on 2 February 1823 at St Mary's Church, Worsbrough. He worked in a colliery and married Mary Broadhead on 3 November 1844 at the same church. They lived in Worsbrough Dale and had four children: Frederick, Albert, Walter and Mary Ann, who died in spring 1852, aged 1. Mary Winter died in summer 1852, aged 27. Andrew got married again late 1858 to Ann Bagshaw, who had two sons, John Bagshaw, aged 5, and 3-year-old Henry Winter

Bagshaw. They remained in Worsbrough, at Kingwell, 'No 54', near Darley Square, then 35 Jarretts Buildings. Andrew had another eight children with Ann: Tom, Mary, Ann Elizabeth, George, Emley, Edward Ezra, Fanny and Thomas. Nine of Andrew's thirteen children became coal miners. After Andrew died in spring 1888, aged 65, Ann was supported by their unmarried son George and two grandsons, both coal miners, who resided with her along with other younger grandchildren. Ann Winter died late 1901, aged 68.

Edward Ezra Winter (1869–1895) was baptised, aged 4, on 4 May 1873 at St Thomas' Church in Worsbrough Dale; he was known as Ezra. He followed the family tradition of working as a coal miner and continued to live with his parents until his death on 7 October 1895, aged 26. Ezra had suffered from various health problems: rheumatism for years, heart disease for three years and dropsy for two months (although it was reported differently in the press). He died in an ambulance car while being conveyed home by his mother from Beckett Hospital. An inquest was held on 9 October 1895 by Pelham Page Maitland, coroner.

The *Barnsley Chronicle* reported details:

> On Monday Edward Ezra Winter, of 42 Jarretts-buildings, Worsbrough Dale, died under peculiar circumstances.

Postcard of the Beckett Hospital. (Author's Collection)

He was only 27 years old but had been ailing eighteen months or more from dropsy. A fortnight ago he was removed to the Beckett Hospital, where it was found that his case was incurable. On Monday he was placed in an ambulance and was being conveyed home, when he died in the presence of his mother, Ann Winter, who was riding with him. Deceased's condition was recognized by Dr Currie, house surgeon at the Hospital, and it was against his wishes that deceased's friends undertook his removal; but they wanted to have him at home that he might die among his friends. At the coroner's inquest held on Wednesday, a verdict of 'Died from natural causes' was returned.

Henry Winter (c.1826–1890) was baptised on 14 May 1826 at St Mary's Church, Worsbrough. In 1851, he was a labourer, residing with his widowed mother, nephew Henry, and two coal miner lodgers. Henry married Ann Senior in summer 1853 and they had five children: Ada M., Clara Elizabeth, John Henry, Sirus/Syrus Senior and Herbert. The family remained in Worsbrough, moving from Pantry Hill to 12 Grove Street; the sons were coal pit labourers. Ann died in 1889, aged 61, and Henry died less than six months later, aged 63.

With thanks to Michael Chance for sharing information about his ancestors.

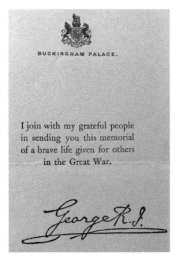

Left: The King's letter for those who died in the First World War. (© Potter Family)

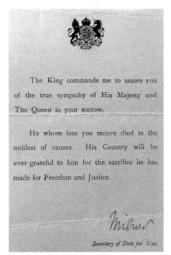

Right: Message on behalf of the King from the War Office. (© Potter Family)

John Woodcock (c.1834–1847)

John Woodcock was lodging at Common Side Houses, Ardsley, in 1841 with Sarah Sedgwick and three children (see chapter for Sedgwick page 218). John was killed, aged 13, in the 1847 explosion and was interred in Christ Church churchyard three days later.

John's widowed mother was initially awarded relief but the Committee decided at their meeting on 4 May 1849 'that the Pay to the following Parties be henceforth discontinued altogether they being merely Widows who lost Children upon whom it is considered they did not much depend viz- to Widows … Woodcock etc'.

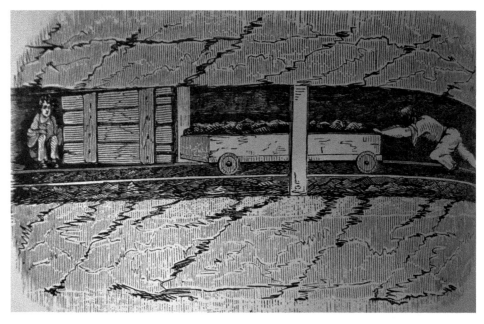

Illustration from the 1842 Royal Commission Report. (Courtesy of the National Coalmining Museum)

Brothers: Joseph Woodhead
(c.1832–1847) and
David Woodhead (c.1835–1847)

David Woodhead senior (1804–1839) was baptised on 22 December 1804 at St Mary's Church, Worsbrough, the son of Benjamin Woodhead. He became the miller at Aldham Water Mill in Wombwell, remaining there until he died. (This attractive sixteenth-century stone complex has survived with an adjacent cottage, separate barn conversion and Aldham Mill Farm, described on its website as the 'home of Yorkshire Dressage').

St Peter's church, Tankersley.

Postcard of the Interior of St Peter's church, Tankersley. (Author's Collection)

David married Ann Fowlstone on 4 February 1828 at All Saints' Church, Rotherham (Minster). They had five children: Benjamin, who died, aged 8 months in Birdwell and was buried on 29 January 1833 in St Peter's churchyard, Tankersley; Joseph, baptised at All Saints' Church, Darfield on 22 July 1832; Sarah Sophia; David, baptised at All Saints on 27 September 1835, and Benjamin (named for his deceased older brother). David died on 5 December 1839, aged 35, of 'consumption' (tuberculosis or TB). He was buried four days later in Tankersley churchyard, where there are other Woodhead graves, some with headstones. Ann was widowed at 33 with four children, the youngest a baby. She had to leave Aldham Water Mill and resided at Lindleys Yard, near Crow Well Hill, by 1841, when she worked as a winder and took in lodgers to support her family.

Joseph and David Woodhead started work at the Oaks Colliery after leaving school and were both killed in the 1847 explosion, Joseph, aged 13, and David, aged 11. They were interred three days later in St Peter's churchyard. A note in the Burial Register states: 'both perished at a Colliery explosion at Ardsley Main together with 73 others'.

Their mother got married again on 14 April 1854 at St Mary's Church to George Wainwright, a widower and agricultural labourer aged 46, with one son, John. They lived at 1 Wortley Street for many years. In 1861, George, a 'labourer (coal mine)', and Ann were there with his son John, aged 11, but he had left by 1871, when George was a carter. George died later that year, aged 63, and Ann Wainwright died late 1888, aged 80.

Joseph and David's Two Siblings

Benjamin Woodhead (1839–1871), a labourer, was boarding at California Gardens, 12 Doncaster and Salterhouse Turnpike Road by 1861. He appears to have relocated to Stanley to work in the Victoria colliery. Benjamin died in 1871 and was interred on 9 March, aged 32, in St Peter's churchyard, Stanley, Wakefield. (This church was rebuilt in 1913, closed in 2004 and the building demolished in 2014. There were plans to make the site into a garden).

Sarah Sophia Woodhead (1833–1897), known as Sophia, was a machine winder and had an illegitimate daughter Elizabeth in spring 1851, when she was only 17. Sophia got married on 24 August 1851 at St Mary's Church, Barnsley, to Charles Wharam, a coal miner aged 21. They began married life in the Courts in Wine Street before moving to 15 Allott Street with their growing family. Sophia and Charles had eight children, baptised at different churches: Emma, William, Richard, Walter, who died summer 1900, aged 31, Mary Ann, Martha, Samuel, and George. In 1891, four children aged 21 to 15 still lived with their parents: Walter, Martha, Sam and George; the sons were working in a colliery. Two grandsons were staying with them: Charles Wharam, a general labourer aged 18, and Alan or Alvin Walker, aged 2. Sarah Sophia and Charles Wharam both died in spring 1897, aged 63 and 66 respectively.

Elizabeth Woodhead (1851– ?), married George Coldwell, a coal miner aged 22, in 1869 and they had one son, Charles, who was brought up by his grandparents. On 28 July 1906 Charles Coldwell 'or Colwell', a woolcomber aged 34, was found guilty of 'attempting to carnally know Lily Midgley, a girl of the age of 12 years, at Bradford on 19 March 1906'. He was sentenced to six months imprisonment with hard labour at HMP Leeds.

Emma Wharam (c.1854–1914) was a mill hand until she married Edward Bennett, a coal miner aged 21, on Christmas Day 1872. They had ten children: William, Sarah A, Florence, Walter, Laura, Emma, Elizabeth, Martha and two names unknown as they died in infancy.

William Wharam (c.1859–1906) was a miner when he married Margaret O'Brien, aged 21, in 1878. They had six children: John, Ann E, John William, Charles, George and Sarah Sophia.

Richard Wharam (c.1862–1928) was a miner when he married Harriet Denton, a widow aged 36, in 1881. They had eight children: Herbert, Charles, William, John, Arthur, Minnie, Sophia and George.

Mary Ann Wharam (c.1866– ?) was a varnisher at the bobbin works before getting married in 1883 at St John the Baptist Church to Matthew Walker, a miner aged 25. They had two sons: Reuben and Alan, who went to live with Mary's parents by 1891. It seems that Mary had died and that Alan died as a baby, leaving Matthew to raise Reuben on his own. In 1901, they both worked in a colliery and resided at 1 Court, 4 Heelis Street. They were each convicted for assault on 29 September 1904 and for this first offence they were imprisoned for one month at HMP Wakefield, because they were unable to pay the fine of £2 17s 9d (worth £1,162 today). The Prison Records stated that Matthew, a 47-year-old 'knocker up' of Barnsley, was 5ft 7¾in tall with brown hair. Matthew Walker died late 1910, aged 53.

Reuben Walker (1887–1940) was a 'pit pony driver' when 14 years old. The 1904 Prison Records recorded that Reuben, aged 'over 16', a pit boy of Barnsley, was 5ft 4in tall with brown hair. In 1911, he occupied two rooms in Heelis Street and was a coal miner's filler.

Reuben enlisted on 25 August 1915, aged 28, at Silkstone as a Private in the 15th Battalion of the York and Lancaster Regiment. He was living at 6 Court, 6 Thomas Street, Barnsley, with his common-law wife Sarah Jane Marsh and their son Thomas William Marsh, born on 4 June 1912. After training, Reuben was posted to France on 9 April 1916 and he served as a private with the First Barnsley Pals. He was discharged as physically unfit on 8 November 1917 with chronic bronchitis caused by active service. Reuben was awarded a Silver War Badge and subsequently received the Victory and British War Medals.

Reuben got married in summer 1918 to Harriet Harrison (née Warren), a widow, aged 31. They had four children, the sons working in a colliery: Florence, Matthew, Harriet and William. By 1939, Reuben, a general labourer, and Harriet had moved to 66 Maple Close, where he died early 1940, aged 53, and Harriet died in spring 1947, aged 60.

Martha Wharam (c.1872–1901) married James Johnson, a miner aged 21, in 1899 and they had no children. In 1901, he was an 'onsetter' and they resided in New Houses, Monk Bretton, where Martha died in summer 1901, aged 29. James went to live with his parents and siblings.

Samuel Wharam (c.1874–1928) became a coal miner hewer and by 1901 he occupied three rooms at 15 Allott Street on his own. He was a bricklayer's apprentice there in 1911. Samuel died late 1928, aged 54.

George Wharam (1875–1946) was a brewer's labourer and he lived with Emma Amelia at 25 Barton Road, Brightside, Sheffield. In 1911, George, foreman cellarman in a brewery, and Emma, aged 35, occupied five rooms at 435 Walkley Bank, Eccleshall, with their four surviving children out of seven: Gladys, Bertram, George and Wilfred. By 1939, he was a brewery lorry driver's mate and lived at 31 South Street with Emma. George died in spring 1946, aged 70, in Sheffield and Emma died early 1950, aged 76.

Doncaster Road, Ardsley. (Courtesy of the Tasker Trust)

Edward Burrows (1831–1899)
(Survivor)

Edward Burrows was the son of Sarah and John Burrows, a weaver then 'callenderer' (operator of a machine used to press and finish paper or fabric between rollers), who had at least five children: George in 1826, Edward, Jane in 1834, Ellen in 1836 and Thomas in 1838.

In 1841, John and Sarah, both aged 45, resided at Westgate with three children: two with the surname Walker: Mary, born c.1821, and Joseph W., a collier born c.1831, and George Burrows, a collier aged 15. Edward, a coal miner aged 10, was one of two lodgers at Old Bleach Croft King Well, Worsbrough, with Thomas Steel (see chapter for Steel page 222). There were close links between the Burrows, Walker, and Steel families.

Edward was injured badly in the Oaks Colliery explosion on 5 March 1847 when he was 16 years old. He continued to lodge with Thomas Steel, who had also survived with serious injuries and had moved to Shambles Street by 1851. Edward's parents were still at Westgate with three Burrows children: Jane, Ellen and Thomas, Sarah Walker, with her two young children, Caroline and Richard plus visitor John Lindley, a coal miner aged 77.

Edward was mentioned three times in the minutes of the Colliers' Relief Committee: on 15 February 1848, they 'Resolved – That the allowance to <u>Edward Burrows</u> be reduced to 2s per Week' (worth £80). On 4 May 1849, they decided 'That <u>Edward Burrows</u> pay be reduced to 1s/- a week 'til Midsummer and that it be then discontinued altogether.' This was confirmed on 11 January 1850: 'Your Committee also at Midsummer last discontinued their Payments to … Edward Burrows in consequence of the Parish Officers having first done so on the ground (he being an Apprentice) that his Master was in a position to maintain him.'

Whatever his apprenticeship might have been, Edward was a coal miner by 1861, boarding at 18 Prospect Street, Barnsley, with Francis Gothard, a

Illustration from the 1842 Royal Commission Report. (Courtesy of the National Coalmining Museum)

coal miner, and his wife. By 1871, Edward was a coal pit hurrier lodging at Court 2, 2 John Street with George Parkes, a brewer, and his family.

Edward, aged 44, was an inmate in 1881 of Barnsley Union Workhouse, where he endured harsh conditions for twenty-four years. William Sowen, aged 51, was the workhouse master and Hannah Wilson, aged 27, was matron; there were ten other staff (a schoolmaster, two nurses, three porters, a cook, a seamstress, a tailor and a cab driver). The workhouse accommodated 394 Inmates (205 males, 189 females) plus fifteen casual paupers (fourteen males, one female).

Edward was still in the Workhouse in 1891, when Samuel Johnson Crawshaw, aged 34, was the master and his wife Emily Mary, aged 35, was the matron. There were eleven other staff: two porters, three nurses, two cooks, two attendants on lunatics, a shoemaker and a girls' industrial trainer. The number of inmates had decreased to 319: 187 males and 132 females.

Edward Burrows died there in January 1899, aged 68, and had a pauper's burial on 7 January in an unmarked communal grave in Barnsley Cemetery,

Edward's Four Siblings

George W Burrows (1826–1857) was baptised at St Mary's Church on 17 October 1824. He became a coal miner and, in 1851, was lodging in Barebones with John Haigh and his family (see chapter for Haigh page 128). George died early 1857, aged 30.

<u>Jane Burrows</u> (1834–1902) married Henry Steel (see chapter for Steel page 222)

<u>Ellen Burrows</u> (1836–1910) was baptised on 24 October 1836 at St Mary's Church. She married William Scholey, a coal miner aged 20, in summer 1855. They lived at 10 Fitzwilliam Street by 1861, when Ellen was a winder in a factory, and they had two children: Hannah in 1856 and George in 1858. Ellen and William separated. By 1871, William, a coal miner, and his two children, Hannah, linen worker, and George, a coal pit hurrier, were staying at 37 Heelis Street, the home of his parents. By 1881, Ellen, listed as 'head' and a linen weaver, resided at Seventh Court 2, Corporation Street, with Hannah, a bunt picker (linen), and a boarder. Ellen, a bobbin winder, was living alone at 10 Pinfold Hill Steps by 1901. William died in Sheffield late 1892, aged 55. Ellen got married again, using surname Burrows not Scholey, aged 59, on 31 December 1894 at All Saints' Church, Silkstone, to Robert Rapson, a labourer aged 58. Robert died early 1897, aged 60. Ellen 'Robson' (née Burrows) was imprisoned at HMP Wakefield for ten days on 28 February 1898 for being drunk and disorderly; she was 62, 5ft 1in tall with grey hair and worked as a mill hand. Ellen Rapson died early 1910, aged 73.

<u>Thomas Burrows</u> (1838–1909) was baptised on 4 October 1838 in St Mary's Church. He became a whitesmith (tin metal worker) and married Martha Ann Batty there on 5 July 1857. They resided in Gas Works Road by 1861 with their daughter. By 1871, they were living at 31 Somerset Court with six children, aged from 13 to 3 months: Sarah J., Clara, Annie, Tom, and twins Polly and Lucy. Ten years later, Thomas was a plumber at Shambles Street, Court 2 Number 38; with Martha and two more children: George and Gertrude. He was 'manager of slag works' by 1891, when he occupied the Gas House with his wife, son George, 'GW rail clerk', and grandson Arthur Burrows. Thomas, 'gas manager', and Martha lived in Cemetery Road by 1901, looking after two grandsons: Arthur, a box maker, and Walter. Thomas died in Sheffield early 1909, aged 71. Martha Burrows died in Rotherham early 1910, aged 72.

Bernard Wogan (c.1830–1885)
(Survivor)

Bernard Wogan's Irish parents were Catherine and James who relocated to Barnsley with at least one child in the 1830s to take advantage of employment in the weaving industry. In 1841, James, a weaver, and Catherine were residing in Copper Street with five children, aged from 20 to 2, born in Ireland and Barnsley: Ellen; Bernard; Elizabeth, who died early 1842, aged 10; John, who died in spring 1853, aged 16; and Mary. James and Catherine remained in the same house until Catherine died in 1862, aged 61, and James died in 1866, aged 75.

Bernard was a linen weaver like his father in 1841 but changed his occupation soon afterwards to work in the Oaks Colliery. He was a miner, aged 17, when rescued after the 1847 explosion. Bernard suffered from burns so bad that he was unable to work.

The Colliers' Relief Committee paid him an allowance of ten shillings per week (worth £400) but this was reduced to 7s 6d per week in January 1848 with a decision to reduce it again to 6 shillings 'so soon as the Committee shall feel warranted in making such a reduction'. On 15 February 1848, they 'Resolved – That the Sum of 11s/6d be paid to George White for teaching Bernard Wogan to write.' On 11 January 1850, the ledger notes that they, 'at Midsummer last discontinued their Payments to Bernard Wogan whom they thought so far recovered from his accident as to be able, with the advantages which had been extended to him by this Charity in the shape of Schooling, to earn a respectable livelihood by his own exertions.'

However, Bernard continued to work as a miner and married Eliza Skelton from Doncaster in spring 1853. They had eleven children: John, Mary, Emma, James William, Catherine, Eliza, Bernard, Isabella, Albert, Mary Ellen and Thomas William. Mary died on 24 May 1872,

The Old Oaks Colliery c.1900. (© Barnsley Archives)

aged 10 months, in Union Street; Thomas died in 1892, aged 17. In 1861, the family resided at Court 1, No. 3 Copper Street, where they had a lodger. They moved to 61 Park Road, Worsbrough, by 1871, with Eliza's widowed mother.

Bernard was assaulted at work in 1872 and details were reported in local newspapers: 'James Beaumont, miner at the Rosa Colliery near Barnsley, was in breach of rules on 31 January and Bernard Wogan, shot lighter, reported him.' Joseph went to Bernard's home five days later 'and struck him and kicked him' for passing on information leading to a summons. Joseph was 'convicted and sentenced to two months with hard labour for breach of safety rules and one month for assault'. The *Barnsley Chronicle* quoted Joseph as threatening, 'The first opportunity I have I will do your job for you', before hitting him 'on the face hurting his eye very severely.' Bernard's son John gave corroborative evidence.

Bernard put his education to good use as revealed by his letter to the editor of the *Barnsley Chronicle* in June 1872 about North Country v. Yorkshire Viewers.

> SIR – In reading your last week's issue, I find George Beardshall's reply to the North Country managers. In one place I find that he says two of the largest explosions in the Yorkshire district took place under North Country men; but he says nothing about any other explosions that took place

before the North Country managers came into Yorkshire. I hope he will look back, and he will find that at pits where other explosions took place there were Yorkshire managers, and not North Country managers. I would name the Oaks Colliery, March 5, 1847, where 73 lost their lives; Darley Main, January 25, 1849, where 75 lost their lives; Rawmarsh, Dec. 20, 1851, where 50 lost their lives; Higham Colliery, February 15, 1860, where 13 lost their lives; Edmunds Main, Dec. 7, 1862, where 59 lost their lives. Has G.B. forgotten the other explosions that took place in Yorkshire? In his reply he gives a long list of managers' names whom he calls Yorkshire men. I wonder if he knows a Yorkshire man when he sees one. I think not, or he would not call Jackson, at Silkstone Fall, one, for he is a Lancashire man; nor is Platts, at Wharncliffe-Silkstone, one either. He says the Yorkshire miners do not put themselves forward to look out for situations as managers. I don't know what he may think; but I find that all who have the chance take it. He perhaps thinks they have no chance, as he says the North Country managers are rooting their noses in. Wishing G.B. sweet success,

I remain yours truly,
BERNARD WOGAN

Grace Street.
(© Barnsley
Archives)

Bernard was injured again in a colliery accident at Swaithe Main in 1878. He was unable to work for nineteen weeks and must have been worried about supporting his large family. By 1881 the family had moved to Court 10, Silver Street 1, the oldest four of seven children were working. Two baby granddaughters were staying with them.

Bernard committed suicide on 12 August 1885, aged 55, at home in Wood Street and was buried three days later in Barnsley Cemetery. Details of the inquest were recorded in the Wakefield Charities Coroners Notebooks:

At the house of Benjamin Fairclough
the Wood Street Hotel, Barnsley, on
Friday the 14th Day of August
1885, on view of the body of
<u>Bernard Wogan</u> dec'd

<u>Eliza Wogan</u> of No. 3 Court 10, Wood Street, Barnsley, widow, sw. says, Dec'd was 55 years old & a coalminer. He was burnt in the explosion at Oaks Colliery in 1847 & was injured 7 years ago by fall of stone upon him in Swaith Main Colliery. He was laid up for 19 weeks from the effects of the last injury. He has only worked 4 months altogether since that time. He has now worked since last November. He has been healthy & tolerably steady. Last month one of our sons was summoned & had to pay 8 shillings [worth £202] & dec'd seemed to become much excited & began to drink. He arrived at home about 2 o'clock in the afternoon & said that the money should not be paid. I told him it must be paid & then he rose from the chair & came toward me & made a stroke at me with his fist. I stept out of the way & he fell forward & struck his face on the corner of a chair. He was raised up & was violent & spat at us but soon laid himself on the bare floor & fell asleep. He got up when he awoke & he walked upstairs to bed. He walked up and down the bedroom for some time before he undressed himself. He seemed to rest well. Last Tuesday forenoon he slipt on his trousers & came downstairs & smoked his pipe for a few minutes then went back. He did not eat anything. <u>Last Wednesday evening</u>

about ½ past 6 o'clock being still in bed he called to my son Tom, aged 11 years, to take him a pipe tobacco & knife & also a pot of water. The boy took the things upstairs then went out to play. I did not suspect anything wrong as dec'd had been in the habit of lying in bed 2 or 3 days after drinking. About 7 o'clock last Wednesday evening my daughter Isabella had a fit & while I was attending to her I heard him walking about. About 10 minutes afterward I went upstairs & saw him hanging from a nail in the wall off which he had removed the clock. I fetched Mr and Mrs Worstenholme.

Thomas William Wogan sw. ways, Dec'd was my father. I took him some tobacco, a pipe & dinner knife & some water last Wednesday evening. He was in bed. He told me to go down as that would be his last. He had frequently said so & I did not tell my mother.

Tom Wogan [*signature*]

John Worstenholme [*his son George married Bernard's daughter Isabella*] of No 2 Court 10 afsd., shoemaker sw. says, Dec'd came to our house about ½ past 10 o'clock last Monday night & asked me whether I had seen his children. He was tipsy. My wife said they were in bed at home & he went home. Last Wednesday evening about ½ past 7 o'clock I cut him down. He was hanging with a rope. He had on his shirt & trousers & had one foot on the chair & the other hanging down by the side of it. He was dead but warm. My wife laid out his body.

Verdict Hanged himself while temporar'y insane.

Paid William Harper £7: 2: 6. Persl exps. [*Worth £3,590*]

Bernard's widow Eliza went to live with her married daughter then son. Eliza died in 1902, aged 70, and was interred on 25 September in Barnsley Cemetery.

The Nine Children of Bernard and Eliza Wogan

John Wogan (1853–1912) was a coal miner and he married Frances (Fanny) Hitchen, aged 18, in 1874 at St John the Baptist's Church.

They lived in Copper Street then Britannia Street and had eleven children, three of whom died young. Albert Ernest, Lily, Annie, Charles and Frances all got married and had children.

James Willie Wogan (1879–1939) was a collier like his brothers and he married Maria Fox in 1901. They had nine children, two of whom died young. According to Wakefield Prison Records, James was sentenced at Barnsley County Court on 31 October 1905 to twenty-one days' imprisonment for debt or a fine of £1 16s (worth £723), which he paid; he was 27 years old, 5ft 2in tall with light brown hair. They occupied four rooms at 5 Court 4 Thomas Street by 1911.

James enlisted as a Private in the 14th (Second Barnsley) Battalion of the York and Lancaster Regiment, but he was transferred to the 2nd Battalion of the Durham Light Infantry. He survived and was awarded the Victory and British War medals. However, his daughter Agnes, aged 8, succumbed to the influenza pandemic while he was in France. The *Barnsley Chronicle* reported in August 1918 her mother's explanation to the coroner that Agnes,

> had not been a healthy child. Since some eye weakness was cured about four years ago she had suffered from abscesses in her head…. She attended St John's School until Thursday last, when the school closed for influenza and on Saturday night complained of headache. During the night she vomited but had a fairly quiet night. When she awoke on Sunday morning she seemed all right but two hours later had two fits, dying in the second one.

After carrying out a post-mortem, the coroner returned a verdict of 'Died from heart failure from commencing pneumonia and convulsions, probably due to an attack of influenza.'

James died early 1939, aged 59, and Maria stayed with her daughter Ida at 69 Heelis Street until she died in 1957, aged 76.

John Thomas Wogan (1881–1918) enlisted in Barnsley on 29 May 1915 as a private in the 14th (Second Barnsley) Battalion of the York and Lancaster Regiment. He was nearly 34 years old, a labourer at Hemsworth Chemical Works, living at 54 Britannia Street, 5ft 2½in tall with a 33in girth. John committed two offences of overstaying his pass: in February 1916 he was two days nineteen hours and thirty-five minutes late, and had not used the train as ordered, which resulted in a punishment of fourteen days' duration and four days' loss of pay; in June 1916 he was over three days late resulting in the same punishment. John was transferred to the Army Reserve on 24 May 1917 and discharged on 8 December following a medical assessment in Sheffield. John's disability had started in May 1916 while training in Sunderland, where he complained of suffering 'pain in chest with cough & shortness of breath, reported sick & excused duty, never in hospital.' The board wrote:

> he states that he had a 'stroke' in June last and lost the use of his right arm & leg, & speech. There is no loss of power or muscular weakness now. Speech is normal. There are some physical signs of Bronchitis, probably of old standing. There is no evidence of organic Heart Disease.

He was awarded a pension based on being 20 per cent disabled. John returned home to 217 Heelis Street but was not as fit as the Army had assessed because he died in summer 1918, aged 37.

Walter Wogan (1891–1917) was a linen mill hand at Beevor Bobbin Works when he married Edith Wood late 1913. They lived at 13 Clifton Street, where their daughter Annie was born in 1915. Walter must have enlisted around this time and he served as a Private in the 9th Battalion of the King's Own Yorkshire Light Infantry. He was killed in action on 4 October 1917 on the Western Front and his name is on the Tyne Cot Memorial in Belgium. Walter had been reported as missing and Edith put a notice in the *Barnsley Chronicle* six weeks later asking for news of her husband. She had to wait until August 1918 for confirmation that he was dead; her tribute was printed in the Deaths Column:

> 'Tis only those who have lost can tell,
> The sorrows of parting and not saying farewell;
> But the unknown grave is the bitterest blow,
> None but an aching heart can know.
>
> Ever remembered by his loving wife and child.

Walter Wogan's name is on the Tyne Cot Memorial

Walter was owed pay of £3 13s 1d (worth £770), which his widow received nearly a year after his death; she received a War Gratuity of £3 10s in November 1919 for his loss. Edith was also sent his medals and the Memorial Plaque and Scroll.

Mary Wogan (1855–1923) married Charles Bray, a pit labourer on Christmas Day 1874 at St John the Baptist's Church and they had seven children, three of whom died young. Charles changed his occupation to glass-stopper maker then a grocer and baker, with assistance from Mary, at 98 Sheffield Road. Mary Bray died early 1923, aged 67, and her husband Charles died about a year later.

Emma Wogan (1857–1923) was baptised in May 1857 at Holy Rood Roman Catholic Church. She married Edward Brotherton, a coal miner hewer, in spring 1882 and they had eleven children, who all survived to adulthood. Emma and Edward lived in Rotherham and their sons were miners. Emma Brotherton died early 1923, aged 65.

James William Wogan (1860–1924) was a lamp keeper in a colliery, aged 11, and a hewer when he got married late 1883 to Sarah Ann Waterson, an Irish widow with three daughters, one of whom was blind from birth but worked as a linen weaver. They occupied three rooms at 33 Longcar Street for most of their marriage and had no children together. In 1891, three of James' brothers shared their home: James died in summer 1924, aged 64.

Catherine Wogan (1862–1925) was a linen power loom weaver, aged 8. She married Albert Chappell, a boot and shoe rivetter born in France, in spring 1881. They had thirteen children, three of whom died before 1911, and occupied four rooms at 44 Union Street. Albert died in 1909, aged 50, and Catherine shared her home with six sons, aged from 29 to 13, whose occupations were varied: a platelayer for Midland Railway, two boot repairers, a miner trammer and two box makers at glass bottle works. Catherine Chappell died in spring 1925, aged 62.

Eliza Wogan (1864–1921) was a weaver and moved to Bradford, where she married George Daybell, a wood sawyer, in 1890 at St Peter's Church (Cathedral). They had four children but the eldest died in infancy. Eliza's mother, Eliza, stayed with them for a period after being widowed. The family occupied four rooms at 82 Seaton Street, Bradford, by 1911, when their three children, aged 17, 16 and 13, were working as a 'learning spinning overlooking Worsted Manuf', a saw sharpener and, the youngest, half at school, half at worsted factory. Eliza Daybell died early 1921, aged 56

Bernard Wogan (1866–1932) was baptised in January 1867 at Holy Rood. He became a coal miner hewer and boarder with James until he got married in 1894 to Elizabeth Ann Waterson, a blind linen weaver, who was one of James' stepdaughters. They had two daughters in Shaw Street then moved to 98 Sheffield Road, where Bernard may have taken over the grocery in 1924, after his oldest sister Mary and husband had died. Bernard died on 10 April 1932, aged 65, and Elizabeth remained at 98 Sheffield Road for at least another seven years; her older daughter being a confectioner there. Elizabeth Wogan died early 1946, aged 73.

Isabella Wogan (1868–1919) was baptised at Holy Rood. In 1886 she married George Worstenholme, a glass bottle maker aged 20, at St John the Baptist's Church. They had nine children and lived in one of the

Courts in Wood Street, then 78 Heelis Street. Isabella died in summer 1919, aged 50, and George continued at the glassworks until at least aged 73. He lodged at 14 Park Terrace, where he died in 1945, aged 78.

Albert Ernest Wogan (1870–1923) was baptised at Holy Rood. He became a coal miner hewer and, after his father died, went to live with James before lodging at 2 H 2 Court, Wilson Street. Albert was convicted for debt at Barnsley County Court in February 1901 and he served twenty-one days in HM Prison Wakefield, unable to repay the 22/9 (worth £462). He was 5ft 2½in tall with brown hair. Albert moved to Bradford where he married Catherine Beatrice Gooch in 1903 and they had four children. Albert, a 'carter general carrier', died in summer 1923, aged 52, and Catherine died in 1947, aged 72.

New Street. (Courtesy of the Tasker Trust)

Glossary

There is a wide range of jobs above and below ground in collieries. Some general terms for workers are coal miner or miner, colliery labourer and mineworker.

BANKSMAN – the person at the top of the pit who removes full corves from the cage and unloads them into wagons, when they are weighed and screened.

BARROWMAN – the person who pulls full corves from Hewers to the shaft.

DATALLER – underground worker paid by the day.

DEPUTY – appointed to manage an area of the pit to ensure safe and efficient working conditions.

ENGINE TENTER (Engine Man) – similar to a Blacksmith repairing machinery, e.g. for winding cages.

GETTER – see Hewer

HEWER (Coal Miner Hewer, Colliery Hewer) – a worker underground, who cut coal from its natural situation, often in cramped conditions, and filled corves or waggons. Aged from 21 to retirement. The usual daily wage in 1849 was between 3s 9d to 4s 3d for eight hours for an average of four or five days in the week. A small house was provided as part of his wages.

KNOCKER UP (Early Risers Caller Up) – before people had alarm clocks they relied on others to ensure that they were awake in time for work.

ONSETTER (Hanger On) – the person at the bottom of the shaft who hooks full corves into the cage to take to the surface and unhooks empty corves on their return.

OVERMAN (Foreman) – a senior worker who inspects the mine each morning before men commence work and who keeps an account of men's labour.

PONY BOY (Pony Driver) – one of the first occupations for a child, who would care for the pit ponies and lead them while pulling corves or wagons underground between the hewer and the lift shaft (full) and back (empty).

PUTTER – see Trammer.

SCREENER – a worker who removes stones and other rubbish as the coal goes over screens to remove the small pieces.

TRAMMER – a child worker who pushed corves or waggons filled with coal from the hewer to the lift shaft, returning it empty.

TRAPPER – a job for the youngest boys, who would spend their time opening and shutting a trap-door when required, working alone in darkness. Wages were 9d or 10d for a day of twelve hours in 1849.

VIEWER – the manager, responsible for underground and surface arrangements, including ventilation. He often had an Under Viewer to help pass on instructions to men.

(From Durham Mining Museum website: dmm.org.uk and other sources).

Bibliography

Oaks Colliery Explosion 1847: Minutes of the Subscription Committee 1847–1857 (Barnsley Archives reference A/3716/G/1/1)

Children's Employment Commission First Report of the Commissioners Mines 1842 and *The Condition and Treatment of the Children employed in the Mines and Collieries of the United Kingdom 1842* (digitised by Google)

Children's Employment Commission Appendix to First Report of Commissioners Mines Part 1 Reports and Evidence from Sub-Commissioners 1842 (Irish University Press Series of British Parliamentary Papers)

Aspects of Barnsley 4 – Chapter 8 Barnsley Comes of Age: the Town in the 1860s

Memories of Barnsley – article on Barebones area

Baines, Thomas, *Yorkshire Past and Present (to 1870)*

Downes, Eddie, *Yorkshire Collieries 1847 – 1994 –* (published 2017).

Elliott, Brian, *Tracing Your Coalmining Ancestors: A Guide for Family Historians* (Pen & Sword, 2014)

Engels, Frederick, *The Condition of the Working-Class in England in 1844* (Republished by Freeriver Community Project)

Gallop, Alan, *Victoria's Children of the Dark* (The History Press 2017)

Heald, Tony, & Chance, Michael, *Ardsley & Stairfoot Revisited* by (Greenman Enterprise, 2008) and *Ardsley, Stairfoot and Hoyle Mill* (Comtec Printing Services Limited, 2018)

Hoyle, Eli, *Old Barnsley Streets and Byways* (from 1777) and *A History of Barnsley etc to 1850*

Jackson, Rowland, *The History of the Town and Township of Barnsley, in Yorkshire (1858)* (Reproduced by Andesite Press)

Machin, Frank, *The Yorkshire Miners: A History Volume 1* (NUM 1958)

NUM and People & Mining Group *The Oaks Disaster 1866: A Living History* (published 2017).

Wilkinson, Joseph, *Worthies, Families and Celebrities of Barnsley and the District (1883)* and *Worsbrough: Its Historical Associations and Rural Attractions (1879)*

Embroidered picture 'Head to Face' by Maureen Livesey. (Owned by the author)

1800 Maps of Barnsley

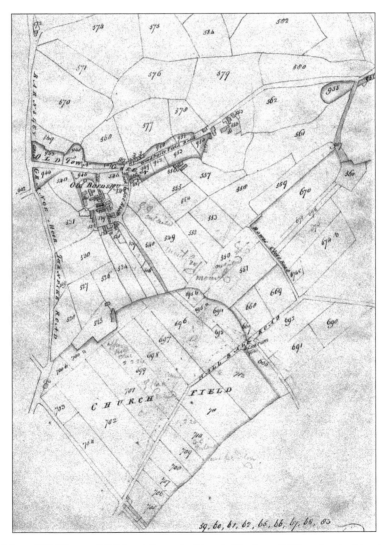

Map of Old Town c.1800 hand-drawn by Francis Kendray. (© Barnsley Archives)

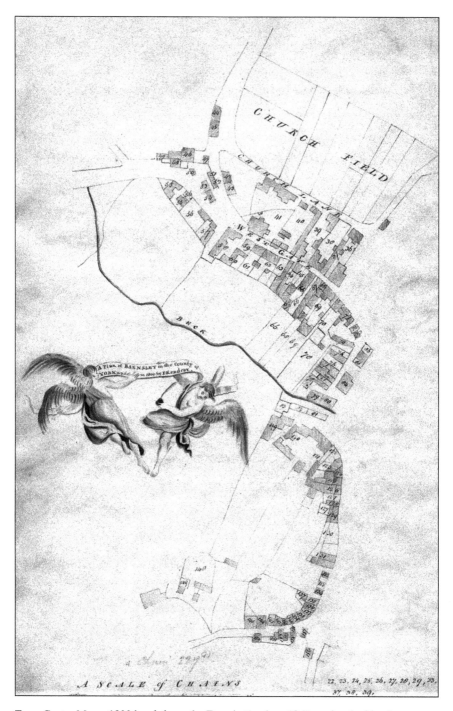

Town Centre Map c.1800 hand-drawn by Francis Kendray. (© Barnsley Archives)

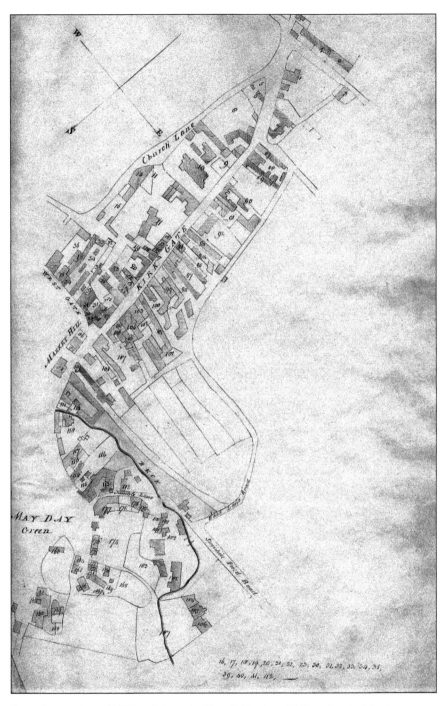

Town Centre Map c.1800 hand-drawn by Francis Kendray. (© Barnsley Archives)

Illustration: View of Barnsley in the early 1800s. (Courtesy of the Tasker Trust)